D1570228

Slaying

THE N.I.M.B.Y.

Dragon

Slaying
N.I.M.B.Y.
T H E
Dragon

Herbert Inhaber

Transaction Publishers
New Brunswick (U.S.A.) and London (U.K.)

Library of Congress Catalog Number: 97-15480
ISBN: 1-56000-219-0
Printed in the United States of America

Library of Congress Cataloging-in-Publication Data

Inhaber, Herbert, 1941–
    Slaying the NIMBY dragon / Herbert Inhaber.
        p. cm.
    Includes bibliographical references and index.
    ISBN 1-56000-219-0 (cloth)
    1. NIMBY syndrome—United States.   2. Land use—United States—
Planning—Citizen participation.   3. Land use—Environmental aspects—
United States. I. Title.
HD205.I54   1997
333.73'17—dc21   97-15480
                                                                        CIP

This book is dedicated to my wife, Donna, who has helped me through thick and thin with great encouragement.

Contents

List of Tables

List of Figures

1

A NIMBY Overview:
How it has Prevented the Establishment
of Needed Facilities

Advanced societies around the world are facing a dilemma of gigantic proportions: What to do with all the facilities that everyone desires in principle, but wants to keep out of their own block? The phenomenon is called NIMBY—Not In My Back Yard.

It may seem to be a far-fetched problem that does not affect most of us. Yet it looms bigger than we imagine. Hundreds of millions of dollars, if not billions, have been spent to overcome it. Some of the most talented engineers and scientists, whose skills could be applied to more productive activities, have devoted years to defeating it. And it still remains.

The dragons of legend used to roam the countryside, wreaking destruction wherever they wanted. Because of the pervasive nature of NIMBY, I have labeled it a "dragon" in the title of this book. It has indeed burned up the detailed plans of administrators, politicians, and scientists.

Nobody knows exactly how much damage the mythical dragons caused. But the problems produced by NIMBY are well documented. In the rest of this chapter, I will give only a few examples. A complete listing might fill a library shelf.

At least one dragon would continue to ravage villages if it had not been for St. George, who slew it. A mere compilation of NIMBY problems would be inadequate without a proposed solution. The modern-day analogy to St. George's sword—the reverse Dutch auction—will be revealed later in this book. Briefly, it attempts to use both environmental science and economics to wipe out NIMBY, conclusively. I believe that it will work, and we can go on to better things.

Acronyms and Definitions

The NIMBY field is full of abbreviations. Let's go over them briefly, so we can understand what people have said on the subject. However, in the rest of this book I will try to keep acronyms to a minimum.

NIMTOO—Not In My Term Of Office—is sometimes used by elected officials confronted by a NIMBY decision. That is, we will solve the NIMBY problem just as soon as I retire from this office. The phrase is a bit unfair to politicians, who are often merely reflecting what their constituents want or do not want.

LULUs—Locally Unwanted Land Uses—is the generic term for all the facilities to which people object: landfills, prisons, radioactive waste sites, AIDS treatment centers, and so on. This acronym is used extensively, since it encompasses all the facilities that create NIMBY opposition.

The nuclear energy field, subject of much NIMBY controversy, has spawned its own jargon. Two phrases are "low-level" and "high-level" waste.

The Nuclear Regulatory Commission and the Environmental Protection Agency have their own precise definitions of these two terms. We can think of low-level wastes as gloves or resins used in a reactor, and needles that might have contained some radioactive tracer material in medicine. These wastes are slightly radioactive—you could be in a room with them without suffering much increased risk.

High-level wastes come only from nuclear reactors. They are mostly the spent nuclear fuel rods from which electricity has been produced. These are highly radioactive. You would not want to go near where they were stored.

What about hazardous wastes, which seem to be related in some way to the two previous terms? Hazardous wastes are specific chemicals and compounds that have been identified by the Environmental Protection Agency and other regulatory bodies as posing some type of hazard to human health or the environment. The hazards vary considerably from one chemical to another.

The risks of all these sources—hazardous, low- and high-level wastes—vary, depending on how close you are to them, and how many of these materials you breathe or drink. Most people are unhappy with *any* wastes in their back yard, whether those wastes are fairly benign or highly toxic.

For those who are unalterably opposed to undesirable facilities, ever, at any time, place or condition, other phrases exist. They are NIABY—

Not In Anybody's Back Yard—and NOPE—Not On Planet Earth. The idea behind these phrases is that the wastes should not have been created in the first place.

Those seeking a solution to NIMBY might say:

• Is it better to build a new prison that offers some chance of rehabilitation of prisoners? Or is it better to confine them to a century-old structure, overcrowded and under court order to be torn down?

• Is it better to keep radioactive wastes in the back rooms of a hospital or a nuclear reactor, storage areas which were never designed to hold them for decades? Or is it better to build a special structure that will meet all environmental rules and regulations?

Calvin Brunner, a Virginia-based waste industry consultant and the author of several books on waste disposal, thinks NIMBY will gradually produce an overwhelming crisis. In an article entitled "NIMBYists Put Society at Risk", he wrote: *Will our inability to come to grips with pollution force revolution on us?* [emphasis in original]...there may be too much democracy in America...this would eventually lead to anarchy...[producing] a lack of respect for institutions, people in power and for everything and everyone."[1]

Could Brunner be exaggerating for the sake of effect? In this book, I avoid the name calling that has characterized much of the NIMBY debate. I avoid labeling as "NIMBYists" those who do not want undesirable facilities near them, even though Brunner does. I have a certain sympathy for them, as will be shown later. Name calling, regardless of the merits of the case, does nothing to produce a solution to NIMBY. A solution is what this book produces.

Being Canadian by birth, I am alert to NIMBY events there. Jim Temple, an official of a Canadian waste handling company, wrote: "A couple of years ago, I had the pleasure of hearing a Mayor from a Nova Scotia municipality tell a most inspiring story of community activism. She told how she and her constituents put up a valiant struggle to keep a regional waste disposal site out of her community. The Mayor and her followers applied political leverage, recruited a sympathetic press and put in a lot of long hours of hard campaigning."[2]

He noted that the Mayor had kept the dump out of her town. But then she gave a public speech in triumph, to tell the world what a wonderful thing she had done. She was asked by a member of the audience: "Madam Mayor, where does your community's waste go [now]?" to which she replied, "It goes into the community that did accept a regional site." Second question: "Can you, Madam Mayor, honestly say that the community that got the regional site is better suited to receiving waste than your community is?" Her answer was, "No. The site ultimately chosen was technically poorer than the site proposed in our community."

Temple concluded, "Ladies and gentlemen, that's what NIMBY is all about."

Recycling

Some demonstrators at battles over landfills have said. "We don't really need this new dump. If we just recycled our wastes, we could put the remainder in the present landfill. This new one is being built just because we're wasteful."

Nigel Guilford, another waste management official at the very same conference as Jim Temple, said:

> I visited a plant in Vienna in 1981. It was brand new, cost $60 million, had twin rotary kilns, twin fluidized beds and sludge incinerators, a heat recovery system, power production, beautiful labs, and physical-chemical treatment. But there were also concrete blocks on the conveyors, tree stumps in [the] receiving area, tires piled up in the receiving area, guys walking around with no hard hats in the areas where they were unloading drums of solvents, no goggles, and smoking cigarettes. Sixty million dollars had been spent on [hardware] but the system as a whole didn't work. When I was back in Europe earlier this year, I learned that the Vienna plant had been closed down.[3]

Suppose that recycling could reduce waste X by half. Would opposition to siting that waste be halved? I doubt it. The biggest nuclear waste riot in the U.S. occurred over low-level waste, much less harmful than high-level waste. Observers conclude that most members of the public do not distinguish between large and small amounts of waste, nor their relative toxicity.

To take another example, some years back Mercedes-Benz, in one of their ads, showed their longest-running vehicle, still rolling along. As I recall, it had gone about 750,000 miles. We could build cars to last longer than present ones, although the average person might not want a vehicle to last fifty years at an average use of 15,000 miles annually. Even if we increased the lifetime of cars substantially, there would still be some auto graveyards. Like death and taxes, at least some wastes will always be with us.

Recycling is part of public policy in many countries. In some areas, it proceeds naturally, without the intervention of governments. For example, photo developers recover the silver they use, because it is so valuable. As far as I know, this has always been done, without any government regulations. On the other hand, some government rules require recycling, regardless of economics. The regulations in some states on bottle deposits probably fall into that category.

When People are Involved, Not Just Wastes

Recycling can improve some parts of the NIMBY problem, without question. This in turn may decrease public battles over undesirable facilities. Yet, there are areas of NIMBY that are not concerned with inanimate objects like wastes, but with people. These situations do not lend themselves to recycling. Consider a few examples.

People walked around in the parking lot of an A&P store in Wanaque, New Jersey.[4] Signs were displayed, "Keep AIDS out of Wanaque!" Another said, "We Need State Aid, not AIDS from the State." One of the protesters, Ken Higgins, described himself as a big believer in the Not In My Back Yard theory: "Those AIDS people come from a degenerate society. I'm talking about sex and degenerates passing drug needles in Newark. They don't want them in Newark. Newark says Nimby. Well, don't put them in our backyard. We believe in Nimby too! Nimby! You said it, Nimby! That's what we believe."

A convalescent home in Wanaque had agreed to take 120 AIDS patients. At the time, New Jersey had the fifth highest number of AIDS cases nationally; Passaic County, in which Wanaque is located, had the third highest AIDS level in the state. But it was clear that many of the patients would be coming from outside the town.

The state of New Jersey decided not to hold public meetings on the move. Paul Langevin, the assistant state health commissioner, when asked about a meeting, said, "Should we have? Perhaps, but we're trying to play it down."

Many of the protesters shouted and screamed. Mike Ryan, a civic leader, said: "If they're drug abusers, they belong in the inner city and who knows where they're from if they're homosexual. I don't have anything against them, but why should they be next to my house? Who's going to visit a drug addict? Who's going to visit a homosexual? Another homosexual! They go after your children."

A local priest, Angelo Gambatese, who was watching the demonstrators, said: "This is Good Friday. Good Friday! This is terrible."

Now on to something more pleasant, the bright and shining faces of little children. Surely those innocents do not have anything to do with NIMBY. Or do they?

Consider someone trying to set up a day care center for the children of her neighborhood, so that working mothers did not have to drag their offspring all over town. She had just finished putting up the new wallpaper, with images of Donald Duck and Mickey Mouse, when she hears some noises outside the window. More demonstrators. Only this time they were not complaining about AIDS. Their object was the day care center: "Kids get out! You'll ruin the neighborhood! Kids get out!"

According to Michael Coughlin of the Massachusetts Office for Children, forty to fifty communities in the Bay State have faced controversies of this type.[5] Sandra Gellert, president of the National Association for Family Day Care, says it's "an ongoing problem everywhere."

This event took place at Elaine Sibley's eight-room ranch house in Westwood, Massachusetts. Mrs. Sibley, mother of two, had wanted to open a center for only six pre-school children. She had a certificate in early childhood education, experience in working with very young children, and a state day care license.

Not enough, neighbors said. They petitioned to block the day care center.

The business would create traffic and noise. The neighborhood would go to the dogs. Their property values would plummet. Of course, good day care from qualified teachers such as Mrs. Sibley was an absolute necessity, but Not In...

There were a few people who did not agree with the marchers, such as Susan Twombley of the Child Care Resource Center in Cambridge. She said, "I understand some concerns, but children need to exist somewhere. If they can't be in residential areas, where can they be? And what does exclusion say about how we as a society feel about children?"

From children we go to those people who, in some instances, have the minds of children. Nobody in the Highland Park Civic Association hates mentally ill people.[6] This part of affluent Nassau County on New York's Long Island was being considered for a small group home for twelve mentally ill patients.

The association did not want these unfortunates confined to the terrible conditions exemplified in such movies as *The Snake Pit* or *One Flew Over the Cuckoo's Nest*. Those bad old days had to go.

As far as putting a handful on Highland Avenue, well, that was another matter entirely. It just happened to be the wrong location for these hapless people. Marilyn Goodman, who has two daughters who are psychologists and thus should know something about the subject, said, "I have great compassion for these people, but this is not the place." Dr. Rocco Cirigliano, a psychologist himself, called putting twelve patients in the proposed house, a home which cost $320,000 and contains twelve rooms and over 3,000 square feet, creating a "slum."

On the other hand, Dr. Roy Speiser, a chiropractor in the neighborhood, feels that the house may not be good enough for the patients. "It's on a very steep hill, a very dangerous hill. The patients may come out of [the house] heavily medicated, very disoriented, possibly out of touch with reality. They will have to walk down this severe hill, walk four blocks and get on a bus. Is that really fair?"

The association felt it was not. Surely these wealthy and highly educated people, who know more about mental illness than most other citizens, would not act that way. Or would they?

On to so-called affordable housing, the subject of much NIMBY ire across the nation. The residents of Cohasset, an expensive suburb near Boston, favor housing that will not bankrupt young couples, but "not here, please."[7]

Crystal Woods complex, the subject of their wrath, is no slum. Part of it would be sold at market value, with units costing $145,000 to $175,000. Part of it would be financed through a government subsidy, and these units would cost $75,000 to $95,000. These "affordable" houses are what drew the wrath of Joseph Barresi, the state inspector general and District Judge Patrick Hurley.

John Durkin, head of a neighborhood group, did not beat around one of the elegant bushes marking his town:

> We have a lot of high-priced homes here and introducing low-priced homes will have a detrimental effect on our homes. We're not opposed to low cost housing. We're all charitable in that regard. Unfortunately, we're spoiled here on Brewster Road. It's a dead-end street and is beautiful. We like to see housing consistent to the community. We like to see homes in the same price range.

Robert Sturdy is head of the Planning Board in Cohasset. He said, "Frankly, I don't think it's fair to put a project like this in a country setting. You don't build Dorchester [a poverty-stricken section of Boston] in Scituate [adjoining Cohasset] or Cohasset. This has nothing to do with snob zoning."

At one point, when children left home they ended up a few years later down the block from their parents, in a comparable house. Now adult children cannot afford to live in the same suburbs as their parents. Crystal Woods—and many other projects proposed throughout the nation—would have allowed this to happen.

So a few spoiled brats, scions of the wealthy, will have to pay more for their housing. So what? But at least a compassionate society like ours can provide for the poorest, those who have nothing.

New York City is home to the largest concentration of liberals in the U.S. Surely this would be a place where the government would take care of the homeless, those who live on grates and under bridges.

The residents of Midland Beach, Staten Island, opposed a homeless shelter.[8] About 400 people were at a meeting on the subject. A nun, whose group, Homes for the Homeless, suggested building a shelter, made her way to the microphone. In ordinary times, a religious sister talking to New Yorkers would be treated with the utmost respect. These were not ordinary times. A police escort was necessary.

By the time she got to the microphone, many in the audience were shouting at her, "We don't want you! We don't want you!"

Could this be happening in New York, with its large Catholic population? It was. Others addressed the meeting. Of the thirty-five who spoke, all but one opposed the shelter. The one who favored it was chased from the microphone.

The people of Midland Beach had good reasons for all of this. They always do. One member of the community board in Staten Island, Phil Scampas, said that the large number of black and Hispanic families that would likely occupy the shelter would not fit into the mostly white community of Midland Beach. "I wouldn't be welcome in South Bronx [a largely Hispanic section of New York]," Scampas said. The nuns were upset. Sister Joan Kirby said that the opposition has left her "depressed and appalled and hurt and frightened for the human race. You really wonder how our society is going to solve our problems."

Some say, "Let's face it—the homeless brought it upon themselves. They drank away all their money, or drugged themselves, or didn't pay enough attention in school. It's all their own fault. They're adults, so they have to face the consequences of their actions." But surely NIMBY wouldn't pick on defenseless babies.

In Fresh Meadows, New York City, one day there was a smoldering house, with the fire chief standing nearby. "Looks like arson to me," he said. Was it another house burned down for the insurance? It had been planned for boarder babies, those infants whose mothers were on drugs or had other severe health problems.[9]

These examples have dealt with people. Can insects be the subject of NIMBY?

The medfly (a small fly that infests citrus groves) could cause disaster to California's agriculture, the largest in the nation. According to experts, aerial spraying of malathion is the only thing that can stop this. The spraying has to cover a large area, not just the few locations where the medfly has been sighted.

In Orange County, California, demonstrators circled round and round a giant papier-mâché figure of a medfly. Signs read, "It's Your Air! Stop Spraying!"; "Honk Your Support!"

Renee Dufresne, a resident of La Habra Heights, says, "Until the helicopters came over our house, it was somebody *else's* problem."

The cast of television's "Cheers" marched in another rally. Surely in addition to their concerns about their own health, they also were thinking about the farmers whose crops might be destroyed by the pesky fly. Or were they?[10]

In rural Georgia, NIMBY about garbage is alive and well. Confronted by the possibility of a regional landfill, J. D. Whidby, a farmer in Cherokee County, says, "We're going to fight this thing to the fullest extent of the law. If we have to get down on our knees and beg them, we'll do that." Debbie Buckner said, "We don't want to become the sacrificial lamb, and we don't want our state sacrificed either."[11]

Some have tried to look at it from another viewpoint. Michael Sheward, an official of the National Solid Wastes Management Association, says, "Not everyone wants them in their community but someone has to have it." He said this from the safety of the Washington Beltway, not in the red clay belt.

Everyone is in favor of recreation, fresh air, and the great outdoors. Could NIMBY creep into visions of bucolic settings?

In Kane County, Illinois, members of STOP, a citizen's group, handed out petitions. They said they wanted to stop the county from acquiring land along the banks of the Fox River for a park and bike trail. The members of STOP approved parks and bike trails, of course, as long as it was not their land that was being expropriated. The county said they were helping the landowners by preventing the flood plain from being occupied. They were not believed.[12]

Steven Thompson knows more than he wants to about NIMBY. Thompson started off in Wheaton, Illinois, by fighting an attempt to put a fast-food restaurant near a nature trail. We need these establishments, but just not there.

Sometime later, his property was proposed by the state to be part of a site for the Superconducting Supercollider, a giant particle accelerator. He joined CATCH—Citizens Against The Collider Here—to stop it. Thompson did not have much against the huge scientific tool, just as long as it was not....

Then a developer wanted to build a subdivision in a cornfield behind Thompson's home. Eventually he became head of the group fighting it.[13]

All the NIMBYs

Eric Zorn described the NIMBY dragons roaming Chicago neighborhoods:

> The Nimbys are really rolling now.
>
> They have just been in Lake County, successfully staving off the creation of a dump near Grayslake and vanquishing a particularly odious sludge depository outside Richmond.
>
> They have been in DuPage County, keeping the White Sox [baseball team] out of Addison, stopping a self-storage facility in Westmont, howling about the proposed widening of 31st Street in Oak Brook and tilting against the new tollway.
>
> They have recently appeared in Crete, blocking the development of an outdoor music theater; in Barrington, fighting the proposed Gateway Mall to its death; in La Grange Park, objecting to the construction of a retirement home, and in Evanston [home of the Women's Christian Temperance Union] trying to make sure the Amvets don't pour liquor in their clubhouse....
>
> Nimby: One of those who likes a few drinks with dinner, but who campaigned against a referendum proposal to allow restaurants in River Forest to serve alcohol; one who likes to watch night baseball, but wants the diamond or stadium to be in someone else's neighborhood; one who throws away trash, but never wants to see the dump.[14]

The Psychology of NIMBYs

Some psychologists have tried to determine what the NIMBY syndrome means. Caplice writes:

> What underlies the NIMBY syndrome? One answer might be found in Maslow's hierarchy of human needs. Maslow placed human needs in an ascending order with basic needs, such as the need for sustenance, shelter and security at the bottom and other less tangible needs at the top, such as the need for self-esteem, respect of your peer group and opportunity for personal growth and self-actualization.[15]

When we find a locally unwanted land use staring us in the face, we are plunged to the bottom of Maslow's hierarchy.

> In our society, the higher level needs tend to be our primary concerns on a day-to-day basis, until we're confronted with something like a nuclear power station or a waste disposal site. Then we're brought right back down to the bottom of Maslow's hierarchy. We fear that our personal and family survival is threatened. We fear what "those chemicals" can do to us, our family and friends...there's nothing more gut-wrenching than to be brought back suddenly to the bottom level of this hierar-

chy of needs. The natural human reaction is to start fighting. You start asking questions but you don't get the answers that you want. The technical people don't deliver. You get frustrated.... When you don't get answers to your questions, your fear and anger increase. It's a perfectly understandable thing.

So psychology may have some solutions to NIMBY. Yet there are still a vast number of unanswered questions.

The above examples may have given the impression that I regard NIMBYists as unreasonable, illogical, insane, or even worse. Nothing could be further from the truth. They are acting logically, in their own interests. While some may regard them with disdain because of their sometimes-violent tactics, most of us would object if an undesired facility were proposed for *our* neighborhood.

The problem is that the NIMBYists are reasonable, and the state and waste generators are also reasonable in trying to find a relatively safe place to put their facilities. The two sets of reasonableness collide, with headlines as the result. My purpose here is to set up a framework so that both sides can continue to be reasonable. At the same time, a facility gets built.

Is There a Way Out?

The above NIMBY news stories are gloomy. Nonetheless, there is a way out, one that I describe in detail later.

To summarize it briefly, it is based on the principle that to find sites for undesirable facilities, the surrounding community has to be a volunteer. Trying to cram these facilities down a community's throat almost never works, as these and hundreds of other examples show.

The assumption in present siting systems is that nobody in their right mind would volunteer, so we *have* to force people to take it.

The reverse Dutch auction allows a way out of the exaggerated claims and counterclaims of high or low risk attached to the unwanted facility. It does use money—perhaps the only universal solvent in this context—but in a novel way. The price paid by the rest of us to take the facility out of *our* backyard gradually rises until a community, after balancing risks and benefits, decides they can live with it.

As well, the community could have as much control over the facility it wants, even owning if it likes. At present, the state or the waste generators try to give as little power over the facility as possible to the surrounding community, fearing that the people will close it at the first opportunity.

The reverse Dutch auction idea is simple, yet it has profound ramifications for the way we handle the NIMBY dragon.

In later chapters, I will go into more detail on the auction. For the time being, it is sufficient to know that the NIMBY dragon can and will be slain.

Notes

1. Calvin R. Brunner, "NIMBYists Put Society at Risk," *Waste Age* (March 1988): 65.
2. Jim Temple, "Remarks." In *The Not-In-My-Backyard Syndrome*, ed. Audrey Armour (Toronto, Canada: York University, 1984), 12.
3. Nigel Guilford, "Remarks," ibid., 125.
4. Michael Winerip, "Nimby View on People with AIDS," *New York Times* (5 April 1988): B1.
5. Marilyn Gardner, "Not In My Backyard: Family Day Care Faces Stiff Resistance in Many Communities," *Christian Science Monitor* (21 January 1988): 23.
6. Michael Winerip, "There's No Room in Neighborhood for Mentally Ill," *New York Times* (11 December 1987): B1.
7. Bella English, "On Fencing the Back Yard," *Boston Globe* (27 February 1989): 17.
8. Sam Howe Verhovek, "Neighbors Now More Likely to Oppose Jails and Shelters," *New York Times* (23 April 1987): A1.
9. Ibid.
10. Kathleen Doheny, "Not in My Back Yard!" *Los Angeles Times* (29 January 1990): E1.
11. Connie Green, "As Garbage and Cost of Waste Management Pile Up, Rural Folks Shout: Not in My Back Yard...," *Atlanta Constitution* (6 July 1989): C1.
12. David Young, "NIMBY Spells Protest in Suburbs," *Chicago Tribune* (2 September 1990): 2C-1.
13. Ibid.
14. Eric Zorn, "Maybe Things Never Get Better because Answer's in Your Own Back Yard," *Chicago Tribune* (8 May 1987): 2-1.
15. Dennis Caplice, "Remarks." In Armour, *Not-In-My-Backyard*, 11.

2

A Personal Story:
How I Went from Nerdism to
Devising Siting Solutions

The Start of an Odyssey

I approach the subject of finding locations for unwanted facilities from an unusual outlook. Hundreds, if not thousands, of articles and books have been written on the subject, often from the viewpoint of those who have fought siting authorities. A typical title might be "How We Stopped the Malathion Sprayers (or Mental Health Facility Builders, or Homeless Shelter Advocates) in Their Tracks."

The authors have varying backgrounds, but they usually share one characteristic: their technical knowledge is small. Many of the writers glory in it. If pressed, they might say, for instance, "I really didn't want to know all the technical details of the plan to site that dump. All I knew was that I didn't want it here."

The stories tell clearly enough how the siting authorities were frustrated because of the authors' tactics and quit. They never say where a prison or mental health treatment center *should* be built—only that it should not be next door.

My frame of reference was not the same. I grew up in the technical community, obtaining a doctorate in experimental physics. From there, I went into environmental studies, doing analysis for the Canadian Department of the Environment. From there, I moved into the risk field, at the Atomic Energy Control Board in Canada. For a period, I was Coordinator of the Office of Risk Analysis at Tennessee's Oak Ridge National Laboratory, a major U.S. Department of Energy facility.

In my work on risk, I developed systems for comparing the hazards of different energy forms, such as nuclear, coal, solar, and wind. The results were published in a well-reviewed book I wrote, as well as scientific journals such as *Science* and *Proceedings of the Royal Society of London*. I became a charter member of the Society for Risk Analysis, the major professional society in the field of hazards understanding, and served for a time as a national officer.

None of this means, of course, that those who have taken courses in physics and chemistry are inherently superior to those that avoided those subjects in high school. In terms of finding locations for unwanted facilities, it merely denotes two different approaches to the subject.

Finding a solution to NIMBY is only partly technical. In the extreme, the technical portion serves only as a smoke screen.

For example, in the U.S. endless dollars have been spent on studying soils, hydrology, and other technical fields in order to find "the most suitable site" for low-level radioactive wastes. In Korea, they skipped all these studies and decided to put it in an almost uninhabited island, many miles from the mainland. They did not feel the need to bring in physicists and engineers. Who is right?

Excess Reliance on Risk Analysis Leads to Techno-Nerdism

My technical background could have led to a fatal illness—techno-nerdism. I could have been so caught up in the numbers, equations, and diagrams that I might not have noticed that eventually *people* are involved. An energy system does not exist of and for itself, but for all of society. And it is society that has to find a place to put the wastes associated with all energy production.

I knew all this in the back of my mind, but it did not come to the frontal lobes until I attended meetings on nuclear waste in Tennessee. It was only after listening to ordinary Tennesseeans that I began to discard the vestiges of techno-nerdism—the assumption that people are little cogs in a machine. Nobody worries about cogs.

Confrontations in Tennessee

I first was put on the trail of a new method for siting wastes in the mid-1980s. The U.S. Department of Energy had proposed to store high-level nuclear wastes—spent nuclear fuel rods from reactors—in Oak Ridge, Tennessee. The government said that the rods would be there only temporarily, until they were moved to a final resting place. This last destination is called a "repository" in the lingo.

The attitude of people in Oak Ridge was generally favorable. The town was created during the Manhattan Project of World War II to deal with things nuclear, and many of the townspeople were knowledgeable about the atom. The proposal passed the Town Council unanimously. Polls showed that most Oak Ridgers were favorable to accepting the fuel rods. If the NIMBY dragon existed in Oak Ridge, he was in hiding.

Under the law, the rest of Tennessee had to approve as well. In other words, Oak Ridge by itself could not say yes. Public meetings were held in other parts of the state to discuss the Department of Energy proposal.

The purpose of these meetings was to be education. The citizens of Tennessee outside Oak Ridge would be told that the risks to health would be small, and there would be some small benefits for non-Oak Ridgers. Everything would be conducted on a civilized plane. There would be respectful questions from the audience, and learned answers from the platform.

That's the way the script read. The play put on was completely different.

People in the audience were almost always hostile to those on the platforms. They booed the speakers when they tried to talk about risks and hazards, and cursed when the ever-present jargon was used. The word "disrespectful" was a mild description of their queries. The Southernism of "sassing" was more accurate.

Listeners asked loaded questions like, "Why should we trust you?" and "Who asked you to come to this state in the first place?" A common theme was "Why in hell don't you go back to Washington?"

I attended my first meeting wearing a tie. When I went to the second one, fearful that I might be mistaken for a scientist who was sitting in the audience instead of the platform, I switched to jeans and a plaid shirt.

The flaring emotions and catcalls during the meeting made me understand why Desmond O'Connor of Canada had called these events "the last of the blood sports."[1] Matadors would have felt at home.

If there was any educating done, it was of the scientists and administrators on the platform. They learned, rather painfully, that their estimates of risk were not trusted by the people. In fact, they as *people* were not trusted.

Was the audience made up of rabid environmentalists? Since no poll was taken, there is no way of telling. However, from the questions at least, they seemed to be, as in the movie title, "ordinary people." But they were deeply unhappy ordinary people.

At first, I thought that the audience had gone completely off the deep end. How could they denounce the respected and often world-renowned scientists who were talking sense to them?

Ordinary People Make Some Sense

After thinking it through—and having a few sleepless nights—I realized that those objecting to spent nuclear fuel being brought into Tennessee made a certain type of sense. Obviously, they could not perform risk analyses on their own. They somehow instinctively knew that somehow their personal risk could rise.

It's true that the increase in their risk was probably not very great. Many in the audience were puffing away on cigarettes, and there were few seat belts in use as the pickup trucks pulled into the parking lot. Yet who was I—or anyone else, for that matter—to say how much bigger their risk should be?

The trouble with that way of thinking, I told myself, was that if everyone avoided even the smallest rise in risk, no wastes would ever be buried, anywhere. This was also an unreasonable situation.

Somewhere in the bowels of Washington's Department of Energy building may be the transcripts of the meetings I attended. At least, there was someone on the platform writing down every word. If the Secretary of Energy ever has any restless nights, he or she might descend to the basement, flip through the file cabinets, and try reading some of these transcripts. No matter how well the words were transcribed, he will not be able to gauge the anguish of those anonymous Tennesseeans. And until he can get a grasp of their anger and frustration, he would not be able to come up with a scheme for meeting their valid concerns.

I am glad I went to those meetings, even though I was a little nervous at the time. After hearing those red-hot words, my mind-set was changed. There had to be a better way. But what was it?

A Riot in Western New York

Dawn broke over an almost cloud-free day in Caneadea, New York, on 5 April 1990. That day would mark the first nuclear waste riot in the United States.[2]

It seemed like an unlikely place. Caneadea is a small town of about 2,300 people in Allegany County in Western New York. The county touches the Pennsylvania state line, and is at the northern end of the Allegheny range that starts in the southeastern U.S. To my knowledge, there had never been so much as a demonstration in the town, let alone a riot.

My place in the story? I had arrived on the scene just a few days before, to take up a position in a large environmental consulting firm. I naturally scanned the newspapers, looking for stories on festivals and other amusements. I got the opposite of what I had expected.

Why a mob scene in Caneadea, of all places? New York State wanted to build a low-level radioactive waste site. They went through the usual scientific procedures, and narrowed down the "best" sites to two counties: Allegany and nearby Cortland. There is no "best" site, although the siting authorities pretend there is.

The next step of the authorities was to inspect some of these potential sites, on the ground instead of on paper. That's when the trouble erupted. Many people in the area wanted the visitors to go back to the state capitol.

Protesters were well prepared. One photograph shows dozens of them, bundled up against the cold, with their faces obscured by masks. The masks read, "Allegany—No Dump." The overall effect was frightening.

In addition, the protesters tried other tactics. Six of them rode horses into state police lines. Night sticks were brought out by the troopers, and a melee erupted between the horseback riders and the police. One rider was pulled off his horse and pinned to the ground before being arrested. According to one report, police hit the man, and his horse, several times with clubs before arresting him.

Protesters realized that not all in their ranks could ride horses. Some were elderly, and would have difficulty exerting themselves against young police officers. Six senior citizens, handcuffed to a heavy chain, formed a human barricade across the steel bridge spanning the Genesee River. Their purpose was to prevent the siting commission from getting across the bridge. A photograph shows a bemused eighty-seven-year-old Alexandra Landis, surrounded by video cameras, having her portion of the chain cut with huge snippers wielded by a police officer.

That did not exhaust all the tactics used by the protesters, who clearly had spent much time deciding what to do. They rolled giant snowballs down from the hills onto their unwelcome visitors. (Allegany County still has lots of snow in early April).

After this reception, commission members realized that trying to get through to the proposed waste site could provoke even more violence. State Police Lt. Charles McCole told commission members, "I'm not going to have a riot over a walk on the land.... We can do it. We can get on the site. But I don't see the sense in it. It could turn into a very ugly situation."

Protesters thought the police had used too much force. Sally Campbell, a representative for the Allegany County Non-Violence Group, said, "The state police, I believe, got way out of line, and they're going to suffer in court because of this. I think it's going to make it very difficult for them [the siting commission] to come in again."

Thirty-nine were arrested during the riot, including the six senior citizens who had blocked traffic. The result? None of them had to spend a day in jail. The county grand jury refused to indict any.

The NIMBY dragon roamed freely in Allegany County. If residents had been quizzed about the necessity for finding a place to put nuclear wastes, they would have approved the idea overwhelmingly. As long, that is, as it was not in *their* back yard.

After reading these reports of a riot just a few dozen miles from where I lived, I said to myself, there has to be a better way to find a nuclear waste site, or any other undesirable site for that matter. Forcing these sites down people's throats will, in the long run, just provoke violence.

Are There Any Answers from Psychology?

Paul Slovic, a psychologist with Decision Research Inc., in Oregon, has done some of the best work on how the mind reacts when confronted with dangers. Occasionally I ran into him at Society for Risk Analysis meetings.

Slovic and his group of analysts are best known for their "true *versus* perceived risk" graph. This chart has been reproduced in many magazines and journals around the world, and is one of the best-known in the field.

To develop the graph, Slovic gave members of the League of Women Voters in Oregon a list of sources of risk: automobile accidents, lightning, nuclear power, dam failures, cancer, and so on. They asked League members what their estimates were of the annual deaths in the U.S. from each source. They then compared the estimated numbers to the actual numbers.

The plot of estimated *versus* actual produced an intriguing result. Some of the largest risks, such as deaths from stroke, were underestimated. But many dangers, such as dying from a lightning bolt, were overestimated. The greatest overestimate from the dozens of sources considered was nuclear power. It stood out from the others like a sore thumb.

Slovic has said that nuclear power's abnormal effect is due to a "dread factor." The atom seems to produce a much higher estimate of risk from the public than from experts.

One day, after a long day at a conference, I cornered Slovic:

> Paul, I can understand why some people have the "dread factor" you refer to in your scientific papers. At one time, it referred only to nuclear power, but now it's been extended to AIDS, prisons, and a host of other problems.
>
> Is there any way to change people's opinions on this? After all, if people over-estimate risk, it's more than a mistake on a questionnaire. Society will allocate too much money to reduce the risks that people don't understand and think are bigger than they really are. Is there any way to reduce the "dread factor"?

Slovic had to admit that he did not know how. One of the leading risk analysts couldn't think of a way to change people's minds. Then how could the "educational" campaigns in areas slated for nuclear wastes and other undesirable facilities have any chance of working?

When a siting authority comes into an area targeted for a waste site or other undesirable facility, the "education" campaign usually flops. This does not mean that education is a bad idea; merely that an approach *besides* education has to be tried. We need something more than pamphlets saying how harmless the AIDS center, or prison, or landfill, really is.

Why Pointing at a Locality Produces Hostility

In 1989, a curious book appeared on the top-selling list. Written by Robert Fulghum, a former Unitarian minister, it was entitled "All I Really Need to Know I Learned in Kindergarten." Millions enjoyed the simple insights it conveyed. It was very different from the usual run of thrillers, diet books, and get-rich-quick volumes that often top these lists.

Reverend Fulghum did not say a word about wastes or where to put them, as far as I could tell. He *did* observe that many of the teachings he had learned at the age of five or so had stood him in good stead in later life. They included pick up after yourself, share, and wash your hands.

If he had had enough space, he might have included one lesson that my mother taught me years ago. I can distinctly remember her saying, in her authoritative tone of voice, "Don't point at people. It isn't nice." I can even recall her slapping my finger in a long-forgotten restaurant when I pointed at a diner wearing his hat while eating.

What is the relation between that long-ago lesson and the protests of people in Tennessee, Allegany County, and elsewhere? Everyone—not just diners who wear hats—*still* resents fingers pointing at them. Regardless of the merits of the situation, people who have wastes headed their way feel that of all the towns in the universe, they had the bad luck to be the one selected. They fight back.

When I gestured at someone at the age of five, all I got from my mother was a slight rebuke. The stakes were small; just a potentially insulted fellow diner.

For everyone targeted for unwanted facilities, the ante is higher. Risk analysts can argue that the stakes are smaller than residents of the affected area imagine, but no matter. The finger is still aimed their way.

The moral? Whatever system is devised to site wastes, it cannot, at any point, have a finger pointed at a specific county, state or region. If we need that finger, the battle is over before it's begun. Reverend Fulghum would approve.

Is NIMBY Worldwide?

Is NIMBY a peculiarly American phenomenon, fueled by the fact that we have more lawyers than any other nation? Or does it reflect a fundamental human urge to keep unpleasant things out of sight? After all, Tevye, the milkman in *Fiddler on the Roof,* had to deal with an undesirable individual, from his viewpoint the nineteenth-century equivalent of hazardous waste. He was fond of a toast to the Russian ruler: "God bless the Tsar and keep him—far away from us."

I once spoke with Commissioner Kenneth Rogers, one of the five members of the Nuclear Regulatory Commission. He had recently spoken with French officials on a trip there, and related how they found a site for low-level nuclear wastes.

French authorities said they had narrowed down all the possible sites to one, and then went to the local office-holders. "You've got to take these wastes for the good of the nation," they said. "You've got to look beyond the interests of your town or *département.* It's for *la patrie.*"

That worked in France, Rogers said. But Americans think differently from the French, perhaps having been fooled too many times by appeals to the flag. He told me, as if I did not already know, that such an attempt would never get off the ground in this country.

Take, for example, the proposed high-level nuclear waste site proposed for Nevada. I will discuss this in more detail later in this book. Silver Staters generally hate the idea with a passion. Does anyone think that if the President himself phoned the Governor of Nevada, and begged him to take the wastes for the good of the other forty-nine states, that the trucks would be rolling any time soon? Not too many people hang up on a phone call from the White House. This might be a first.

If the French can get volunteers by flag-waving, more power to them. In the U.S., the time that would have worked—perhaps during the early stages of the cold war—is long past. If we are going to develop volunteer waste sites, we will have to do better than flutter Old Glory.

NIMBY among the Amish

I was on my way to a conference on the NIMBY question and picked up the airline magazine. These publications are usually crammed with light stories on how to achieve success and the latest dance festivals in Dubuque. An article on the Amish people of Pennsylvania had a different twist.[3]

Writing about these God-fearing "simple folk," William Hoffman said, "To their credit, the Amish do not have the 'NIMBY—not in my back yard'—philosophy. While an Amishman might not want a new road on his land, he would not feel relieved if it were rerouted onto his neighbor's property instead. The sense of community is one of the most highly prized values in Amish culture."

Most Amish—there may be exceptions—do not shun responsibility by passing problems onto their neighbor down the road. If an inconvenience has to descend on them, they accept it as God's will. They all could have Harry Truman's sign on their desk, if they had desks—"The Buck Stops Here."

The Amish turn the other cheek. As for the rest of us, not only do we not turn the other cheek when someone slaps us, we are apt to sue all the way up to the Supreme Court.

This attitude is reflected in NIMBY. The old slogan underneath a snake on American Revolutionary-era flags, "Don't Tread on Me," comes to life when we say, "Not In My Back Yard."

If we were all Amish, presumably the NIMBY dragon would curl up and die. There would be no need for new and innovative systems to eliminate him. But they number only a few thousands in a population of a quarter-billion. The dragon is safe for the time being.

The Four Factors to Overcome NIMBY

By this point, the strands of my thinking were fusing. I had finally sorted out the conflicting opinions and studies on NIMBY into some sort of rational order. As a techno-nerd, I had thought that those who did not want these undesirable facilities next door were peculiar at best, and against progress at worst. Now I believed that they were rational, in their way, in spite of not their knowing all the latest techniques in risk analysis.

As a nation, we have to develop waste sites to store our detritus. We must find specific locations for AIDS treatment, day care centers and a host of other facilities that we want in the abstract, but get nervous about in the specific. We cannot just adopt the "leave it where it lays" philosophy, hoping that a future generation will be smarter than us and find a solution.

The time to solve the siting problem is *now*, not next year, not ten years from now. If we had come up with an answer years ago, we would not be caught in the present endless cycle of confrontation and postponement.

I decided that any improved system for siting otherwise unwanted establishments had to be based on a few major factors. First, there had to be a *volunteer* community. Any general knows that an army of volunteers will fight much better than a collection of sullen draftees. For those who doubt this, the experience of the U.S. military in the Persian Gulf conflict (a force made up solely of volunteers) and Vietnam (mostly draftees) is instructive. I did not have to be a military expert to determine that.

Second, the system had to be simple and understandable to all citizens. I had come across the risk analyses performed for the Tennessee nuclear waste site and other unwanted materials during my employment. I could understand parts, but not all. If the Coordinator of the Office of Risk Analysis at a major energy laboratory had some trouble with the risk analysis, how could Joe Six-Pack cope with it?

Third, there had to be compensation for the affected community. I was not saying anything really new here. Many, if not all, books and papers on NIMBY advocate this. They rarely say exactly how big that compensation should be, leaving it for others to solve. If my system was to be better than the present one, it had to have a method for setting compensation that would satisfy most people in the affected community.

Fourth, the people in the affected community had to be able to control the facility as much—or as little—as they wanted. Psychologists and social scientists have often pointed out that the battles over NIMBY are, in a sense, arguments over control. A community wakes up one morning and finds a finger pointing at them from a state capitol or a waste generator, accompanied by "You're the one. It doesn't matter what you think. We've decided for you." If anything can demonstrate to a community that it is powerless, it is the present system of siting unwanted facilities.

So any viable system has to allow the affected community to control the facility, completely. They may wish to subcontract its operation out to private industry. They may want to operate it as a city or county department, just like the water department or the tax collector. It will be completely up to them.

At present, operators of undesirable facilities often set up elaborate systems of advisory boards and the like, saying that this gives the community control. The people are not fooled by this. The boards meet and discuss, discuss and meet. They do not have any real control, as anyone who has sat on one of these boards knows full well. I have known people who have served. Without exception, they told me that their degree of control over the facility was minimal, and close to nonexistent.

Using these straightforward principles, I devised a method that should work. I call it the "reverse Dutch auction." It is an auction of waste sites and other hated works, but of a different type. It should finally slay the NIMBY dragon. I will explain its pros—considerable—and cons—minor—in the rest of this book.

Notes

1. Desmond M. Connor, "Public Consultation—Necessity or Frill," presented at Hazardous Materials/Wastes: Social Aspects of Facility Planning and Management, Toronto, Ontario, September 1990.
2. Peter Simon, "Troopers Arrest 39 at Allegany Site as N-Dump Protest Takes Ugly Turn," *Buffalo News* (6 April 1990): Al.
3. William N. Hoffman, "Window on the Amish," *USAir Magazine* 12 (10) (1990): 68.

3

What Doesn't Work in Siting Unwanted Facilities

A wide variety of techniques have been used to generate public approval for siting wastes and other undesirable facilities. Some of the most prominent have been various forms of risk analysis. I feel regret in saying this, since I have published risk analyses myself. Why have these techniques not succeeded?

Just How Big are the Risks of Undesirable Facilities?

For some engineers and scientists, the risk size is the most important factor. They regard these calculations as scientifically determined.

Risk calculations form the basis for many of the other devices—environmental impact statements and the like—used to persuade people that a nearby controversial site will not harm them. As a result, I will spend much of this chapter on risk.

There are risk analyses for nuclear repositories, hazardous waste sites, chemical plants, and a host of others. They are used to assess the size of the hazards to potential neighbors.

In principle, all that has to be done is publicize the generally low risk numbers. According to the script, people will then be convinced that the facility in question is not so dangerous after all.

There is a gaping problem with this way of proceeding. The implication—rarely stated explicitly—in many risk analyses is that the numbers generated are much the same as the other numbers with which we deal in everyday life—the size of the budget deficit or the speed our car is going. While the size of the deficit changes every day, and our speedometers are probably a little off, numbers of this type are reasonably accurate.

Almost all reputable risk analyses of undesirable facilities have a range of uncertainty attached, and the detailed assumptions are usually explained in excruciating detail. Someone with enough time, patience, and mathematical skill could understand all the unknowns. Yet many of these associated *caveats* are lost in the heated debates over the facility. I do not fault the risk analysts here, because usually their warnings of uncertainties are put down in black and white. But the discussion of the risk analysis often comes down to a single number, and opponents of the facility often say, "Why weren't any uncertainties published? Where is the list of assumptions?" The risk analysts sit silently, gnashing their teeth.

Tens of millions have been spent on risk analyses in the last two decades. Few would claim that its results have changed a thousandth that number of minds. If there is one gong that resonates through the NIMBY battles, it is that *ultimately, the perception of risk may be more important than its calculation.* It was a personal struggle for me to stress the preceding phrase. I have been engaged in doing the calculations for over a decade now. But how people make use of the numbers, rather than the numbers themselves, is the key to risk analysis.

Consider a phone book. I have no interest in flipping it open and running through numbers at random. When I am interested in making a phone call, I look up just one, and dial it. I may misuse the number, just as risk data can be tortured, by misdialling it. That is my problem, not the phone company's. I have no interest in the numbers I do not use.

Risk Perception is a Cultural Phenomenon

Why have risk calculations done so poorly in keeping the NIMBY dragon away? As Brian Wynne, a British risk analyst, has noted, what we do about risks is a cultural phenomenon. An acceptable risk in one place and time is regarded with horror and loathing in another, for a complex set of historic and philosophical reasons.

Consider a few examples. In the U.S., building of new nuclear reactors has stopped over the past decade and a half. This halt is primarily due to fears of increased risk, especially after Three Mile Island and Chernobyl.

In France and Japan, construction goes merrily on, although citizens of these countries know about as much about nuclear accidents as do Americans. The French now produce about three-quarters of their electricity from the atom, a proportion about four times as great as the U.S. Apparently the French and Japanese are less concerned about the risks of this energy source.

On the other hand, Americans usually drink tap water with their meals. Water from a faucet is regarded by most French as a source of danger and contamination. Along the banks of the Loire and Dordogne, wine is regarded as much better for you.

Are the French and Japanese wiser or more foolish than Americans about risk? They are just different. There is no system of logic that can prove the relative wisdom of different sets of risk standards or acceptability.

Within a nation, there can also be varying attitudes. In 1974, as a result of the oil embargo, President Nixon set a national speed limit of 55 miles per hour. He justified it on the basis of saving oil, but also because it would preserve lives. Excessive highway speed kills.

This was not accepted in the Western U.S., though. Almost all of its representatives in Congress lobbied for years to repeal the law, even though they knew that some of their constituents would be killed in extra highway accidents when the rule was lifted. Eventually, in the late 1980s, a compromise was reached. Some Federal roads would have their speed limits raised; others, mostly around cities, would not. As expected, most of the ones with exemptions were in the West.

Does all this mean that Westerners are smarter or less wise than Easterners? They are neither. Westerners can read about highway accidents just as well as Easterners. They balanced the undoubted risk of moving faster with the longer distances they travel, and came up with a different conclusion from Easterners. They were willing to take a greater chance of dying to overcome those distances. A national law looked good on paper. It could not handle different attitudes towards risk of high-speed auto travel.

Even if we knew the risks to within a percent, that knowledge would not be sufficient. Different people, different communities, different nations would act in varying ways on that information. And nobody can say which action is better or worse than another.

Cultural attitudes toward risk can differ within a community. A county or town will accept one risk and reject another that seems smaller, on the surface at least.

Comparison of Risks in Allegany County

An example of this took place in Allegany County, in Western New York, in 1990. Shortly after their riot against a low-level nuclear waste site, described in chapter 2, they agreed to accept a medium-security prison from the state.[1]

Was a risk analysis done? After a fashion. Amy Colodny, director of public information for the state Department of Correctional Services, said that New York's prisons have "less than a handful of escapes per year." The basis for this statement, as well as any crimes committed near the prisons by this "less than a handful" of inmate departures, is not clear in the news reports.

Residents of Allegany County clearly felt that the risks of being terrorized by escaped inmates was less than that of radioactive wastes, even though the latter would never receive a saw concealed in a cake. They made a rough-and-ready risk comparison in their minds, and the radioactive wastes ranked higher.

Part of the reason was that they had *volunteered* for the prison. They thought they had been dragooned on the radwaste site. As state assemblyman John Hasper said, "The prison is a different issue entirely. It was a local decision to seek [it]. Nobody has a gun to their heads on this." That is, unless an escaped prisoner puts it there.

The residents of Allegany County had juxtaposed the two risks, accepting one and rejecting the other. They clearly did not use a sophisticated method of weighing them.

A More General Model of Comparative Risk

All disease causes over one million deaths in the U.S. annually; all cancers of the order of 300,000. The list can be extended down to small numbers of deaths from tornadoes, botulism poisoning, and other unusual causes.[2]

As mentioned in chapter 2, people tend to underestimate risks from some large sources, such as stomach cancer (which gets much less publicity than lung cancer from cigarette smoking) and diabetes. People tend to overestimate risks of unusual occurrences, such as botulism, tornadoes, floods, and vaccination.

Some of these risk comparisons are contained in risk analyses presented to potential neighbors of undesirable sites. I have done risk comparisons myself on relative energy risk. The data I calculated has sometimes been discussed at public meetings. I would like to say that my data and other risk comparisons have carried the day, but I am not certain of this.

The way in which risk juxtapositions are debated in a public meeting follows an almost rigid pattern, like a Japanese Noh play. The experts say that the risks of the landfill (or half-way house, or nuclear facility) are low compared to the risks to which all of us are exposed, such as driving. The surrounding community thinks the risk of the proposed site is much higher than their day-to-day activities like eating high-cholesterol foods or smoking. The abstract numbers come to life in the plaintive complaint often heard from the floor in these public meetings: "Dr. X, we just do not believe you!"

If everyone knew precisely how many died from various diseases and accidents, we could make an accurate comparison of different risks. Then society would allocate money to relieve these problems in a more rational manner than it now does.

Everyone agrees that we often allocate money and technical risk-reducing skill in an often arbitrary manner. If Rock Hudson dies of AIDS, much time and money are showered on the disease. If Rock Smith perishes of the same disease, nobody outside his family and friends pays much attention.

The Society for Risk Analysis, one of the leading scientific groups studying hazards, is not likely to send bulletins like the following to TV and newspaper editors across the nation: "It has come to our attention that people overestimate the risks of floods. The actual deaths from this source annually are about 200; our survey indicates that people generally estimate about 1,000. This means that flood deaths are overestimated by 500 percent. Therefore, you should have only 20 percent of the coverage you now give to floods. Please decrease your coverage of these events by 80 percent in the next year."

However, minds *can* be changed under certain circumstances. Take Perrier water, for example. Twenty years ago, if someone had suggested that shoppers would pay about a dollar for a small bottle of water, imported from thousands of miles away, they would have been regarded as a bit unbalanced. Yet today water, brought at great cost from France and other countries, occupies a niche on the grocery shelves. When circumstances were right—increased emphasis on health, concern about residues in ordinary tap water—bottled water sales boomed. (Sales nose-dived when it was determined that Perrier contained microscopic amounts of a toxic chemical).

Admittedly, some feelings are easier to change than others. I do not know if there is a Liver Board, set up to promote eating that organ, like those that try to promote beef, pork, catfish, and probably even broccoli. A Liver Board would have an enormous challenge. But the fact that some hazardous waste sites have been set up with the assent of surrounding communities shows that the NIMBY dragon is not always around.

The Weight of the Wastes

One traditional way of getting some understanding of risk around undesirable facilities, at least for those that involve wastes of some type, has been to estimate the weight of the garbage. This is a form of comparison, since we implicitly contrast this weight with what we put out on the curb. For example, one estimate of nonradioactive hazardous wastes generated in the U.S. annually is 55 million tons.[3]

But this naked number means very little. First, the number itself has great uncertainty. It might be a factor two or five too low or high, and only a handful of us could catch the error.

Second, few of us understand the value by itself, even if it were highly accurate. Is it 100, 1,000, or 10,000 tank cars?

Third, the risks of these wastes depend on their constitution. Some hazardous wastes belie their name, being fairly innocuous. Others are highly toxic. Without knowing the constituents of these 55 million tons, we cannot say much about their hazards.

Fourth, and most importantly, *where* the wastes are is the crucial factor. If somehow they could be transported safely to the moon, most of us would agree that their risks were not worth considering. Conversely, if they were spread near schools and playgrounds, everyone would admit that they posed a hazard. Merely repeating "55 million tons," like a modern-day mantra, does not tell us *where* this mass is or could be.

For all these reasons, we have not learned much about the risks of waste sites by weighing what goes into them. We will have to do better if we really want to understand risks.

The Size of the Risks

Comparisons of risk can be useful, but at some point we have to look at the hazard numbers themselves. How big (or small) are they?

The undesirable facility that has had, by far, the most risk studies is, of course, nuclear waste. As early as 1983, at least 5,700 studies of nuclear waste had already been undertaken.[4] Neither I nor anyone else on earth has, or ever will, read them all. What do the risk analyses say?

Invariably, the hazards per site, at least in official publications, are estimated as microscopic, of the order of a few tenths, or thousandths, of a health effect such as cancer, annually. I will not quote the exact numbers because that would lead to debates about calculations and assumptions about how and where the nuclear wastes would be stored. Even if the assumptions were changed somewhat, it is unlikely that the calculated risks would be substantial. Yet millions, especially those around potential waste sites, believe these numbers to be much higher. Scientists can measure certain physical quantities to eight or ten significant figures. That is, they may know the value of an electron mass to one part in a million or billion.

In many aspects of risk, if we know the value to within *one* significant figure we are doing well. Knowing that the value is two and not five (whatever the units) can be an accomplishment.

The Environmental Protection Agency is Specific about Hazardous Waste Site Risks

Most reports of the Environmental Protection Agency are printed carefully. The words are typeset, and they are often accompanied by colorful photos and graphs. So when an EPA publication is reproduced cheaply from typewritten material, even though it is supposed to deal with momentous matters, we wonder what is happening.

Yet the publication *Unfinished Business* gives one of the few estimates of the risks of hazardous waste sites that are backed up by a regulatory agency. At the same time, it shows why risk analyses of many waste sites are so difficult to perform.[5]

The incomplete look of *Unfinished Business* might suggest that it was thrown together after midnight by one or two EPA scientists. A staff of seventy-five worked on it, and it has a preface by Lee Thomas, then the EPA Administrator. The risks of waste sites were sketched only roughly not because of lack of effort, but because they are so difficult to capture mathematically.

There are many types of risk: Health, environmental, and others. The simplest to calculate is health, yet even here there are almost as many uncertainties as there are reports. Most discussions of these risks center on cancer. More is known about cancer effects than any other disease from these sites.

Unfinished Business divided the problem areas it considered into five sizes of cancer risk. A total of twenty-nine conditions or sources of exposure to carcinogens were ranked. In category 1, the most dangerous, were such effects as worker exposure to chemicals, indoor radon, and consumer exposure to chemicals.

Attached to most, though not all, of the problem areas are estimates of the annual number of cancer cases and deaths. The two aspects of cancer are not identical. For some cancers, such as that of the skin, the number of deaths is much smaller than the total cases.

For example, worker exposure to chemicals is expected to generate about 250 cancer cases per year. The number of deaths would be lower. For indoor radon, about 5,000 to 20,000 cases of lung cancer are expected annually. Most, although not all, lung cancers are fatal.

These numbers may not be as precise as they seem. First, they are only given to one or two significant figures, as the statistical jargon has it.

Second, there is no documentation for the numbers. One scientist may estimate 250 cancer cases from worker exposure to chemicals; others may estimate 100 or 500. Who is right? *Unfinished Business* says that the right answer is 250, but there is no way of tracing their calculations or postulates. If there is one certainty about risk calculations, it is that the assumptions can shape the final numbers.

Inactive versus Active Waste Sites

In spite of these uncertainties, how do hazardous waste sites rank on the EPA list? The EPA divides them into two categories: inactive and active.

Inactive sites are those that have been abandoned. Money from Superfund taxes and from companies that owned, operated, or sent waste to the sites is supposed to clean them. The main sources of cancer are chemicals such as trichloroethylene, vinyl chloride, arsenic, benzene, and others.

The EPA says that "incidence [of cancer] from six chemicals is estimated at just over 1,000 annually. [There is] considerable uncertainty, since nationwide risk estimates are based on extrapolating from 35 sites to about 25,000 sites nationwide. Individual risks can be very high."

The EPA ranks risks from inactive waste sites as category 2, in the second-highest of their five groups.

The second group of hazardous waste sites are those which are active, still accepting wastes. The EPA ranks active sites in category 2 (second-highest), but lower than inactive sites. They are ranked thirteenth out of twenty-nine problem areas, approximately midway down the list.

Why are inactive sites ranked as more dangerous than active sites? The EPA does not give a specific reason, but it may be because active sites usually try to prevent leaking; inactive and abandoned sites, almost by definition, do not. Old waste sites were usually just dumping grounds, with few if any controls on what was poured over the fence. New sites are subject to a host of Federal and state regulations.

How big are the risks from new or active sites? The EPA says that the data are very spotty, but they think there are likely fewer than 100 cancer cases annually. This would make cancer cases from this source about one-tenth that of inactive or abandoned sites, and about one-thirtieth of one percent of all cancer deaths. These numbers are national totals, not the risk per site.

Public opinion of these risks is another matter. In a poll, Americans thought that the two major environmental problems facing the nation were active and abandoned waste sites, with about two-thirds of the populace being troubled about their real or perceived risks. All the scientific papers and symposia suggesting otherwise were ignored.[6]

Now that we have some EPA estimates on cancer risk from active or abandoned waste sites, what do they mean? It all depends on where you sit. A risk analyst might say, "forget about the 1,000 cancer cases from inactive sites. Those dumps were created many years ago, and we are not building them today. All we are talking about is new, active sites. They're subject to careful regulation and inspection, not like the old days. One hundred cancer cases is 100 too many, but it is only a tiny proportion of the hundreds of thousands of cancers every year suffered by Americans."

A resident of a proposed site might respond, "Fine for you to say. You do your studies and then go back to the university. I do not want to increase my chances of getting cancer by even a thousandth of a percent, even though I do smoke like a chimney. Besides, I am not all that sure that your numbers are right in the first place. That environmental group who spoke to us thinks that your estimates are way too low."

The EPA knows more about the environment than any other agency. Yet when it ventures to make a specific numerical estimate of cancer risks from undesirable facilities, different uses will be made of the numbers. It is the old story of the half-full, half-empty glass. We can never fill (or empty) it by generating ever more numbers.

Calculating risks is a useful activity, one in which I have personally engaged for years. Without the numbers it generates, we would be completely in the dark.

However, the numbers produce, at best, dim light. Some of the hazards of waste sites are clear enough for us to discern their size, but others remain in gloom. Our flashlight of risk analysis just is not big enough to illuminate them all.

Environmental Impact Statements

If risk calculations do not convince people, environmental impact statements will not either. These documents were first written in response to the requirements of the 1970 National Environmental Policy Act. Originally, they operated only on the federal level. Now they are required, in one form or another, by states and even counties.

They are supposed to list all the impacts of a proposed course of action, such as building a hazardous waste site, and show the alternatives to the action. Prior to passage of the law, this information was often hidden from the public.

Risk analyses are a vital part of many environmental impact statements, so almost everything I have said about these former studies applies to these latter documents as well. Even if an environmental impact statement were absolutely accurate in every respect, the way in which its conclusions were perceived would vary from person to person, and from community to community. Environmental impact statement perception is about the same as risk perception.

These documents are, by their nature, much more complex than risk analyses. They supposedly encompass the entire range of a waste site's effects, not just the hazards aspects.

Because they can be so complicated—some run to thousands of pages, in multivolume sets—few people, if any, have the skill and technical training to understand them all, cover to cover. Yet for those with some patience, it is simple to pick out a point or two, buried in the verbiage and tables, to stop or slow down the siting process.

In a typical scenario, a group opposed to a waste site hires someone to read the environmental impact statement prepared by the siting authority, and to search assiduously for errors or contradictions. Given that the study is almost invariably prepared by a committee, the result is a camel, not a horse. Some have three or even dozens of humps, all too easy to spot.

The searchers find a specific point that can serve as the basis of an objection. For example, they might say, "The research says, in volume 17, page 471-A, that cretaceous soil will never leak. This is contradicted in volume 14, page 1791-B, where it is stated that in certain circumstances, this type of soil might do that. As well, the environmental impact statement fails to cite the work of Belushi and his co-workers in the most recent issue of *Journal of Dirt*. They found that this soil will leak when subjected to a pressure of 100 atmospheres. The work is faulty, and has to be redone. Come back in a year."

I myself have read parts of environmental impact statements, and within half an hour found a few points that could serve as the basis of a lawsuit or appeal. It does not take much effort.

For these reasons, these studies usually do not convince people of the acceptability of a waste site. They have probably been used, on balance, more to stop than start them.

Presenting Risk Analyses at Public Meetings

The results of risk analyses and environmental impact statements are often presented at public meetings, where citizens are supposed to calmly weigh all the pros and cons of the siting proposal.

Reality is different. The heat generated during the thousands of these meetings would probably be enough to keep all of New Hampshire toasty warm during a frigid New England winter. But not enough light is produced to illuminate a dog house.

In a typical meeting, the crowd gets increasingly agitated, until the chair has to bring the meeting to a hurried close. Whether anyone really learns anything through the hail of catcalls has never been determined.

These meetings have been promoted as an alleviation of, if not a panacea for, the siting problem. However, this is based on the assumption that participation is equivalent to cooperation. As Richard Bord, a professor of social psychology at Pennsylvania State University, says, "[T]he public tends not to interpret participation programs as exercises in democratic decision making, because they do not trust sponsoring agencies or the technical experts representing industry and government regulatory agencies."[7]

A newspaper report described a 1989 meeting on a proposed New York waste site, "About 5,000 people, many of them chanting 'no dump,' [who] hooted and hollered their opposition."[8]

This was undoubtedly one of the major examples of public participation in the state's history. It certainly was not cooperation.

Why do these people feel this way? Their attitude might be explained by the story of Arthur Dent, the protagonist of Doug Adams' *The Hitchhiker's Guide to the Galaxy*, one of the funniest books of the 1980s. Dent's house is about to be bulldozed to make way for a highway bypass. He knew nothing of this until the day before. Mr. Prosser, the bulldozer operator who also happens to be a lineal descendent of Gengis Khan, is amazed:

> "But Mr. Dent, the plans have been available in the local planning office for the last nine months..."
>
> "On display? I eventually had to go down to the cellar to find them."
>
> "That's the display department."
>
> "With a flashlight."
>
> "Ah, well, the lights had probably gone."
>
> "So had the stairs."
>
> "But look, you found the notice, didn't you?"
>
> "...Yes I did. It was on display in the bottom of a locked filing cabinet stuck in a disused lavatory with a sign on the door saying, 'Beware of the Leopard."

Information on forthcoming projects is not always as hidden as it was to Arthur Dent, but undoubtedly many of the participants in the New York meeting felt that it *had* been. Public participation programs may result in even *more* hostile attitudes than existed before the program began, according to some experts.[9] They say it can actually increase awareness of risks, convince the public that either the will or the skill to eliminate the hazards are unavailable, and generate a negative attitude out of formless opinions.[10]

Citizen involvement is crucial to finding acceptable waste sites. But public participation in the present system of siting frequently generates, not alleviates, opposition to the plans of siting officials.

As with risk analyses and environmental impact statements, public meetings would work if people were not involved. When humans show up it makes life more complicated.

Educating the Public About Risks

A messenger bearing bad news once was liable to be strangled or shot. About the same situation has developed about risk education—do not even talk about safety, because that might make people suspicious.

Education about hazards and risks should make people more accepting of a low-risk waste site. That is not what happened to Ed Brethour, of the Hamiota, Manitoba Community Advisory Committee. Officials asked this small Canadian town to consider a hazardous waste facility. The usual arguments and eventual defeat of the proposal ensued.[11]

Risk analysts sometimes believe that a siting proposal went down in flames because the people did not get enough information. They might say, "If only that last report had been distributed in time, all would have been well."

The opposite occurred in Hamiota. Brethour writes, "[T]oo much emphasis was being placed on the technical merits of the site…the question was also raised as to why all the emphasis on the safety of the site."

In other words, technical people are damned if they discuss safety issues, and damned if they do not. The prescription for misunderstanding of risks has always been more and more education, but Hamiota shows it can fail.

About the same thing happened in Taiwan when a new nuclear plant was proposed. Taipower, the Taiwanese electric utility, had announced plans for the nation's fourth nuclear plant. When decisions had been made about the previous nuclear plants, they had been announced from on high, in keeping with the authoritarian nature of the Taiwanese political system. Now some democratic winds were blowing. The people had to be consulted, at least in part. Some of that consultation would be "educating" them.[12]

A national risk communication program on nuclear power was undertaken, with a budget of almost half a million dollars. The program included debates, discussion group sessions, lectures on safety, and a series of TV programs and newspaper articles that emphasized the merits of the proposed plant.

What were the results? Before the educational program, 42 percent favored the plant, 31 percent opposed it, and 27 percent had no opinion. Afterward, 46 percent were in favor, 34 percent against, and 20 percent retained no opinion. It seemed that the major result was that the ranks of the undecided diminished, presumably because of the information they had gotten. Taipower clearly wanted the formerly undecided to move into the ranks of those favorable. Instead, they moved in almost equal proportions to the pro and anti ranks.

Putting it another way, before the debates and articles, the pro majority was 11 percent. Afterward it was 12 percent—not much of a change.

Taipower could say, "We spent only about half a million, so our loss was not all that great. After all, the plant itself could cost hundreds of millions or even billions. Half a million is only a drop in the bucket."

That begs the question of the effect of this education. If education produces no result, why bother with it at all?

A curious result of the educational campaign was that it *increased* concern about the risks of the plant. Before the campaign, 48 percent of those who were asked about the risk of the proposed plant rated it as slight. Those who had little idea of the risks constituted 29 percent, leaving 23 percent who rated the risks as above "slight," on a scale from two to five.

After the debates, those who said they knew little of the risks dropped from 29 percent to 8 percent, indicating many felt they had learned something about this topic. But the fraction that rated the risks as very serious—five on the scale—rose from 8 percent to 39 percent. That is, those most troubled about risk rose by 31 percent. I doubt that is what Taipower had in mind when they began the educational campaign.

Education produced a Mexican standoff between proponents and opponents of the proposed Taiwan reactor. It had a perverse effect, producing much more concern about risks than had existed before.

How Much Education About Risks Should There Be?

What is the correct amount of information to supply to a community? Books have been filled with claims and counterclaims. Nobody really knows.

In the right siting system, the process should be self-adjusting. Communities that are not really interested in having the facility near them need not be bombarded with probabilistic risk analyses. No need to stuff *their* mailboxes.

Those that have a slight interest will order some pamphlets and books. Towns and counties that are strongly considering the offer of their land will devour every bit of information they can find. For once, the detailed hazard analyses will be read, not used as doorstops. The mismatch between facts wanted and facts supplied will be ended.

Why does not education, in the broad sense, work when siting of undesirable facilities is part of the curriculum? It does its job when students *want* to learn. Any teacher knows that unless a student is motivated, the facts he or she gleans during class evaporate like a drop of water on a hot stove.

In most waste siting situations, the people affected are not interested in learning. They feel, perhaps rightly, that if they became acquainted with the facts, they might be sucked into the entire siting process. So from their viewpoint, the most logical step is to chuck the informative pamphlet, prepared at great expense, into the garbage, and hoot and holler at the desperate scientists at the public meeting next week. Education, while a noble and uplifting idea in other contexts, usually does not work when an undesirable facility is in the wings.

Forcing a Waste Site Down People's Throats

When all else fails, authorities are tempted to use force. That fails, too.

After the "rational" alternatives like meetings and pamphlets have been abandoned, siting authorities sometimes use the police or army. They do not employ force indiscriminately, of course. It's often wielded to clear out demonstrators who are blocking the proposed site.

In all cases I have read where force is used, I am not aware of a single one that has succeeded (e.g., got the facility built in that very site. It has sometimes been built elsewhere as a result of the violence.)

A typical example occurred in South Korea in November, 1990, where 3,000 riot police battled 10,000 demonstrators over a nuclear waste site. This was probably the largest waste riot in history. The plans were canceled.[13]

I suppose that in each of the many cases where strong-arm tactics was used, some police chief or general muttered, "At least we have shown those jerks just who is in charge." In truth, it was the "jerks" who controlled the situation. The presumed object of the show of power, to get the undesirable facility constructed, never is achieved.

After this litany of failed approaches to chasing away the NIMBY dragon—risk analyses, environmental impact statements, public meetings, education, and force—an observer might wonder, What is left? If most attempts to rout the dragon end in failure, how can any system be devised to satisfy both neighbors of a waste site and society?

I have carefully omitted a few factors, such as volunteerism and setting one's own compensation level, from this list. When these and other factors are carefully combined in just the right form, the NIMBY dragon will flee the scene. I discuss the solution, the reverse Dutch auction, in the next chapter.

Notes

1. Peter Simon, "Curiosity Unlocks Prison's Potential," *Buffalo News* (2 May 1990): B1.
2. B. Fischhoff, P. Slovic, and S. Lichtenstein, "Knowing with certainty: The appropriateness of extreme confidence," *Journal of Experimental Psychology: Human Perception and Performance* 3 (1977): 552–64.
3. Peter Sandman, "Getting to Maybe: Some Communications Aspects of Siting Hazardous Waste Facilities," *Seton Hall Legislative Journal* 9 (1985): 437.
4. Carl Walske, "Burying the Nuclear Waste Issue," *Public Utilities Fortnightly* (3 February 1983): 6.
5. Environmental Protection Agency, *Unfinished Business: A Comparative Assessment of Environmental Problems, Volume I, Overview* (Washington: The Agency, February 1987), report EPA/400/02.
6. L. Roberts, "Counting on Science at EPA," *Science* 249 (4969) (10 August 1990): 616–18.
7. Richard J. Bord, "The Low-Level Radioactive Waste Crisis: Is More Citizen Participation the Answer?" In *Low-Level Radioactive Waste Regulation: Science, Politics and Fear*, ed. Michael E. Burns (Chelsea, Michigan: Lewis Publishers, 1988), 193.
8. "Allegany Crowd of 5,000 Assails N-Waste Plan at State Hearing," *Buffalo News* (27 January 1989): 1.
9. D. A. Deese, "A Cross-National Perspective on the Politics of Nuclear Waste." In *The Politics of Nuclear Waste,* ed. E. W. Colglazier, Jr. (New York: Pergamon, 1982), 63.
10. D. W. Orr, "U. S. Energy Policy and the Political Economy of Participation," *Journal of Politics* 41 (1979): 1027.
11. E. Brethour, "Adapting a Siting Process to Fit a Rural Community," presented at Hazardous Materials/Wastes: Social Aspects of Facility Planning and Management, Toronto, Ontario, September 1990.
12. Jan Tan Liu and V. Kerry Smith, "Risk Communication and Attitude Change: Taiwan's Experience," *Resources* (published by Resources for the Future), 14 (102) (Winter 1991). The data on which the article is based was published in the December, 1990 issue of *Journal of Risk and Uncertainty*.
13. "Rioting Over Alleged Radwaste Disposal Plans in Korea," *Nuclear News* (December, 1990): 19.

4

What Can Work—The Reverse Dutch Auction Slays the NIMBY Dragon

A Battle over Hazardous Waste in Braintree, Massachusetts

On 3 April 1991, the Public Broadcasting System telecast a three-hour special on risks. The last half-hour dealt with waste sites. It showed a confrontation in Braintree, Massachusetts, described as a working-class community. The show probably reached more people in its description of a siting battle than all the books and articles on the subject put together.

Clean Harbors Incorporated proposed to build an incinerator in addition to its existing hazardous-waste handling facility. The proposal was met with considerable opposition by the community.

Clean Harbors proceeded in the usual scientific mode. Their toxicologist was shown as saying that the increased risk of cancer due to the incinerator probably would not be more than one in a million. Since one person out of four or five already dies from cancer without a nearby incinerator, this added risk probably would not be too much, he thought.

The next scene showed the massive risk analysis, in 7,500 pages, that had been prepared. The announcer intoned that it had met federal and state regulations.

The following scene showed the president of the company talking with employees about what material should be given to the public. The scene might have been a surprise to some viewers. Rather than a tough-talking and cigar-smoking male executive, the president turned out to be an attractive and rather young woman. As it later turned out, the public's reaction was about the same as it would have been with the prototypical beefy male administrator.

The president said that the information had to be described in one page, a challenge to employees who had just used 7,500 pages to understand the problem. When one employee used the word "emissions," he was stopped. "We want the public to understand the concept in simple language. That is not simple language," the president told him.

Later came an interview with two local activists. They were not too concerned with the risk analysis performed by Clean Harbors, although the 7,500 pages were supposed to impress people like them. It's easy to poke holes in it, they said. We are not scientists, and even we could do it, they noted.

The next scene was a mock "wedding" between the two activists (one male and the other female), in which the woman represented Massachusetts and the man Clean Harbors. The bride was shown as ignoring violations by the groom. The groom then bribed the bride to accept the incinerator. While bribes are, by definition, a bad thing, I will show later that the compensation system I propose for handling situations like this is not bribery. In any case, all this was greeted with chortles from the assembled crowd.

The final climactic scene was a public hearing on the incinerator. As I mentioned in chapter 2, these meetings have been referred to as "the last of the blood sports." This was a typical example. The citizens refused to stop talking when cautioned to do so by the chair, presumably some government commissioner. The meeting was completely disrupted with the arrival of the "Anti-Toxic Ranger." He wore a bright blue cowboy outfit, complete with mask and wooden horse made from a pole. The "Ranger" denounced the incinerator, and shouted that the voice of the people would be heard.

By this point, the meeting had broken down completely into chaos. The camera panned to the president of Clean Harbors, who sat tense in her seat. If the citizens had known she was there, violence might have ensued.

The chair tried to end the meeting, saying it would be continued in nearby Boston. The final scene was of a stocky woman confronting the chair, saying that no vote had been held on ending the meeting. She wanted the chair to hear more complaints from the community.

The battle of Braintree displayed all the defects of the old system. The site was imposed from above. The "consultation" was, in the opinions of residents, just a sham. While a risk analysis was performed, few if any residents could understand it. The analysis, supposedly for the benefit of the citizens, could only be understood by the siting commission, if that. Finally, if any mention of compensation was made during the dispute, it did not register at all with the citizens.

It's all too easy to criticize those crying "NIMBY," as in the battle of Braintree I have described. Writing in Boston, not far from Braintree,

James Goldberg noted that "if the [Massachusetts] State Department of Leprechaun Affairs wanted to site a pot of gold, the war-cry would go up, 'Not In My Back Yard.'"[1]

What was seen in Braintree and many other communities is, in my estimation, a perfectly natural reaction. As Gail Bingham writes,

> Although it may sound heretical or obvious, *local residents are acting rationally in opposing hazardous waste facilities* (emphasis in original). Those wishing to site new hazardous waste facilities must begin by acknowledging (at least to themselves) that even good proposals are likely to impose more costs than benefits on local residents. The reason local residents oppose new facilities is that they have every incentive to do so—the new facility makes them worse off. Thus, the most direct way to respond to such opposition is to change the incentives that motivate people's behavior.
>
> Direct compensation—but not necessarily money—to offset the concentrated local costs of hazardous waste facilities appears to be a promising approach for changing the incentives to oppose such facilities. The rationale for compensation is threefold: [it is] pragmatic, equitable and efficient."[2]

The reverse Dutch auction that I will describe below differs from previous compensation schemes in that it allows the residents of an affected area to *set their own levels of compensation*. It thus contrasts strongly with present systems, where a central authority sets the level from on high.

Seven Stages of Protest

Years before the Braintree battle, it had been foreseen by officials of a Texas radioactive waste siting authority. They identified seven stages of opposition to a facility siting process:

1. Contacts are made and letters written when the public discovers their area is under consideration.
2. Petitions and resolutions oppose the activity.
3. Special interest groups form and outside groups take an interest.
4. An attempt is made to halt the process by legal actions.
5. Political threats are made against licensing and siting authorities.
6. Formal intervention in the licensing process takes place.
7. Public disobedience breaks out.[3]

The reverse Dutch auction solves these problems before they occur. At the same time, it preserves environmental and safety standards and safeguards. It will produce a volunteer community, county, state, or other political jurisdiction willing to accept the facility, whether it's a prison, waste site or oil refinery.[4]

The Reverse Dutch Auction Began on Airlines

A fair and equitable siting system would eliminate most of the deficiencies of the present system, and alleviate almost all the rest. The reverse Dutch auction does this.

This type of auction sounds exotic and mysterious, but it is not. Almost everyone who has ever flown on an airline has encountered it, but it is never announced as such. The key fact about this airline example is that the reverse Dutch auction *works*. It is proven every day in practice.

Because what happens on airlines is familiar to many who have never heard of a Dutch auction, I will present it here.

Consider an airline operating on a small profit margin. It knows that some of the passengers on a specific flight will not show up when the aircraft is ready. It then may sell more seats on the flight than are available, in the expectation that the usual proportion of "no-shows" will hold. For example, if the expected fraction of no-shows is 20 percent, it may sell 110 percent of the seats on a given flight. If this is a typical flight, then 90 percent (110 percent–20 percent) of the seats will be filled.

All this is based on statistical averages. On a given flight, the no-show percentage may be higher or lower than the average. For example, on one specific flight the no-shows may constitute only 5 percent. If the airline has sold 110 percent of the seats, its usual rule, then 105 percent (110 percent–5 percent) of the seats have been allocated. What to do about the excess 5 percent?

At first reading, this may appear to have no relationship to the problem of finding waste sites. But there is. In both cases, some detriment— loss of time for "excess" airline passengers, possible health risks for neighbors of waste sites—is imposed on unwilling citizens. The detriment is different, but the principle is the same.

Consider how the airline situation is handled. The flight attendant announces, "Is anyone willing to take the next flight to the same destination for a payment of $50? No volunteers? Well, how about $100? $150?"

Having witnessed some of these auctions personally, I can testify that they are invariably over in a few minutes, often before many of the passengers are even aware of what is happening. A volunteer or volunteers comes forth, at a price that is acceptable to that person.

The airline auction did not come about by a finger descending from the clouds through which the airplanes fly. Julian Simon, a professor of business management at the University of Maryland, labored for years to convince the airlines and the Civil Aeronautics Board (CAB, since abolished) to use it, even for a day. They continuously refused. Finally, for the first time, President Carter appointed an economist, Alfred Kahn, to head the CAB. Professor Simon realized that an economist would see the merit of his system. Professor Kahn did. While the auction was never mandated by federal regulation, the system was arranged so that airlines would at least try it. They did, and found that it solved their overbooking problems quickly and cheaply—an American success story.

How the Airline Overbooking Problem Would Be "Solved" Using Waste Siting Techniques

Consider what would happen if the command-and-control system, used for finding most hazardous waste sites in the U.S., were employed. In this system, there is almost never a volunteer; someone, usually unwilling, is selected by a higher authority.

How would it work in the case of airline overbooking? Presumably some type of objective data would be gathered, such as the value of time to each passenger. The flight attendants would have to go up and down the aisles, getting passengers to fill out lengthy and complicated questionnaires. They could contain such questions as: "Rate how desperate you are to get to the destination, on a scale from one to ten. How many people are waiting for you? Have you considered taking the train? List your age, sex, social security number, automatic teller machine code and all other pertinent data bearing on the question of who should be ejected from this aircraft."

Some of these replies could be falsified to avoid being the one selected. For example, a passenger might respond, "I'm desperate to get to Dayton to see my dying mother," when in reality all he would do when he got there would be to drink beer at his girlfriend's house.

So there would have to be some type of psychological verification, perhaps by lie detector machines, to ensure that the passengers were not lying. This in itself would add another layer of complexity to the already abstruse system of filling out forms. Exactly how we could determine just who was or was not lying is far from clear, but let's suppose that it could be done.

Finally, some type of ranking of the answers to all these questions would have to be employed, by which the person or persons to be ejected from the aircraft would be chosen. Suppose that after this lengthy procedure, the flight attendants concluded that the bald-headed man in row 15 had to depart.

"Now Mr. Jones, don't make any trouble. We have shown objectively that of all the 100 passengers, you will suffer the least if we put you off. Just look at this four-inch high computer printout. It proves it. Take your time reading it. The equations and the charts should convince you."

Does anyone really expect that Mr. Jones would get off without a protest? There would be threats to write to the airline's president, promises to see them all in court, intervention by other passengers sympathetic to Mr. Jones, and perhaps even a wrestling match in the aisles. In short, the situation would be similar to the arguments that rage about siting hazardous wastes, although on a smaller scale.

Anyone who proposed such an "objective" system as I have described would be regarded as slightly balmy, or at a minimum someone who wants to spread the efficiency of a government bureaucracy to other areas of life. Their proposal would get about a microsecond of consideration by airlines.

The airline reverse Dutch auction works well because each passenger decides for himself just how valuable his time is. Nobody else, no matter how well-meaning or scientific, can do this for him.

Second, no passenger is required to participate in the auction. If they want to, they can just sleep through it all, without anything adverse happening to them. Finally, no specific action is needed to avoid being ejected. Someone solely interested in getting to the destination as soon as possible need only sit tight and do nothing.

What is a Dutch Auction?

The standard auction, much beloved of Saturday mornings in the front yards of farms, is known technically as the English auction. There is almost always more than one bid, and the price rises.

In a Dutch auction, the price *falls,* at a rate determined by the auctioneer. The Dutch auction started in Holland, naturally enough, to sell cut flowers. Since the flowers were highly perishable, the auction had to proceed quickly. The leisurely English auction was too slow.

The amount of time saved in each auction by using the Dutch as opposed to the English auction was probably only a few minutes. However, over perhaps hundreds of auctions in a day the time savings were considerable.

The Dutch auction (sometimes called Chinese and used in churches to raise money) moves fast. Sometimes to speed things up even more in commercial auctions, the auctioneer is replaced by a backward-running clock.

There is only *one* bid in the Dutch auction. When the bidder raises his hand, the goods are sold. There is no competitive bidding, as in the English auction.

For example, the auctioneer might mentally value some flowers in his mind at 500 guilders. He might start the clock at 800 guilders. It then drops to 750, 700, 650, 600, 550, and so on, until someone bids. That bidder gets the flowers.

In the reverse Dutch auction, the price rises, but again there is only one bid. Why a reverse Dutch auction, making life more complicated? The cut flowers sold in the ordinary Dutch auction are desirable. Everyone knows that sites for wastes, prisons, and refineries are undesirable. So the Dutch auction has to run opposite to the regular way. That is, it becomes a *reverse* Dutch auction.

How Would a Reverse Dutch Auction
Work for Undesired Sites?

How would a reverse Dutch auction work? The mechanisms are shown in figures 4.1 and 4.2. The first graph indicates the steps taken until the one and only bid is made; the second, the subsequent steps.

In the following example, it is assumed that a state wishes to site a specific facility, a low-level radioactive waste site, somewhere within its boundaries. The counties are the ones to decide whether to take it. The principles can be applied to any other LULU—landfills, penitentiaries, group homes for the mentally ill, and the like. We can also have other combinations of siting authority and communities, such as sections within a town, county, or state.

The auction begins with an announcement, by the siting authority, of the environmental and safety criteria. These could include, for example, the maximum population density, the minimum distance to a water table, endangered species considerations, and types of acceptable geology. These ground rules are circulated to all counties and interested parties. *There is no reduction of environmental requirements* from the present system.

A county might say, "We might be interested if the price rises high enough, but we do not have the money to gather all the scientific data needed to make an evaluation." To make a bid by a county as cost-free

FIGURE 4.1

Prebid Steps in the Reverse Dutch Auction for Noxious Facilities

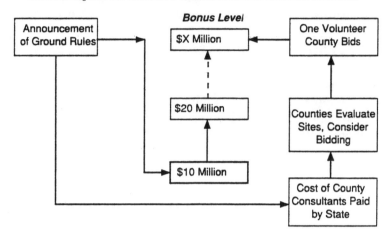

The process begins with announcement of the environmental criteria or ground rules. After each county evaluates these regulations, the auction begins, at a pace to be set by the siting authority. As the price rises, a volunteer county will "bid."

FIGURE 4.2

Postbid Steps in the Reverse Dutch Auction

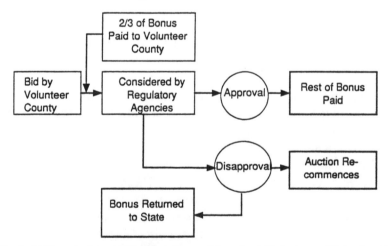

After the bid is made, it must still gain environmental approval. To ensure confidence from the volunteer county that the money for the bonus is really there, most of it is transferred to a temporary trust fund immediately after the bid is made. The bid is then evaluated using the preannounced environmental criteria, and either approved or disapproved. If the latter occurs, the auction recommences, at the bonus level previously reached.

to its residents as possible, the state will pay for the hiring by counties of consultants to find a suitable site, consistent with the ground rules.

The counties can hire the consultants without having to pay the bills. They can also fire them for any reason. This way a county can decide whether to bid without worrying about the cost, or imposing a burden on its taxpayers.

In the past, consultants have been used in the siting process. But the advisers hired were invariably used to show the siting authority that the location on which the agency wanted to build was completely wrong.[5] Finding a place to put the wastes was a good idea, the consultants admitted. But somehow, the siting agency invariably seemed to pick precisely the worst possible spot, according to the consultants hired by the chosen county.

This war of the consultants will not happen in the reverse Dutch auction. There is no need for a community to demonstrate that it is unsuitable, that is, to prove a negative. If its residents have come to that conclusion, they simply do not submit a bid. No proof by consultants or anybody else is required.

Remember the passenger on the plane who wants to get to his destination at any cost? He does not have to lift a finger to achieve this.

Most counties will not consider bidding. However, a handful will. To bid, they must propose a specific site. A general statement that the county would merely try to find a site within its boundaries is not acceptable in the reverse Dutch auction. If this statement were allowed, the door would be open to further controversies, as different potential sites within a county were considered.

How the Reverse Dutch Auction Works—The Auction Begins

How would a reverse Dutch auction operate? We begin after the ground rules, noted above, have been set. The next step is determining the amount of money that a willing county would accept.

Figure 4.1 shows the bonus rising in increments of $10 million, but the difference could be any amount decided by the siting authority. The timing of the increments is also under the control of the authority, as it is in the case of all Dutch auctions. The interval between bonus increments should be long enough to allow counties that hitherto sat on the sidelines to hire consultants to find a site. A county that was blasé at $X million may suddenly become interested at $2X million.

Eventually, a county will come forward, with a specific site, when the *true social cost* of the facility is reached. That is the cost that the rest of us have to pay so the wastes are not in *our* back yard.

The procedure differs radically from the present system, in that a county, not a siting agency, selects a site. In other words, the finger-pointing is gone—forever.

Why should the auction system have a rising bid and not a falling one? We could start off with a high level of compensation, and have it drop gradually. However, if we begin at a steep price—say $1 billion for certain wastes—many people will think their locality should get that bundle of money. As bids come in from states or communities for lower amounts—say $900 million, then $800 million, and so on—it will be a hard sell to get people to agree to the lower amounts. Some will feel they have been "cheated" of the original big bundle of cash. In other words, as Michael Gerrard of the New York law firm of Arnold and Porter has noted, the process of rising or falling bids is not psychologically symmetrical.

Is the fact that a county, as opposed to a siting agency, will choose a site radically new and different? Not really. The procedure is analogous to that employed by the Nuclear Regulatory Commission and its predecessor, the Atomic Energy Commission.

These federal agencies are and were responsible for reactor safety. They *never* chose a site for a nuclear plant. Any electric utility wishing to build one submitted a proposed location to the Commission, and it was either approved or rejected. Presumably, the utility foresaw advantages in building a nuclear plant as opposed to a fossil-fueled facility. The financial consideration formed much of the basis for the siting of nuclear reactors, and plays an analogous role in the reverse Dutch auction.

The Second Stage of the Auction—The County Gets the Money

Figure 4.2 shows the second stage, after a bid has been made. Right after the bid is submitted, most of the bonus (perhaps two-thirds) is transferred to the volunteer county. It is placed in a temporary trust fund until the process is complete. The reason for this has been described by Gretchen Monti, a former official of the League of Women Voters, who has dealt with many waste controversies:

> Once a community has said yes to being the host of a low-level waste facility, it could be under considerable stress...there are likely to be some residents, or maybe outsiders, who will be watching the watchdogs and working to reverse a

community's decision. Worse, in some states it looks like a community will not receive any economic benefit from a facility commonly portrayed as a burden for three or four years after being chosen as the host. What kind of a deal is this?

It may be possible for a community to negotiate some up front payments for needed improvement....[6]

Immediately passing most of the bonus to the volunteer community through a temporary trust fund takes care of these concerns. People in the volunteer community have to know that the bonus is really there, that it's not a smoke-and-mirrors type of financial instrument. The appropriations process of a state legislature or Congress is too lengthy and too prone to detours. Potential hosts are unlikely to have much faith in it.

The implications of the "instant funding" step is that bonds in the amount of the bonus will have to be issued when the amount is known. Who will pay for these bonds? The money can come from only one source—taxes on the waste generators, if we are talking about a waste site. Ultimately, most of the cost will be borne by consumers of the products that generate the wastes—electricity, chemicals, plastics, medical tests using radioactivity, and the like. This means almost all of us.

What about the source of the financial bonus for siting non-waste facilities, such as AIDS group homes or homeless shelters? There again can be only one source—the government, either local, state, or federal. This should not come as much of a surprise. Governments already pay almost all of the cost of caring for these victims. What they have not paid for is finding a place for them to stay.

The Third and Final Stage—Environmental Rules are Enforced

Pre-existing environmental or safety rules will be retained in the reverse Dutch auction. This provision leads to the third stage of the process. The proposed site must be approved, on environmental grounds, by the appropriate regulatory agencies. This step is shown in the middle of figure 4.2.

Will a county try to pull a fast one, like proposing a swamp for a radioactive waste site? Since the volunteer county will have had unlimited access to consultants, it is highly unlikely that it will submit a bid that fails the environmental tests. There is little to be gained by submitting a flawed bid, except embarrassment and being made to look like a fool. The county that submits the bid will be careful, very careful, that it's chosen a valid site.

If the bid is approved, then the temporary trust fund is placed under the control of county officials. They can spend it, as the legal phrase goes, in any lawful manner. The rest of the bonus is paid out as the facility is constructed.

In the unlikely event that the bid is disapproved on environmental grounds, the trust fund is returned to the state. This step is shown at the bottom of figure 4.2. The auction begins again, at the bonus level where it was halted. The process continues until a site is finally approved.

The Voice of the People in the Reverse Dutch Auction

Almost by definition, no county will bid unless it has a *consensus* willing to do so. While some opposition will undoubtedly occur, it will be in a minority.

Opposition to a proposed site has been a majority, not a minority, in almost all towns, counties, and states considered for waste sites and other undesirable facilities. For example, an October, 1990 report said that in Allegany County, the scene of a nuclear waste riot described in chapter 2, 91 percent of the inhabitants were opposed to waste being stored there.

One of the major advantages of the reverse Dutch auction is that it has a system of checks and balances, much like the American Constitution. This analogy is based on how scientific knowledge played a part in developing the ideas behind the Constitution.

John Diggins, a history professor at the University of California, Irvine, notes that while the drafters of the Constitution were not scientists, they used many of the concepts of philosopher David Hume. In turn, Hume thought that he had derived some of his hypotheses from the work of Isaac Newton. Newton being long dead by the time Hume wrote, it is not known what he would have thought of the philosopher.[7]

One of Hume's major conclusions was that sound government comes about because of observations of human behavior, not because of some abstract theories. He thus followed the precepts laid down by the experimental scientists, starting with Galileo, who had overthrown the Aristotelian world of theoretical fixed dogma.

What does this have to do with the reverse Dutch auction? The present siting system is overlain with the dogma that communities slated for a waste site are made up of perfectly rational beings. These citizens are expected to study risk analyses, note that the new facility increases their risk by perhaps one part in a thousand or a million, and conclude that this rise is of little consequence.

Because this dogma does not agree with the way that people think, we get vicious and drawn-out siting battles that make headlines. Diggins writes,

> Hume argued that the aim of government should not be to exhort citizens to attain grace or virtue, but to accept man as a pleasure-seeking creature. Rather than leading to political instability, man's pursuit of material gain will induce productive work habits…as long as government is designed to offset opposing actions. This picture of mankind accorded well with the world view of eighteenth-century science, which was based largely on Newton's three laws of motion, in particular, the third: for every action there is an equal and opposite reaction.

How does this seemingly abstruse view apply to the reverse Dutch auction? Consider a community considering bidding in the auction. At first, when the bonus level is low, there is almost universal hostility to the waste site. This might be called the anti-site *action*. At that time, there is no pro-site *reaction*.

As the bonus rises, some of the hostility diminishes. There are now some people that would grudgingly accept the facility in that community. The increasing bonus has created a reaction to the original virtually unanimous anti-site action.

The bonus keeps rising. Eventually, in one community there is a reaction—the development of a pro-development group. This reaction, over time, overcomes the action—the previous creation of the anti-site forces. That community will be the one that bids. We cannot foresee which one it will be, of course; all we can do is to set the framework to allow the volunteer to come forward.

In the same way, the framers of the Constitution divided government into three branches, knowing full well that there would be conflicts from time to time. They expected that an action by one branch could set up a reaction by another, with the result to be decided as the factions contended. The framers could not predict how the inevitable clashes would end. All they could do is write the Constitution to let the inevitable factionalism and divided loyalties have full play without suppression.

Why the Auction Must be an Integral Part of the System

Why go to all the trouble of an auction if the siting problem can be solved in a simpler fashion, just by asking for volunteers? Consider the experience of Ed Brethour, of the Hamiota, Manitoba, Community Advisory Committee. He had started a volunteer system for a hazardous waste site in that Canadian province. He got some volunteer communities to investigate, but soon found that many of the towns were "de-volunteering," that is, quitting the process.[8] "This ease of with-drawal (from the volunteer process started by the Manitoba Hazardous Waste Management Corporation) became a weakness in the process later on as there was not any commitment on behalf of the community to the process or its completion."

About the same statement was made to me by James McTaggart-Cowan, one of the officials in the Government of Canada siting process for low-level radioactive wastes. He told me that while a number of communities had volunteered for the first stage or two of their siting process, most had fallen by the wayside. He seemed perplexed why this should be so, especially since his program had made it very clear that compensation to the volunteer community was going to be supplied. The word "compensation" is used many times in the literature they have supplied to the communities.

Why, then, this falling away? The people in the volunteer communities are acting quite logically. They read the word "compensation" in the literature, but that is *all* they read. There is no indication of just how large this compensation will be, whether it will be decided by the community, or if the siting agency will retain the final power of the purse. Merely using the word "compensation" in literature is obviously not enough.

Suppose someone is being hired for a job. He talks with the employer, who shows him the office in which he will work. The interviewee asks, "What is the rate of pay?" The answer is, "Not to worry. We'll talk about it later."

The next week, the prospective employee shows up again. This time he is taken around to all the other employees with whom he will work. Again he asks, "What is the salary range for this job?" He is told, "Well, we're working on it. We'll let you know."

If this goes on for one or two more times, the average person in this position would say, "These people haven't really decided what they will pay me. They may *never* decide. It's time for me to look for a job elsewhere."

Because in neither the Manitoba nor the Canadian system is the methodology of compensation specified up front, communities have no incentive to go forward. They will not know how much they will receive until they are almost completely committed to the system. Naturally, there is a tendency to pull back.

The problem can also be put into an economic context. The first phase of volunteering is what the economists call "demand-pull." The siting agency asks for volunteers. Some communities are interested because there is no cost to them. The siting agency supplies any literature and experts that they want, they can withdraw at any time, and other attractive features appeal to them.

What is lacking from the process is "supply-push." There is no push on the communities to go forward. Incentives will be supplied at some stage, but exactly what they will be and when they will appear is left deliberately vague. The communities that either withdraw completely or lack the will to go forward with the process are then acting quite logically. There is nothing pushing them forward.

The Role of Consultants

I mentioned above that any county or state that wanted to hire consultants to look over a potential site could do so at no cost to themselves. At first glance, this might seem to be only a minor part of the reverse Dutch auction idea. As Suzanne Garment, formerly an editorial writer for the *Wall Street Journal* and now with the American Enterprise Institute, pointed out to me, it is not. Consultants may help to solve the entire NIMBY problem.

The role of consultants in the present system is simple: They are brought in by communities and counties to show siting authorities that their area is the worst possible place. The most prominent example of this is Nevada, which has paid many consultants millions of dollars to show that the Silver State is completely wrong for the proposed high-level nuclear waste repository.

Curiously enough, under the federal Nuclear Waste Policy Act, the money for this comes from the U.S. Department of Energy. Congress and DOE had naively hoped that Nevada would spend the money "objectively," that is, weigh both the good and adverse factors.

If there are any good reasons for Nevada to have the waste site, the consultants that they hired seem to have overlooked them. Frustrated, the DOE has accused Nevada of spending money on consultants illegally.[9]

Under the reverse Dutch auction, their role could be precisely the opposite. Suppose a county brings in a consultant. The county is not really sure that they should go ahead. The consultant sees a location that could be suitable. They will naturally take the lead in trying to convince the people of that county to go forward. If the county does so, the consultant will almost certainly get more contracts. The consultant, in most cases, will serve as an advocate for a site it has considered.

The best part is that the consultant has no ties to the siting authority. The siting authority pays for the consultant, but has no control whatsoever over the latter's conclusions. In other words, an independent company, not an agency from the state capitol or Washington, is making the case for building the waste facility. From the viewpoint of the local people, this will be much more acceptable.

Of course, they do not have to take the consultant's advice. If they do not, there will be another county that *does*.

The Present System is Unworkable

There is a long series of deficiencies in the present system of siting waste facilities, halfway houses for prisoners, oil refineries and a host of other unpleasant entities.[10] The reverse Dutch auction resolves most, if not all, of them.

First, the focus of the present siting system is on administrative or procedural issues, rather than the substantive concerns in the minds of potential site neighbors. For example, a siting commission will typically point out that it has met every legal requirement laid down by the state legislature or Congress. Likely neighbors of the proposed site tend to care little for these administrative rules. This becomes painfully evident at public meetings held to discuss the waste site, where discussions of what the laws and regulations say are usually met with hoots and whistles.

Second, public participation is usually postponed until major decisions have been made by the siting or licensing agency. This makes it difficult for competing views to be heard. In a typical process, a siting agency will narrow down the choices to a few, and then tell the public in these areas they are on the final list. Residents of those regions often contend that the purpose of participation, to have the voices of affected citizens heard at all stages, not just the last one, has been defeated. They are right.

Third, the above two approaches tend to emphasize "adversarial, rather than consensual, relationships aimed at proving the other side wrong."[11] It all becomes a battle, rather than a meeting of minds. The meetings and demonstrations in or around Allegany County are representative of hundreds, perhaps thousands, that have taken place nationwide in the 1980s and 1990s. Heat, rather than light, is produced at these types of meetings and demonstrations.

Fourth, the laws and regulations tend to be highly complicated and detailed. This in turn reduces public participation to a contest between opposing legal teams. Citizen involvement can be primarily to fund one of these teams.

Bill Colglazier, formerly professor at the University of Tennessee, notes that the two-page, low-level radioactive waste act passed by Congress in 1980 apparently required "a more complex type of fairness" when the twenty-four-page agreement for the Southeast Regional Compact was written. This was a group of states that was supposed to get together to find a radioactive waste site somewhere within their region.[12]

The law then evolved to "minutely detailed attempts to maintain procedural fairness in the face of an inevitably unequal distribution of perceived risk, as evidenced in the Massachusetts low-level radioactive waste bill, 49 pages long."

As another example, the complexity of the 1985 amendments to the 1980 federal law on low-level radioactive waste was illustrated by then-Congressman Manuel Lujan, later Interior Secretary. He noted that the "only living human being who completely understands exactly" how the new public law would work was the Congressional staff person who aided in drawing up the bill."[13] Timothy Peckinpaugh, a lawyer in Washington, D.C., writes that "this remark is a sad commentary on the way Congress makes public policy. It is certainly disappointing that the only individual who understands this legislation is a staff aide who was never elected and [who] did not cast a vote on passage of the bill."[14]

From the viewpoint of public opinion, a logical question then is, "If members of Congress who have dealt with this bill do not understand it, how are citizens expected to do so?"

Fifth, the approach to siting has been scientific and technological. But as Richard Bord, a professor of social psychology at Penn State, writes: "Bringing in more scientific experts will do little to allay public fear; while it cannot be unambiguously proven that low doses of radiation cause specific problems in large populations, it likewise cannot be proven that it does not contribute significantly to health problems. Fear in this case is certainly rational.... Given the lack of expert consensus, the safest response is to avoid the material if possible."[15]

Fear of waste sites may be, as Alvin Weinberg, former head of Oak Ridge National Laboratory, wrote decades ago, "trans-scientific," that is, beyond the capacity of science to address it. Yet the present approach on siting has been to deal with the subject as if it were *solely* scientific.

Scientific studies of risk are certainly necessary, and form the basis for many siting regulations. To take a phrase from high school geometry, to prove a theorem, logic that is both necessary *and* sufficient is required. The scientific approach, by itself, has not been sufficient.

End Runs

Sixth, it has often seemed to many politicians that it would be impossible to get public acceptance of unwanted facilities. As a result, a number of attempts to circumvent the elaborate procedures laid down in legislation and regulations have been made. When these have failed, they have tended to bring even the reasonable aspects of the present system into disrepute.

A major end run example, one that shook the nuclear waste community, was the Monitored Retrievable Storage system, proposed by the U.S. Department of Energy.[16] I attended some of the raucous public meetings that were part of the siting process.

The MRS was envisioned as a way station along the road to an eventual high-level nuclear waste site somewhere in the western U.S. It was approved by the Oak Ridge City Council and the Roane County Commission, both in Tennessee. This apparently was the first time that elected bodies had voted unanimously to accept high-level nuclear wastes under *any* circumstances.

This acceptance was voided by the state of Tennessee, which had the ultimate political authority over approval. The Volunteer State (ironically nicknamed in this context) saw few, if any, benefits for the state as a whole. Tennessee thought that getting the nod of the local communities without its own OK was an "end run" by DOE.

Adding to the aura of an end run was the elaborate court case mounted by the Department of Energy against Tennessee. It tried to show that the state did not really have a veto, even though the legislation stated so clearly on its face.

Some good may have come out of the MRS fiasco. Although not planned by any of the officials pushing it so vigorously, the riotous scenes at the public meetings that I attended got me to thinking about the entire siting mess. The reverse Dutch auction is the result.

More recently, the New York State low-level radioactive waste siting commission suggested a site at the former West Valley, New York, reprocessing facility.[17] This thought came to them after the riot in nearby Allegany County I described in chapter 20. However, this site was already barred by state law from accepting further wastes. West Valley people saw this as an end run around state regulations. "We don't want any more wastes brought into the site," said one member of an opposition group. "Nothing new has been brought in for 15 years."

These and many other aborted end runs have decreased the viability of the present process. If the existing system is indeed workable, as its proponents state, there should be no attempts to circumvent established political authority, or to try to get around existing laws and regulations.

The Present System is Highly Centralized

Seventh, the centralized system in use "distorts information and suppresses independent evaluation," according to Charles Malone of Nevada.[18] That is, site-finding headquarters will inevitably possess more data and experts than citizens near a potential site. Typically, a siting agency will spend millions (or billions, in the case of the proposed high-level nuclear waste repository) on its own studies. It will dole out only a few thousands to local communities to hire their own experts.

These communities, because their budgets are so small, can make only the weakest of efforts to evaluate the deluge of data supplied by the siting agency. This leads to frustration and, finally, denunciations of all the data that the siting agency has collected.

Eighth, much of the present system works in secret, at least from the viewpoint of the affected community. Public participation in decision-making is usually postponed until late in the process. Until that point, key choices are frequently made behind the closed doors of siting agencies or legislative committees.

In principle, the legislation creating waste siting authorities is avowedly open. Citizens' committees upon citizens' committees are piled up in the lengthy clauses. The reality is different. Ask any affected community about the degree of democracy in most siting decisions, and you are likely to get a hostile response. "They said they would supply us with the documents at the right time," a typical answer might begin. "But the real documents on which they made their plans were kept from us."

Ninth, any existing level of compensation is set unilaterally by the state or federal government. New York said it would pay $1 million in lieu of taxes annually to a county that would accept low-level radioactive wastes. If any counties were asked what they thought of this, there is no record of their response.

The amendments passed by Congress in 1987 to the Nuclear Waste Policy Act specify payments of $10 million or $20 million annually to a state accepting high-level nuclear waste. The amount would depend on the extent of construction of the facility. No state was consulted on the amount.

No Nevadan (the Silver State is clearly the target of the legislation) was on the conference committee that produced the final law. In almost every other law strongly affecting a specific state, a representative of that state is in the group that reconciles the House and Senate versions. Not this time.

The question can be put simply: How can a bargain be struck if only one side talks about the price?

In summary, the existing process for choosing sites has a multitude of defects. Can the reverse Dutch auction overcome them?

Advantages of the Reverse Dutch Auction

In the following, each of the deficiencies of the present system that I have described in the sections immediately preceding is addressed.

Administrative and procedural issues are much reduced in importance with the reverse Dutch auction. When it's in their interests, citizens of a potential volunteer community will evaluate risks and the environment carefully. Until then, it's a waste of time to ask them to do so. Their most logical response is to tell a siting agency to go away.

Public participation, an ostensible goal of the present system, is now vastly increased. Residents of each county must decide if they will make a bid, and if so, at what stage. The decision will be completely in their hands.

Because of its inherent scientific nature, devising environmental ground rules or criteria has only minimal public participation. While the public will not take a major role in formulating detailed rules, members of a specific community need not worry about being targeted by these regulations. Previous attempts to tamper with ground rules to exclude or include specific counties or regions will not be repeated under the reverse Dutch auction.

For example, when the Monitored Retrievable Storage System for high-level nuclear waste was first being considered the Department of Energy (DOE) came up with a mathematical model. It supposedly showed that Tennessee was the most logical site from the viewpoint of minimizing transportation costs.

Senators Al Gore (later Vice-President) and Jim Sasser from Tennessee denounced DOE, saying that the math had been altered to ensure that the Volunteer State was the victim.

The government denied this, But it was later admitted by Ginger King, representative for the Department, that Ohio would really have been the best choice to produce the lowest transport costs. Senators Gore and Sasser, while not mathematicians themselves, could easily figure out that the laws of mathematics had been twisted.

The adversarial role of the present system will be substantially lessened, although not eliminated. The contest between the siting authority and potential hosts will disappear, since the volunteer county will be self-selected. However, there will likely be residual differences *within* a county. Unanimity can never be achieved by any conceivable siting system.

The entire system will be much simpler. Much of the existing complexity has derived from attempts to be fair to all parties, and yet at the same time ensure that a site is built. Under the reverse Dutch auction, each county will decide for itself what is equitable. If it decides the procedure as a whole is unfair, or the price is not right, it will not bid. Since the decision is placed in the hands of the counties, there is much less need for a complicated balancing of interests.

Science will Still be Part of the System, but Only Part

The objective approach will still be retained, at the beginning and end of the process. At the start, the environmental regulations are publicized. In the final stage, we make sure that these standards are met. All this is clearly necessary.

Remember the criterion for a geometric proof: necessary *and* sufficient. The sufficient aspect of the system is supplied by the auction, during which residents of various communities will balance objective, subjective, and financial aspects of the site, and come to conclusions.

There should be no reason for a siting authority to attempt an end run on the process. All steps, including the increase of the bonus, will be taken publicly, so any attempt to influence unduly a specific community could not be mounted. Since a site is assured if the bonus rises to a sufficient level, an end run would be counter-productive.

Information would not be centralized under the reverse Dutch auction. Data on possible sites would be gathered by consultants hired by communities. The citizens, not just a few experts, will know what is happening. The siting commission will respond to requests for information by the counties, but these transfers of data would be initiated by the counties (or their residents), not the siting authority.

Secrecy would be abolished. The rising level of the bonus would be widely known. If one county was on the verge of bidding, that fact could be determined by others. The remaining counties would have to decide whether they would bid at that point. There would be no stores of private data and analyses at a central authority. Since the ultimate bidder would be the counties, they would gather information themselves.

Finally, the level of compensation would be set by the volunteer county, not a siting commission. A county regarding the bonus as too low would not bid.

The reverse Dutch auction then meets all the deficiencies of the present siting system. It eliminates most inadequacies completely, and reduces the importance of the remainder substantially. The "top-down" approach is reversed to a "bottom-up" system, in which the eventual recipients of a waste site can weigh costs and benefits without external interference.

Disadvantages of the Reverse Dutch Auction

All potential siting systems have drawbacks. Those peculiar to the reverse Dutch auction are as follows.

The final price in any auction cannot be predicted exactly. However, a number of economists, led by V. Kerry Smith of North Carolina State University, have analyzed likely prices. There is thus some basis for estimating the final bonus payment.[19] A study by Hubbard in the Pacific Northwest, described in chapter 7, can be used to calculate some maximum bids.

The unlimited liability to the state and, ultimately, waste generators, could be corrected by a slight variation of the Dutch auction—a *cap* on the bonus. In this variation, the state would announce in advance, for example, that it would pay no more than $X million as a bonus. If that level were reached and no acceptable bids were made, the bonus level would begin to *decrease*, rather than increase. There would still be an incentive for a county to bid, before the bonus disappeared completely. There would be no incentive for a county to wait until the level reached the maximum, since a competing county could bid at any time.

The reverse Dutch auction system could, in some cases, add to the total cost. However, these costs have mounted substantially in the past,

FIGURE 4.3

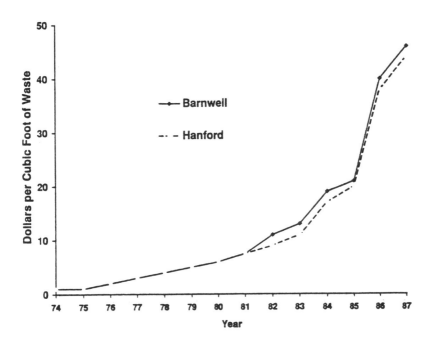

Low-level radioactive waste burial charges at Hanford, Washington and Barnwell, South Carolina, disposal sites. The cost per cubic foot has increased greatly since the mid-1970s.

long before an auction system was proposed. For example, figure 4.3 shows how low-level radioactive waste burial charges varied from 1975 to 1988 at the two major national sites.[20] There is an approximately fifty-fold increase over slightly more than a decade. From 1983 to 1987, the cost increased about 30 percent annually. Because these two sites were a monopoly, prices escalated substantially.

None of this enormous increase was because the waste itself became any more dangerous. It was merely *perceived* as more hazardous. Thus, the price skyrocketed.

Now suppose the reverse Dutch auction had been in place in 1975. New sites for radioactive wastes would have been found. There would have been no reason for the cost to soar out of sight. In other words, the sooner the reverse Dutch auction starts to work, the lower the total cost will be. It can *reduce* the system's total cost.

Some contend that soaring disposal costs have been a good thing, because they encourage less production of wastes. However, in this book I have not tried to determine how wastes can be minimized, but rather how to find sites. There will always be some wastes from civilization, and we will have to find sites for them. I do not believe that the need for any waste site can be pre-determined. The market has to determine that, not an expert or me. In chapter 5, I quote from a seminar held by Prof. Mary English, of the University of Tennessee, in which siting experts noted that past attempts to estimate "needs" for waste sites had been failures.

Elimination of the differences of opinion between counties and a central siting authority will not abolish differences within a county or community. However, in the volunteer county, opposition will be in a minority, by definition. The minority could be negligible or just under 50 percent depending on the approval process chosen by the volunteer county. A county wanting to be really sure could set the approval level at 90 percent, for example.

In addition, as Michael O'Hare states,

> The smaller the group, of course, the more likely that psychological pressure can force cooperation. A neighbor considering opposition to a dump site must think about how the people he meets on Main Street will react to what they see as his selfishness, while they are equally motivated to propose a well-managed dump and perhaps some new street paving. All can look ahead to future opportunities to balance losses and gains in the same small population.[21]

If one and only one site were viable, then the community in which it was located could practice extortion. Almost all siting authorities have considered sites in more than one community, stating that there is more than one suitable site. For example, the original siting plan for the high-level nuclear waste repository evaluated about a dozen sites, later narrowing them down to three. The combination of more than one site and an auction eliminates the possibility of extortion.

The Rich and the Poor

It is possible that a poorer community will bid, although environmental criteria may alter this. Because this is such an important question, I reserve chapter 10 for it. Briefly, I find that rich communities, regardless of the siting system used, will almost always be able to escape facilities they do not want. The auction system will not change the relative position of rich *versus* poor all that much.

As the bonus level rises, waste generators may be distressed by the headlines about the increasing amount. However, the reverse Dutch auction *guarantees* a site. Under the present system, news stories appear every day on the difficulties of finding a site. The Braintree battle and the Allegany County altercation are only two of many. Even with this turmoil and argument, waste generators still do not know if they will get a site. Once the installations are built, the frequency of adverse news stories is likely to decrease.

A number of studies have mentioned compensation as only one of a possible number of incentives to waste site neighbors.[22] These studies suggest that compensation is less important to citizens than other nonfinancial factors, such as having the legal right to shut down the undesirable entity at any time, and the ability to choose (or dismiss) its operator.

If these studies were taken at face value, a reverse Dutch auction, or any other monetary compensation scheme, would be of little benefit in finding a site. This conclusion would be incorrect, for a number of reasons.

First, the *level* of financial incentives is rarely specified in these studies. It is often referred to merely as "compensation". But the size of the compensation determines, in large part, its acceptability.

For example, consider the case of Allegany County. New York State offered to pay $1 million annually to its 50,000 residents to accept low-level radioactive wastes.[23] This works out to $20 a year, less than the cost of taking a family of four to the movies once. For Allegany Countians, the payments are obviously too small.

Second, offering financial incentives does not preclude non-financial ones. For example, requiring the site operator to hire locally, having local personnel participate in health monitoring, and so on, could still be employed besides a reverse Dutch auction. These nonfinancial incentives would have to be negotiated, not auctioned.

Third, many financial incentives can be included in the total bonus of the reverse Dutch auction. For example, money to hire independent experts, compensation for loss of property values, permanent trust funds, scholarships for the children of site neighbors, tax relief and a host of other financial-based measures could be funded from the bonus.

In summary, the disadvantages of the reverse Dutch auction are minor compared to its advantages. Even where deficiencies exist, some can be rectified by small modifications of the procedure.

If one word had to describe the reverse Dutch auction, it would be "incentives." The broadest definition of incentives is:

mechanisms by which affected communities and their residents are assured of being at least as well off, if not better, than before the undesirable land use was sited in their midst. Incentives, as with environmental mediation in general, would not pre-empt present laws, nor replace them; rather they would simply go beyond current practices of conflict resolution.[24]

When the question of incentives arises, the next question inevitably is, "Are they bribes?" John Sorensen wrote they "cannot be viewed as bribes that serve only to undermine pluralistic ideals. Incentive systems are not a means of buying off the opposition, but rather a device for reaching a compromise on substantive environmental conflicts."[25]

Financial incentives are used by the state in a wide variety of endeavors, although they may not always be labeled as such. For example, Post Office walls show portraits of actual or alleged felons. Rewards are offered for their apprehension. While a civic-minded citizenry should, in principle, capture these individuals without thought of money, the state has found that it can achieve its ends by supplying rewards.

If government can use incentives to attempt to solve difficult problems like crime, then they can be employed for the equally troublesome challenge of siting nuclear and toxic waste sites. Bribes differ inherently from incentives, because the former are always given and accepted *sub rosa*, or secretly. In the reverse Dutch auction, all steps would be public and open to scrutiny. The possibility of a bribe does not arise.

Purposes of Incentives

Incentives serve at least three functions:

1. They *preserve* the status quo by reducing negative impacts and compensating for psychological damages.
2. They *improve* the status quo by rewarding site neighbors for assuming risks through which others benefit. Most of the sites planned for low-level radioactive wastes generate little if any of the material themselves. Nevada, planned as the site of a repository for nuclear fuel rods from power plants, has none of these plants itself.
3. They *give access* to the decision-making process, an access that would otherwise be denied. This could include independent monitoring of physical and biological effects, for example.

Monti wrote:

[Economic incentive packages] are a very necessary part of the siting...effort—the chance to publicize the one reason any...community would want a disposal facility. There is a fine line between...selling a package of benefits and selling a bill of goods, however. I've seen some tendencies towards the latter, such as...deciding *for* a community what it will want in the way of incentives or compensation.[26]

Incentives will be successful or fail not merely on their financial level, but on the form in which they are offered and presented. In the reverse Dutch auction, communities set their own level of compensation, rather than having it decided in a state capitol or Congress.

States already offer some incentives to accept undesirable facilities. Massachusetts, Wisconsin, and Rhode Island have passed statutes that incorporate financial incentives and other types of negotiations between the local community and the developer.[27]

In Massachusetts, the key permission under the statute is that between the operator of the undesirable facility and the "second-tier" siting authority—the local committee formed after an operator proposes a facility.[28] A community adjoining the potential waste site may object to noxious material passing over its roads, even though it is not deposited there. Thus both the proposed host and abutting communities are represented on the second-tier siting authority. A wide variety of incentives, both financial and nonfinancial, may be offered by the developer to the second-tier siting authority. The state acts as a facilitator, not a body that imposes its will.

International Incentives

In France, people living around nuclear power plants for years got cheaper electricity than those who lived further away.[29] This accounts in part for the approximately three-quarters share of total electricity generation that nuclear power produces there. Constance Hornig, a lawyer and Fulbright scholar in Japan, has studied that nation carefully. She writes:

> The Japanese government's primary strategy for overcoming NIMBY [about solid waste landfills and trash-to-waste facilities] is to give community benefits to balance the drawbacks.... Waste-to-energy plants have sunken truck ramps and extra thick walls to reduce noise. In some areas, even the steam is treated so that it is not mistaken for smoke. Monitors with large numbers are posted in public view to demonstrate compliance with environmental laws....
>   A combustion facility is built as part of a community center, offering hot baths, gymnasiums, meeting rooms, swimming pools, baseball fields, gardens, goldfish ponds, greenhouses or centers for the elderly, often heated by steam produced by the burning trash."[30]

These amenities could be constructed by U.S. facilities if the financial incentives were high enough, or the reward could be channeled to other purposes. In other words, the auction would give communities enough money to buy new band uniforms, build goldfish ponds, reduce taxes, and produce a host of other benefits.

Incentives can be considered as a total payment, to the present and future generations, for all costs of an unwelcome facility, real and speculative. As the National Conference of State Legislatures writes,

> The actual sociological, psychological and economic effects of a [low-level radioactive waste] facility on a community is difficult to quantify. Thus an incentive program should be considered. Compensation of the host locality and state should be considered for actual harm and perceived harm. A comprehensive incentive plan...should redress impacts on local property values, taxes and public services.[31]

Conclusions

The reverse Dutch auction allows a market-based solution to a seemingly insoluble problem, at the same time protecting environmental standards. There are no other proposals for siting uninvited sites that combine these features.

Because it is market-driven, rather than bureaucracy-driven, it removes the alleged coercion—or attempted coercion—that has marked most attempts to site these facilities. As a result, potential host communities can make decisions in a calmer climate. The NIMBY syndrome has been useful in alerting policymakers of public concerns, but it is now time to send the dragon packing.

Notes

1. James F. Goldberg, "Beyond NIMBY," *Boston Globe* (22 December 1987): 19.
2. Gail Bingham and Daniel S. Miller, "Prospects for Resolving Hazardous Waste Siting Disputes Through Negotiation," *Natural Resources Lawyer* 17 (3) (1984): 473.
3. R. V. Avant, Jr. and L. R. Jacobi, Jr., "The Conflict Between Public Perceptions and Technical Processes in Site Selection," paper presented at "Waste Management '85", Tucson, Arizona, March 1985.
4. It was first described in Herbert Inhaber, "Triple Obstacles to Power Generation: Risk, Greenhouse Effect and Nuclear Wastes," in *Power Generation Technology* (London: Sterling Publications, 1989), 15.
5. Charles Malone, "Ethics and Organization," *Environment* 31 (4) (May 1989): 3.
6. Gretchen D. Monti, "The Role of the Public in Siting and Regulatory Issues." In *Proceedings of the Ninth Annual DOE Low-Level Waste Management Program*, (Idaho Falls, Idaho: EG&G Idaho, February 1988), 1.
7. John Patrick Diggins, "Science and the American Experiment," *The Sciences* 27 (6) (November/December 1987): 28–31.
8. Ed Brethour, "Adapting a Siting Process to Fit a Rural Community," presented at "Hazardous Materials/Wastes: Social Aspects of Siting Planning and Management", Toronto, Ontario, September 1990.

9. "GAO Accuses Nevada of Misusing Grant Money," *Nuclear News* (September 1990): 97.
10. John H. Sorensen, Jon Soderstrom, and Sam A. Carnes, "Sweet for the Sour: Incentives in Environmental Mediation," *Environmental Management* 8 (4) (1984): 287.
11. Ibid.
12. E. William Colglazier and Mary E. English, "Low-Level Radioactive Waste: Can New Disposal Sites Be Found?" In *Low-Level Radioactive Waste Regulation: Science, Politics and Fear*, ed. Michael E. Burns (Chelsea, Michigan: Lewis Publishers, 1988), 215.
13. *Congressional Record* (9 December 1985): H11411.
14. Timothy L. Peckinpaugh, "The Politics of Low-Level Radioactive Waste Disposal." In *Low-Level Radioactive Waste Regulation*, ibid., 45.
15. Richard J. Bord, "The Low-Level Radioactive Waste Crisis: Is More Citizen Participation the Answer?" In *Low-Level Radioactive Waste Regulation*, ibid., 193.
16. Herbert Inhaber, "The MRS—Issues in High-Level Waste Storage," *Journal of Hazardous Materials* 15 (1987): 241.
17. Jon H. Sorensen, "Panel Eyes W. Valley to Store N. Wastes," *Buffalo News* (6 May 1990): B1.
18. Malone, "Ethics and Organization."
19. V. Kerry Smith and W. H. Desvousges, "Value of Avoiding a Lulu: Hazardous Waste Disposal Sites," *Review of Economic Statistics* 68 (2) (May 1986): 29.
20. Robert A. Shaw, "Low-Level Radioactive Wastes in the Nuclear Power Industry." In *Low-Level Radioactive Waste Regulation*, ibid.
21. Michael O'Hare, "'Not in *My* Block, You Don't!' Facility Siting and the Strategic Importance of Compensation," *Public Policy* 25 (1977): 407
22. Sorenson et al., ibid; Bord, ibid.; and A. Dan Tarlock, "Siting New or Expanded Treatment, Storage or Disposal Facilities: The Pigs in the Parlor of the 1980's," *Natural Resources Lawyer* 17 (1984): 429.
23. "State Must Impose Waste Site, but with Payback to 'Host,'" *Buffalo News* (13 September 1989): B2.
24. Sorenson et al., ibid.
25. Ibid.
26. Monti, ibid.
27. O'Hare, ibid.
28. Tarlock, ibid.
29. Remy Carle, "Why France Went Nuclear," *Public Power* (July/August 1981): 58.
30. Constance Hornig, "Japanese Have Working Plan to Handle Trash," *Buffalo News* (26 April 1990): C3.
31. J. M. Jordan and L. G. Melson, *A Legislator's Guide to Low-Level Radioactive Waste Management* (Denver, Colo.: National Conference of State Legislatures, 1981).

5

What the NIMBY Literature Tells Us

Of making books there is no end, so Voltaire assures us. While he did not live to see the explosion in articles and books on the NIMBY phenomenon, his aphorism lives on.

I will not attempt to discuss all the NIMBY-related literature that has appeared in the last few years. Rather, I have subjectively selected a few that seem more important than the rest. As well, in the following I have not attempted to evaluate all aspects of the books and papers I consider. I look at them primarily from the view of compensation and the reverse Dutch auction, which are the focus of this book.

English on Low-Level Radioactive Wastes

Mary English's book concentrates on one of the main sources of NIMBY controversy, low-level waste (LLW) from nuclear power plants and medical procedures. This is primarily gloves, clothing, needles, and the like, that contain small amounts of slightly radioactive material. About 100 pages of the book are devoted to the 1980 Federal law, the 1985 amendments, and the various state programs on the subject.[1]

The frustration felt by many people on the subject is exemplified by the title of her first chapter, "Getting to 1993." The book was published in 1992, and English apparently felt that by the deadline of 1 January 1993, LLW would be barred from the two national waste sites still accepting it. It was not.

An example of the ever-increasing complexity of the subject is illustrated at the beginning of Appendix A. The original 1980 federal law on the subject covered the grand total of slightly over two pages. By 1985, when it was clear that the 1980 law was not working, the amendments passed that year covered about twenty pages, ten times as much. A decade later, the 1985 amendments also have not succeeded.

71

While English gives a relatively dispassionate view of the dismal history of LLW siting, she tends to ignore economic aspects. For example, the words "economics," "incentives," "compensation," and "auction" do not appear in her detailed index. She devotes (p. 131) a total of two paragraphs to what she calls the "volunteerism/incentives" approach, without supplying any references to the vast literature on the subject. She notes that the Southeast Compact (a group of states in that region trying to find a site) called for volunteers, and none came forward. Compact member North Carolina, searching for a site, offered $2.5 million annually to a potential host community. However, she does not observe that this amount was selected from the state capital, and not by a potential host. As I note elsewhere, the entity that selects the compensation amount in effect has control over the process. And control is probably the major factor in the entire NIMBY process.

She does state (p. 160): "Attempts to buy people's consent are not the answer. Certainly, those being asked to take on for society things or tasks that are generally accepted as burdens should be well-recompensed. But even so, offers of handsome compensation packages may, quite reasonably, be refused."

The first sentence of this quotation seems to be in contradiction to the second. If compensation is deleterious, it should be denounced everywhere it rears its ugly head. Yet English says that those who accept LLW sites should be "well-recompensed." It is true that even supposedly "handsome" offers may be turned down by communities. This is the essence of the reverse Dutch auction. As the bonus level rises, many communities, perhaps most, will not show interest. In that sense, they are turning down handsome compensation. They are well within their moral, legal and ethical rights to do so. But eventually one community will come forward, finally agreeing that the compensation is handsome enough.

English notes (p. xviii) that "since we have LLW, we must also have LLW facilities." This then disposes of the arguments of some in the NIMBY debate who say, "Let's not create the waste in the first place." This is a tempting slogan for a banner, but is not part of reality.

Her longest chapter (no. 4) is devoted to risk. I am in accord with her conclusions. She notes in voluminous detail that the way risk analysis is performed and presented—by highly paid consultants and in raucous public meetings—rarely convinces anyone that the risk is indeed small, even though it probably is. She notes (p. 100) that risk "is a concept that is in part socially constructed," as I have stated in perhaps less sociological language.

English clearly has great knowledge of LLW laws and programs, as exemplified by her 100-page compilation. However, while pointing out the innumerable difficulties and battles that have raged on LLW, she does not construct a model law, regulation or program in her final chapter. As a result, some readers will be disappointed.

English's last chapter is entitled "The Quest for Legitimacy." This implies that the authorities trying to find LLW sites have not been legitimate, at least in some eyes. Yet all the laws, regulations, and programs have been passed by legitimate authorities like Congress and state legislatures. The chapter title suggests that it is not sufficient to have the President's signature on a bill; as the old saying has it, "How does it play in Peoria?" The answer, according to English, is not very well.

Rabe's Analysis

Barry Rabe, a professor of health politics at the University of Michigan, has produced one of the best books on the politics of waste siting. He uses a case history approach, much like business schools.[2]

Given all the failures in hazardous waste siting, Rabe spends much space on one of the few successes, Swan Hills in Alberta (p. 58). As well, while most books on NIMBY published in the United States concentrate almost exclusively on American problems, Rabe extends his gaze beyond the border. Some of this may be because Michigan adjoins Canada; if Rabe had been a professor in Kansas, we may have heard less of Canada.

Rabe's book is different from others in this field in that he spends considerable space discussing different aspects of compensation. He notes (p. 76) that "a community is highly unlikely to volunteer to host a treatment or disposal facility in the absence of tangible economic rewards or clear assurance of long-term safety in facility management." In terms of hazards reduction, since the reverse Dutch auction would allow a community to operate the facility itself if it desires, it can make the installation as safe as it wants. This of course depends on how much money it is willing to spend to that end. On economic development, the Swan Hills waste site, the centerpiece of the book, is described as follows: "It has clearly stabilized our town...[g]iven the depletion of the oil fields and layoffs, we might be a ghost town by now if it were not for the plant" (p. 76).

In one of his two figures, Rabe divides nations, provinces, states, and localities according to the approaches they have taken to waste siting: regulatory, voluntary, centralized, or decentralized (p. 30). According to Rabe, ten jurisdictions, ranging from Arizona to Saskatchewan, have taken the "market" approach to siting at one time or another.

However, the word "market" does not necessarily mean an auction or anything like it. Rather, Rabe seems to take it to mean "private," that is, a waste disposal firm attempts to find a site on its own, and often may offer some type of compensation. Browning-Ferris Industries has been active in trying to find sites in New York, as I note elsewhere. Yet New York is listed as a regulatory state. The Browning-Ferris effort is not recorded.

Rabe analyzes the market approach carefully, discussing both positive and negative aspects. He gives a number of state-by-state analyses, starting with Massachusetts, perhaps the first to write compensation directly into state law in 1980. Ironically, Michael O'Hare, the father of the auction concept in 1977, took part in its writing. However, he was unable to get that concept enshrined into law, settling for funding of advisory groups in local communities.

Of course, these communities used the state money to battle sites proposed for them, instead of softening up their citizens. This could have been predicted, since there was no guarantee of final financial compensation by the state or a private waste disposal firm. Rabe notes that the much-ballyhooed Bay State law created "an even more treacherous climate for facility siting than was already in existence."

It is true that in the case of Braintree, to which I refer in chapter 3, Clean Harbors, the proponent, offered compensation. But this was in earmarked dollars, for example, purchase of certain fire fighting equipment. The compensation was not unrestricted, as it would have been under a reverse Dutch auction.

Rabe notes (p. 38) that "In all these cases, communities expressed outrage upon learning that *they had been selected* to bear the burden of hazardous waste management for Massachusetts" (emphasis added). The key is in the emphasized words. In spite of the supposed market approach of the Bay State, someone on high, either in the state or a private firm, pointed a finger. This is impossible in the reverse Dutch auction.

The centerpiece of Rabe's book is the successful Swan Hills, Alberta hazardous waste siting in 1987. He devotes thirty-two pages to it. While it would take too much space to evaluate its success completely, some brief comments are in order.

The people of Alberta are not necessarily patsies for wastes, having rejected a previous proposal for the small town of Two Hills some years before Swan Hills. The Two Hills case was a classic one, where the company met town officials behind closed doors. When the news got out, the jig was up.

In leading up to Swan Hills, Alberta emphasized that only volunteers would be considered. This is also a feature of the reverse Dutch auction. Alberta also abandoned large town meetings, which I have noted elsewhere usually turn out badly for site proponents.

Three volunteer towns approved going forward in a vote, which would also be an essential component of an auction. The present system muffles the voice of the people. Swan Hills citizens did not accept the facility because of patriotic duty to other Albertans, but because they saw financial benefits. While a variety of citizens and liaison committees were set up in Swan Hills, similar committees have been organized in other communities where siting proposals have failed. So the organizational structure was not peculiar to Swan Hills.

Since Rabe does not discuss auctions directly, despite the concept having been in the literature for almost two decades before his book appeared, it is difficult to determine his attitude towards it. Nonetheless, he notes on a number of occasions that some type of compensation is essential for the siting process to move forward. He does not, however, draw the appropriate lessons from the many cases where ordinary, not auction-related, compensation has failed.

Mazmanian and Morell

Daniel Mazmanian, at Claremont Graduate College, and David Morell, president of a consulting firm in Oakland, California, wrote one of the major articles on NIMBY. In the following, for brevity I will refer to them as M&M.[3]

The authors discuss the economic aspect of siting only in passing, and they are skeptical of it. They write,

> While auctioning development sites may sound attractive, especially in this period of siting gridlock, the process would inevitably be weighted in favor of those with the most money, not in favor of health, ordinary citizens, or the environment. Furthermore, auctions would resolve siting controversies one at a time. The approach is not well suited to coordinated regional programs for hazardous waste and materials management, nor does it fit in any obvious way with the drive for source reduction and waste minimization (p. 136).

These are major criticisms, and deserve a response. First, consider the question of "those with the most money." There is no siting system devised anywhere that would ensure that the rich will get their "fair share," however it is calculated, of waste sites and other undesirable facilities. M&M certainly do not come up with a scheme to do so.

Saying that the auction system would be weighted against "health, ordinary citizens and the environment" sounds as if it came from a political rally. It essentially means nothing. M&M nowhere define what they mean by "weighting," so it is impossible to determine what this would mean in practice. An auction system does not require any dilution of environmental standards, and M&M supply no proof that it does. And as far as "weighting" something against "ordinary citizens"— the fog is so thick about this that it cannot be penetrated.

M&M are correct in noting that an auction system would solve controversies one at a time. But the present system solves them zero at a time. One is better than nothing.

M&M are also correct in saying that an auction system would not be "well suited to coordinated regional programs for hazardous waste and materials management." If these coordinated programs were in place, that would be a serious drawback to auctions. But the programs do not exist. As will be noted in the following section on a Tennessee seminar of NIMBY experts, programs of this type have been attempted for about three decades. Reports have been written and filed, and millions of dollars spent. Little or nothing has been accomplished. Given the nature of wastes, it is highly unlikely that such programs will *ever* exist.

The final point in the M&M quotation above is that auctions might not fit in with recycling and reduction of wastes before they go to the landfill. However, these are two separate issues. There is no evidence that auctions *per se* will reduce recycling. M&M supply no evidence to back their claim. As well, if the other proposals for overcoming NIMBY that M&M advocate come true, presumably the same pressure to reduce recycling efforts will take place. M&M cannot have it both ways.

M&M are familiar with the auction and privatization literature, quoting, for example, Ervin and Fitch.[4] These authors wrote some of the earliest works on zoning auctions. However, M&M seem not only to have read the literature, but to have misread it.

M&M quote approvingly the work of Piasecki and Davis, who advocate a "public utility model" for waste management.[5] Briefly, P&D advocate independently operated and managed profit-making corporations to build waste sites. However, they would be regulated in the same way as electric utilities. In the United States, most commercial wastes are disposed of by private companies. They are not regulated except when they have to meet environmental standards for waste sites, so what P&D are proposing is different from the present system.

P&D write, "In exchange for treating all of the waste generated in an area, including hard-to-treat waste and household toxics, at set prices and using specified technologies, the private firm would have no competition in its service area and would receive a guaranteed return on its investment in treatment facilities."

Electric utilities are what is called a "regulated monopoly." P&D propose the same for waste companies.

However, this would not solve the NIMBY problem. Electric utilities have great difficulties in siting power plants and transmission lines, difficulties comparable to finding waste sites. The literature is rife with stories of how local opposition overcame proposals to build a plant producing something that everyone needed, electricity. There is no indication in the P&D proposal that the NIMBY dragon would roar any less strongly.

M&M (p. 139) discuss at length the California hazardous-waste planning and siting process, started in 1986. At the time they wrote, it seemed quite promising. It would take a regional approach to waste siting, thus in principle producing more regional equity and fairness. M&M go on for a number of pages stressing its advantages.

However, by the time that Gerrard's book (see below) came out in the fall of 1994, there was no mention at all of what was supposedly the death of the NIMBY dragon. As in many other cases, a solution on paper, without taking people's feelings into account, failed when put to the test.

To summarize M&M, they are unenthusiastic about auctions, but they supply no evidence why they would not work. In contrast, they tout the California regional equity model, which disappeared without a trace. The NIMBY dragon survives.

University of Tennessee Seminar

Besides the books and papers I quote in this chapter, there have been many panel sessions and conferences on NIMBY. Sometimes the words are spoken and never heard from again. Other times, there is an effort made to record what was said.

The latter event took place in a seminar held at the University of Tennessee in June 1993. Seventeen participants from academia, state agencies and private firms took part, and a summary was produced in a major environmental journal.[6]

Since there apparently were few participants who had thought deeply about the economic aspects of NIMBY, it was hardly surprising that compensation was misunderstood. The authors of the summary state, "Others believe...[overcoming NIMBY] is simply a matter of providing more economic incentives, and that providing compensation for hosting a solid waste facility is all that is needed."

I have combed the literature on compensation over the years, and to my knowledge nobody has ever advocated this in these terms. The seminar attendees seemed to have confused discussing or advocating compensation, either by auction or otherwise, with claiming that it will single-handedly solve the NIMBY problem.

While this dismissal, in the second paragraph of the article, seems to imply that most were united behind this stand, Thomas Aarts, of the waste management firm Browning-Ferris (BFI), was not. He pointed out that BFI advocated massive compensation for a large proposed landfill in Eagle, Western New York. The benefits to Eagle were estimated to be $2.2 million annually, several times its present tax revenue.

The seminar participants asked a number of questions about the BFI proposal. They discussed whether a single volunteer town or county should be sought, or if it should be a competitive process. The reverse Dutch auction is such a competitive process, with each community weighing the benefits and drawbacks. They debated whether the benefits package should be negotiated, or explained up front. The Dutch auction allows varying benefits, with the volunteer community buying in at a point they think is right.

The seminar also evaluated a key point in arguments over NIMBY, the "residual effect." Some observers have claimed that if the amount of wastes could be reduced through conservation or other means, the controversies over NIMBY would also decrease. The seminar disagreed. They noted that "regardless of how successful [recycling and conservation] efforts are, a residual amount of waste requiring treatment and/ or disposal will remain."

Related to this question is what can be called "capacity planning." The subject is described more fully in Gerrard's book, to be analyzed below. Some have claimed that the root of the NIMBY syndrome comes from the perceived inequity between one region and other. State A may produce thousands of tons of wastes. But most of it may be shipped to State B, where landfills are located. State A has avoided burying it in *its* back yard.

If some type of overall national planning could be carried out, in principle each state and region would have to accept its "fair share," whatever that might be. But the participants did not hold out much hope for this happy day coming any time soon. They noted the disastrous experience of the 1960s and 1970s, when the federal government required plans of this type for solid waste (i.e., garbage). As the summary notes, "While many states complied in order to receive grant funding, it was generally recognized that the plans often were paper studies...many also thought that today's capacity plans [also] have little substance to them. One participant put it bluntly: 'Today's capacity planning is an illusion.'"

The workshop spent some time talking about environmental justice. A proposed Environmental Justice Act was described. It would publish a list of the 100 counties with the highest "total weight of toxic chemicals." However, there is nothing in the bill (which never became law) that would prevent more landfills and waste sites being opened up in these 100 counties. Presumably merely being on that list might act as a magic charm to keep chemicals away. The bill was silent on which counties should get waste sites in the future, so it had little do with neutralizing the NIMBY dragon.

In summary, the seminar seems to have missed the point over the meaning of siting compensation, although the matter was discussed in the Browning-Ferris context. They did recognize that the strictly technical approaches to siting, whose defects I point out at some length here, "have not worked."

Environmental Justice and Injustice

Robert Bullard is a sociology professor at the University of California, Riverside. While many others have evaluated what is sometimes called environmental racism in terms of waste disposal sites, his pen has probably been the most prolific. He has written a series of articles and books extending over almost a full bibliographic page in a 1993 book. In them, he has eloquently noted that many disposal facilities tend to be located in minority areas, poor areas, or both. As far as I can tell, he does not address the question of "social service" facilities being located in these areas: the day-care facilities I noted in a previous chapter that were being denounced, AIDS shelters, homes for mentally ill people, and so on.[7]

As often happens in situations of this type, Professor Bullard was not the first on the scene. Apparently the Reverend Benjamin Chavis,

Jr., later briefly head of the National Association for the Advancement of Colored People, broke the ground with a United Church of Christ study in 1987. The study, discussed more fully in chapter 10, noted much of what Professor Bullard later amplified.

In a broad sense, little of what Professor Bullard and Reverend Chavis say should be shocking. Poor people and minorities throughout the world, probably from the dawn of recorded time, have always gotten the short end of the stick in virtually all ways. While there are few records of this aspect of the Middle Ages, I suspect that the wastes and offal of a medieval lord were dumped just outside his castle window. They were probably transported to the farm of some hapless serf. The peasants had to smell its pungent odors.

On a more personal note, I can remember walking through an American college city in my graduate student days in Illinois, noting that the sidewalks disappeared once I got into the black part of town. This came as a surprise to me then, but seemed to be an accepted part of life in that supposedly sophisticated community.

Professor Bullard is probably best-known for his book, *Dumping in Dixie*, dealing in part with the situation in Emelle, Alabama. I will treat this subject later in this chapter, based in part on a report in the *Wall Street Journal*.

It should be noted that much of what Bullard writes is highly polemic. He says, "The history of the United States has long been grounded in white racism" (p. 16). My object here is not to debate this or related points, but to determine how Professor Bullard's proposals relate to "equitable" siting, whatever that may mean.

Bullard's attitude toward the economics of waste siting is ambiguous. On one hand, as exemplified by the above quotation, he seems to blame all, or almost all, the problems of pollution on racism. However, this implies that middle-class and upper-class minority neighborhoods, of which there are some around Atlanta and other big cities, would have as many waste dumps near their carefully manicured lawns as those in inner-city ghettos. Bullard never quite deals with this point, tending to lump all minorities in the same poverty-stricken, under-educated bag.

The key problem in Bullard's writings is that, as far as I can tell, he does not say exactly how undesirable facilities should be located in the future. He favors fairness, equity, and other good things, but precisely how these concepts are to be applied remains in the clouds. Given that, as he says, many of these facilities have been excessively concentrated in minority areas, should all future waste dumps be located only in places that are almost all white? This might be a logical implication to be drawn from Bullard's work, He nowhere states this, or supplies any workable system for achieving equity.

Professor Bullard views the economic side of siding primarily in terms of what he calls "economic blackmail" (pp. 22–23). Other economic aspects are ignored. Under this type of blackmail, minorities are promised jobs if they accept a waste site in their community. However, in most instances waste sites were located in minority communities without any promises of jobs or other economic benefits. The advantage of the reverse Dutch auction in this context is that a community can decide for itself if it wants the benefits. In the past, that rarely occurred, as Prof. Bullard would readily admit. The site was usually imposed from on high on the minority community.

Professor Bullard attempts (p. 203) to formulate an "environmental justice framework," presumably to develop a better siting system than now exists. Unfortunately, this framework is punctuated with the same windy phrases and meaningless terminology that the developers of existing waste facilities use in *their* literature.

For example, he wants this framework to "incorporate the right of all individuals to be protected from environmental degradation." Fine words, but what does it mean in practice? Does "degradation" mean one atom or molecule of a waste chemical entering into someone's body? Or is it ten atoms, or a million? Bullard seems to be unaware of the battles over how safe is safe that have formed the basis of Environmental Protection Agency standards and court rulings over the past few decades. In any case, much the same language was used in the National Environmental Policy Act in 1969, so Bullard apparently has missed the boat by about a quarter-century.

The second plank in his platform advocates a "public health" model of prevention that eliminates the risk before harm occurs. Again, fine words, but models of this type are used every day in government regulations and court cases. Professor Bullard may not like the results of some of the models, but they are being employed as he advocates.

Little of this has anything to do with how new undesirable facilities could or should be sited. Much of Professor Bullard's argument is based on the demonstrably unfair way in which they were sited in the past— none of it due to the reverse Dutch auction. But when it comes time for him to state how those facilities are to be sited in the future, he is struck speechless.

In summary, while Professor Bullard deserves credit for calling more academic attention to the unreasonable concentration of waste sites in or near minority and poor communities, he presents no plan for a more equitable distribution. Without a plan of this type that can be analyzed and debated, the past is likely to continue into the future.

Some of Professor Bullard's points about environmental injustice were incorporated in a new Georgia law, passed in the spring of 1995. State Senator David Scott, representing a middle-class, predominantly black part of Atlanta, noted that six garbage dumps were within a forty-mile radius of his constituents.[8]

He got the notoriously conservative Georgia legislature to pass a bill restricting the density of landfills within a neighborhood. This would answer Bullard's main complaint, that there are unnatural clusters of undesirable facilities.

However, the legislation does not specify exactly how new landfill sites are to be chosen, the essence of the NIMBY problem. It merely prevents them from being located in certain areas, and so does not inflict even a glancing blow against the NIMBY dragon.

Another notable aspect about this legislation was that it was fought tooth and nail by large waste firms, such as Browning Ferris (BFI). I noted earlier in this chapter that BFI had adopted an enlightened approach in Western New York, asking for volunteers and promising large compensation. Apparently that attitude faded as the company moved South, where they were concerned that their choices would be limited if Senator Scott's bill was passed. They lost the battle.

Negotiation

James Boren, the satirist of bureaucracy, used to offer this advice to civil servants, "When in doubt, mumble." When it comes to siting, the analogy is "when in doubt, negotiate." This is the gist of a major book by Lawrence Susskind, a professor at M.I.T., and Jeffrey Cruikshank, entitled *Breaking the Impasse*.[9]

As might be expected in a book devoted primarily to techniques of negotiation, Susskind says little about the financial aspect. The index has no listing for "compensation" or "auctions," for example. The only discussion of auctions is the "dollar bill auction," a psychological experiment (not a negotiation) in which people bid for a dollar bill and find themselves paying more than $1.00.

Negotiation has certainly solved some NIMBY problems, and will undoubtedly solve more in the future. However, it is highly dependent on the situation. If the right negotiator is chosen, and if he or she uses just the right techniques to suit the parties in contention, it is possible, just possible, than an agreed-on site will be chosen. But we tend to read only of the success stories. The failures are not blamed on the negotiating process itself, but on the stubbornness or stupidity of the participants.

For example, Susskind describes (p. 165) an apparently successful negotiation about fishing rights between Indians and white people, not exactly a NIMBY dispute. He goes into great detail, including the mock tantrum that the negotiator threw. Because there was agreement, we are told of it. If there had not been, it would have been just another case settled by a judge, or never resolved at all.

One of the major problems with negotiations is that they almost invariably take place behind closed doors. Even if the motives of all the negotiators are as pure as the driven snow, those waiting outside the door, especially those in a community affected by a NIMBY dispute, will often be suspicious. The techniques advocated by Susskind, which work in other areas, will often fail when the NIMBY dragon rears its head.

In a NIMBY dispute, it is often the best strategy for the protesters not to negotiate at all. The dispute over whether Nevada should be the site of a high-level nuclear waste repository has dragged on for over a decade. To my knowledge, Nevada has never sat down with the Federal Government to negotiate the repository, timing, payments, or any other aspect. Any lawyer would tell them (and undoubtedly many have), "Do not talk to the Feds. That will just entrap you in the process. Never say a word to them outside of a court."

Even in a reverse Dutch auction, there will be some negotiation. However, the force impelling sitting down at a table is the compensation. Without this type of force, even the sophisticated methods described by Susskind will often fail to overcome NIMBY. This history of the field is all too painful evidence of this.

Gerrard's Effort

Michael Gerrard is an attorney who represented localities in Western New York against several waste handling companies—Waste Management, Inc., Chem Nuclear Services, Wheelabrator Technologies, and others. He later became part of the prestigious law firm of Arnold and Porter.

With a background like that, one might assume that he would be at the head of the NIMBY line, saying that waste sites should be located by the NOPE process—Not On Planet Earth. However, in his book he has produced a short but thoughtful look at NIMBY.[10]

While his proposals would take too much space to describe in detail, they are based on his observations (p. 170) that opposition grows from both the culture of the community and the host state's sense of national fairness. His solution is summarized in the title of Section III: Local Control, State Responsibility, National Allocation.

I agree with Gerrard that local control of an undesirable facility is needed. All too often the facility is foisted on the town or county—or so it appears—producing the sense of outrage. The community should have the right to operate the facility, or contract it out to someone else.

The state obviously must meet state and national environmental standards, so Gerrard is also correct about its responsibility. However, the heart of his proposal is a system of national allocations of both waste and sites, through what he calls a Federal Waste Disposal Commission (FWDC). (It is unclear how other undesirable but non-waste facilities, ranging from transmission lines to AIDS centers, would be allocated under Gerrard's suggestions).

The FWDC, as Gerrard notes, "would have a thankless task of allocating hated facilities among reluctant states." It would plan the distribution of all hazardous wastes, from nuclear reactor fuel rods to chemicals. Gerrard views the proposed sending of the first high-level waste repository to Nevada as a promising model, and expects the FWDC to follow in this path.

In the proposal, the FWDC would give each state a given number of sites, based on how much waste the state produced, transportation factors, and the like. Then the state itself would choose the site within its boundaries, possibly by using a reverse Dutch auction. States would be allowed to trade sites among themselves, by using a mechanism like that suggested by the National Governors Association (p. 192).

Gerrard tries to get around the inevitable gigantic controversy that will ensue when the FWDC publishes its list of which states will get which waste sites by using the Defense Base Closure Commission (DBCC) as a model. For many years, until the late 1980s, no military base had been closed in the United States, although many had outlived their usefulness. The problem was that when the military proposed closing a base, members of Congress representing that area would cry "foul," and keep it open just a while longer. The problem was NIMBY in reverse.

Representative Dick Armey of Texas, later a leader in the House, realized that the problem came about because the military acted on one base at a time. Each could be easily defended by a few Senators and Representatives. He proposed the DBCC, which would publish a master list of base closures. The master list as a whole would have to voted up or down, and could not be amended. In that way, the special interests for each base would be at a disadvantage. Congress could say, in effect, "we're spreading the pain. We're not just singling out Montana, or Oregon, or Pennsylvania."

The closure commission worked. In a series of actions, it closed dozens of obsolete bases. Representatives from the affected areas protested mightily, but were overridden by the seemingly politics-free atmosphere of the commission. The nation was saved billions of dollars, and the affected areas accepted the decisions, albeit grudgingly.

Would such a commission work for wastes? The base closure commission offers some precedents. Congress rarely passes a bill, like the DBCC, that works effectively and is praised from almost all quarters. In that sense, the FWDC has a chance of success.

However, the FWDC may be too much of a "master brain" in Washington to meet with public acceptance. The Republicans achieved their greatest Congressional success in forty years in the fall of 1994 by saying that too many decisions were being made by the banks of the Potomac. A poll in the spring of 1995 said that most people thought Washington was the source of problems, not its solution.[11] As a result of these attitudes, the FWDC would have two strikes against it when it when it stepped up to bat.

As well, the exact mathematical models that would allocate the wastes and waste sites are not specified by Gerrard. He refers to "sophisticated computer programs" (p. 187), but this is far from explicitly laying out how the calculations are to be made. The defense base commission has the advantage of having a general or admiral testify, "this base is no longer needed." There is no comparable set of individuals with this prestige in the waste field. And by now, even the most nonmathematically inclined know that "sophisticated programs" can be manipulated to prove almost anything that is wanted. I refer in chapter 4 to the complaints of Albert Gore and Jim Sasser, then the Senators from Tennessee, that their state had been selected by a Department of Energy mathematical model (presumably sophisticated) to receive high-level nuclear wastes. It was later brought out that if a more reasonable model had been used, Ohio would have been the lucky state.

Gerrard spends more time on compensation and auctions than practically any other book on NIMBY. He notes that compensation has never been primarily used to site a hazardous or radioactive waste site in the United States, although compensation, direct and indirect, has been given. However, since these sites have not been built in recent years, their lack of existence can be attributed to factors other than compensation. He does not discuss the literature, mentioned elsewhere in this book, of how compensation has been and can be used to solve a wide variety of environmental problems.

Gerrard does discuss auctions at some length (p. 179). He asks a series of questions about the reverse Dutch auction, questions that are answered in this volume. For example, the extent of the electorate that could or should vote in a referendum on siting is a key question. Gerrard concludes that the auction system deserves further study and possible trial implementation.

Gerrard has performed a master service to students of siting, NIMBY and waste disposal by (p. viii) attempting "to find and read just about the whole body of literature on the siting of hazardous and radioactive waste disposal facilities (requiring a new pair of glasses in the process)." Gerrard's references fill almost 100 pages, adding about 50 percent to the main text. He has performed a superhuman task, and his notes will be consulted for many years to come.

Gerrard has written one of the seminal books on NIMBY. His proposal for a Federal Waste Disposal Commission deserves serious consideration. However, in the present national climate the addition of a new Federal superagency seems unlikely.

Summary

All the books cited, as well as dozens that I have not had the space to discuss, have some grains of truth in them about the NIMBY crisis. Because they usually do not adequately cover the economic aspect of siting, they wound the NIMBY dragon a bit, but do not slay him.

Notes

1. Mary R. English, *Siting Low-Level Radioactive Waste Disposal Facilities: The Public Policy Dilemma* (New York: Quorum Books, 1992).
2. Barry G. Rabe, *Beyond Nimby: Hazardous Waste Siting in Canada and the United States* (Washington: Brookings Institution, 1994).
3. Daniel Mazmanian and David Morell, "The 'NIMBY' Syndrome: Facility Siting and the Failure of Democratic Discourse." In *Environmental Policy in the 1990s: Towards a New Agenda*, eds. Norman J. Vig and Michael E. Kraft (Washington: CQ Press, 1990) 125–43.

4. David E. Ervin and James B. Fitch, "Evaluating Alternative Compensation and Recapture Techniques for Expanded Public Control of Land Use," *Natural Resources Journal* 19 (January 1979): 21–44.
5. Bruce W. Piasecki and Gary A. Davis, *America's Future in Toxic Waste Management: Learning From Europe* (New York: Quorum Books, 1987) 229.
6. Mary English, Jack Barkenbus, and Catherine Will, "Solid Waste Facility Siting: Issues and Trends," *Air & Waste* 43 (October 1993): 1345–50.
7. Some books and articles are: Robert D. Bullard, *Dumping in Dixie: Race, Class and Environmental Quality* (Boulder, Colo.: Westview Press, 1990); *Confronting Environmental Racism: Voices from the Grassroots*, ed. Robert D. Bullard, (Boston: South End Press, 1993); Robert D. Bullard, "Introduction." In *Confronting Environmental Racism*, ibid., 7–13; and Robert D. Bullard, "Conclusion: Environmentalism with Justice." In *Confronting Environmental Racism*, ibid., 195–206.
8. Frank LoMonte, "Unlikely alliance passed landfill restrictions," *Augusta (Georgia) Chronicle* (14 May 1995): 4A.
9. Lawrence Susskind and Jeffrey Cruikshank, *Breaking the Impasse* (New York: Basic Books, 1987).
10. Michael B. Gerrard, *Whose Backyard, Whose Risk* (Cambridge, Mass.: MIT Press, 1994).
11. As reported on *All Things Considered*, National Public Radio, 18 April 1995.

6

Perception and Psychology of Unwelcome Guests

Today, locally unwanted land uses such as hazardous and radioactive waste sites are regarded with as much fear and loathing as all of Hunter Thompson's gonzo books put together. A proposal to build a nuclear facility would now be met with a blizzard of lawsuits. It would be perceived by some as dangerous, unsafe, perilous, and all the other adjectives culled from the thesaurus.

In World War II, the situation was different. According to one story, the senior senator from Tennessee, Kenneth McKellar, was called into President Roosevelt's office early in the war.

FDR was planning the secret Manhattan Project to build the first atomic bomb, and he had to have the support of influential senators such as McKellar. The crusty Senator listened carefully to the assembled generals and scientists talk about the need for the weapon, and why no word must leak out to the enemy. They went on to describe plans for a vast plant, employing thousands, that would be built to separate uranium-235 from its other isotopes.

Senator McKellar paid close attention to the lengthy presentation, but said nothing. Finally, after realizing that the President expected him to respond, he leaned back. As a representative of one of the poorest states in the Union, he was continually on the outlook for ways to improve its economy. He glanced at the assembled brass hats and turned to Roosevelt: "Mr. President, just where in Tennessee are you planning to put this plant?"

Times have changed. The NIMBY dragon breathes fire. We have to understand just how we perceive abhorrent facilities, and why we think the way we do.

NIMBY and Polls

According to O'Hare, "Some things are always in the wrong place. Litter and weeds have this characteristic, according to popular wisdom[;] so do taxicabs and policemen." But few of us would riot or complain bitterly to elected officials if a taxicab was not in view.

A desirable facility in the wrong place *does* inspire these feelings. Emotions run strongly. Earlier, I described a radioactive waste brawl in New York State. Violence about waste siting has occurred in other states as well. In Georgia,

> Five years ago, in a peaceful part of Georgia where cows graze and Baptist churches stand proud, residents of Heard County took up arms to keep hazardous waste out of their community.
>
> The memories of those days are indelibly inked on Moses McCall's mind: a public hearing where a gun-toting crowd crammed into the local high school auditorium to pray and jeer at McCall and other officials of the state Department of Natural Resources; steel drums marked with skull and crossbones hurled from passing trucks; a rally and cross-burning by the Ku Klux Klan; a family grocery store selling "Dump the Dump" T-shirts; and most of all the violence— firebombings, arson, bullet-riddled pickup trucks.
>
> The tactics eventually worked. The Pennsylvania-based company that had hoped to build a hazardous waste disposal site there packed up and went home.
>
> A similar scenario was staged in Wilkinson County, where in 1978 the state's first licensed disposal site was opened for business, and then closed six months later under public pressure."[1]

We have to fathom these powerful passions before the NIMBY dragon bites the dust.

When it comes to determining what people believe, the American way is to conduct a poll. The temptation is to flatly ask what people think. Unless the questions are framed carefully, we will learn only the obvious—NIMBY is alive and well, practically everywhere. We will not get to the underlying psychology.

The universality of NIMBY is evident in a poll such as that described by the Battelle Human Affairs Research Center, a think-tank in Washington State.[2] Both the general public and leadership groups were asked, "Would you be more or less likely to support an acceptable method for permanent storage and disposal of high-level nuclear wastes if it were not in your state?"

Of the general public, 34 percent were more likely to accept the disposal system if it were out of state. Only 13 percent were less likely to accept it. There is a revealing statistic about the 56 political leaders polled. Of this group, thirty-two wanted it out of their state; *not one* wanted it in his or her state.

O'Hare explains the divergence between what people say they will do and what they actually do after the poll taker leaves: "We might be inclined to interview local residents of a facility-threatened community and ask them how much money they think eliminating a power station's smoke or an airport's noise is worth to them. Obviously the expected use to which such answers would be put imposes strategic considerations that make the response useless as indications of price."[3]

If we ask people how much removing the smoke from a stack is worth, they might say thousands or even millions, when they know that they will not see a bill for that amount in their mail. If they are told that their taxes would go up by the amount they specify, the amounts they tell the pollster will be substantially less. This is what Professor O'Hare means by "strategic considerations." If it does not come out of your pocket, then one amount is as good as any other.

Other observers have noticed this effect. Richard Schuler is director of the Waste Management Institute at Cornell University, and a professor of economics and civil and environmental engineering. He says,

> One solution [to the problem of determining the right amount of compensation for causing environmental problems] is to ask people what magnitude of compensation would offset their anger. Previous experiments, and common sense, suggest that such a question creates a new dilemma. When people in the Southwest were asked how much their electric bills would have to be reduced before they could bear the visual insult of a new power plant and its smoke on the horizon, the average response was $10 per month. A similar group of customers, asked how much additional money they would be willing to pay each month to *avoid* seeing the new power plant, gave an average answer of 10 cents![4]

These considerations apply to nonfinancial questions as well. Ask people if they would move away if a waste site came to their town, and many will say "yes." Ask the mayors of the few communities where these sites have been built in the last few decades how many of their residents left town. The fractions estimated by the mayors will be much smaller.

Responses to a poll often do not correspond to actions because it costs little or nothing to give an answer, any answer. Actions can be expensive.

Any workable siting compensation system has to correspond to actions, not words. Residents of a community have to know exactly how much they will lose if they avoid the facility. That loss will be real, not make-believe poll questions.

Does this mean that polling has little value in determining feelings? We have to differentiate between what people are merely thinking of doing and their actual actions. Polls of voters' intentions sometimes make large errors. The November, 1948 picture of a grinning Harry

Truman holding up the *Chicago Tribune* with the headline "Dewey Elected" is on the wall of more than one poll taker.

Contrast that result with exit polls, taken *after* citizens have performed an action—voting. These invariably predict the result to within a percent or two. When action has taken place or is imminent, respondents of polls give accurate answers to questions.

Risk-Averse versus Risk-Tolerant People

The psychology of risks is reflected by the many people who go out of their way to avoid them. We all know these individuals—they will not start their car with you in it unless you put on a seat belt. They leave the room when someone starts to smoke. They do not venture downtown after dark. An extreme example was Elizabeth Gray:

> I have dealt with the situation basically by trying to drop out. I go to my doctor as seldom as possible; I take as few medications as possible. I…go to my supermarket, buy non-additive bread, take my vegetables and fresh fruits home and scour them to attempt to get the pesticides off. We have become just about vegetarians.
>
> Now when you come at me with a nuclear decision, I think a person like me is…going to be propelled into the picket lines when you want to invade the very precarious private space that I am trying to forge…to protect myself from…[the] very dangerous effects of my society.
>
> And when you begin to invade my space with nuclear plants, people like me will say, "No way. Someplace else."[5]

Some of us know the other extreme: heavy smokers and drinkers, who drive when intoxicated because, "listen, don't tell me how to drive," those who have undertaken a personal crusade to eat most of the world's supply of red meat. These people are obviously risk tolerant.

Those who want to site wastes would like to have fewer like Elizabeth Gray and more of the second category. However, there is no simple way of achieving this goal. In each of us, there is a unique mixture of risk aversion and risk tolerance. Someone who demonstrates about a potential hazardous waste site nearby may smoke three packs a day.

Risk Tolerance in the Context of Automobile Noises

Another way of illustrating risk aversion and tolerance in a broader way is when I hear a strange noise under the hood of my car. Neighbor A says, "I can probably solve the problem by fiddling a little. It's just a matter of working toward the solution. Even if I can't figure it out, you can take it to the mechanic down the street. *Somebody* should be able to solve it."

Neighbor B says, "I wouldn't fool with that if I were you. With all these new devices on engines, nobody understands them anymore. Just meddling will make it worse."

The case has nothing to do with physical risk; that is, the engine is not likely to blow up in someone's face. But neighbor A is willing to take the chance of trying to repair a problem. Neighbor B does not want to know about it.

In the *New York Times Magazine* of 18 November 1990, a story dealt with a geologist who claimed that the rock formations around Yucca Mountain in Nevada were unsuitable for the high-level nuclear waste repository proposed there. In Jerry Szymanski's view, the geology showed that the repository would eventually leak.

Here was a man clearly concerned about safety, although it's difficult for nongeologists to tell if he is right or wrong. He risked his career as a government employee to bring what he thought were important facts on hazards to public attention.

Yet he is described in the article as chain-smoking Winstons and drinking Scotch, hardly risk-free activities. As Walt Whitman wrote,

> Do I contradict myself?
> Very well then, I contradict myself.
> (I am large, I contain multitudes).

While we can measure risk aversion and tolerance to some degree, there is no simple method of changing the proportion each of us has in our minds. I would not go so far as to say that it's in our genes, but who knows what future DNA research will show?

Is there a Completely Harmless Facility?

Most of the arguments I have described in preceding pages have been about waste sites that at least some people regard as harmful. But our attitude toward them has blocked the construction of projects that practically everyone thinks of as benign. This spillover effect was never intended by those demonstrating against facilities they feel are dangerous. It has still occurred.

Frank Popper writes:

> In many states—Virginia, for example—it is not possible to locate a new marina. The theme-park industry no longer attempts to build large amusement parks and is

convinced that neither Disneyland in California nor Disneyworld in Florida could be built today. It would be impossible for a contemporary Gutzon Borglum to carve the four gigantic presidential faces into Mount Rushmore, for the mountain is sacred to the Sioux and today's laws—for instance, the 1978 American Indian Religious Freedom Act—protect such lands.[6]

If Mickey Mouse cannot find a place to stay, society does not suffer all that much. Popper points out that consequences for other blockages can be more serious:

> If new hazardous waste facilities cannot be sited, the waste must still go somewhere—to existing overburdened facilities, or often to organized-crime fronts, to midnight dumpers, or to the kind of company that has a truck driver open the stopcock and dump waste along 200 miles of rural roads (a real case in North Carolina).
> Similarly, if oil refineries cannot be built...the United States will remain dangerously dependent on foreign suppliers. If low-income housing cannot be constructed, the poor will have to live in even worse places; and as the problem of homelessness mounts, large numbers of the poor will end up living nowhere at all. If sites for jails cannot be found, more convicted criminals will go free.

While Popper describes the situation accurately, he does not analyze why people have these feelings. He offers only the prescription of "planning" to solve the NIMBY problem. That's natural enough, since he is a city planner himself. Yet this is precisely what got us in trouble in the beginning. When people are boiling with emotion, they do not want to listen to planners any more than risk analysts.

Risk from Undesirable Facilities Outrages Us

Peter Sandman, the director of the Environmental Communications Research Program at Rutgers, has explained why experts and the public disagree so vehemently.[7] To experts, risk has a simple definition. It's the number of deaths (or accidents, or injuries) per year, or per unit of energy output, or some other convenient unit. This is the type of calculation I and others have performed many times, and have published in scientific journals.

The public is aware, at least in a general way, of some of these numbers. To them, that's not all there is to risk. There are many other factors, such as voluntariness and control, that go into their risk equation, aspects that are usually non-numerical. Because they cannot attach numbers to them, risk analysts, myself included, have tended to ignore them.

Professor Sandman lumps all these aspects into what he calls "outrage." That's the equivalent of the TV journalist, in the movie *Network* some years back, bellowing out, "I'm mad as hell, and I'm not going to take it anymore."

So for the risk analyst, risk is primarily the calculated numbers. For the public, risk equals the calculated numbers *plus* (or times) outrage, the sum of the other factors. Small wonder that the two sides usually do not agree.

The factors that make up total outrage are numerous. As many as twenty—some overlapping, admittedly—have been tabulated. Here are some of the major ones.

Voluntarism versus Compulsion

In the United States, voluntarism is highly prized. President Bush's "Thousand Points of Light" was just the latest in a long national emphasis on voluntarism.

Almost everyone favors risks being voluntary, not coerced. This is in contrast to European attitudes, where the tradition of orders being handed down from on high is much stronger.

In a sense, no installation is ever completely voluntary. Most people might welcome a successor to Disneyworld—call it Disneyuniverse—near their town, but there might be one old curmudgeon who does not. He hates the thought of mouse ears in the neighborhood. Minnie Mouse and Pluto hold no charms for him. If the amusement park were built, it would be over his objection.

Voluntarism contrasts with compulsion in geopolitics as well. In early 1991, war broke out in the Persian Gulf between a large coalition of nations, headed by the U.S., and Iraqi forces. After about 100 hours of combat, the Iraqi forces quit.

Commentators noted that there was extremely little protest in the U.S., although the number of troops deployed was as great as at the height of Vietnam. Most observers attributed this to the fact that all the American soldiers, sailors, and air forces in the Gulf were volunteers. Not one had been forced to go there.

Around the same time, riots were breaking out in many parts of the Soviet Union on the draft that had been a fixture there for decades. Draft call-ups were handled by its fifteen republics. Until the arrival of glasnost, draft officials in these republics (corresponding to U.S. states) took their orders from Soviet Army officials without questions. In the late 1980s, many republics, such as the Baltic states, refused to cooperate with draft officials.

As a result, the draft quota for many republics was not being met. The Soviet Army reacted in the usual ham-fisted way. They sent soldiers to round up draft dodgers, provoking violent brawls in the street, with some loss of life.

The contrast could not be greater. The U.S. sent troops half-way around the world, to a place that most Americans could not even spell before hostilities erupted. Antiwar demonstrations were at a minimum. The Soviet Army had to drag men off the street, generating battles between them and bystanders, just to ship them to a training camp a few miles away.

The reason for the difference? One system relied on voluntarism; the other on compulsion. The U.S. proved it was possible to have a strong military made up solely of men and women who come forward on their own. That lesson never sunk in on the banks of the Volga.

There are limits to voluntarism. Suppose a risk or hazard had to be *completely* voluntary, that is, have the agreement of all concerned for it to be accepted. Then nothing would ever be built, no matter how necessary it was.

As Al Smith, governor of New York State in the 1920s, used to say, "The solution for the problems of democracy is even more democracy." Any siting procedure has to have the *imprimatur* of a democratic vote, either by referendum or by elected representatives. The minority has rights, but ultimately the majority decides.

Diffusion of Hazards in Time and Space

A second source of outrage deals with time and space. Suppose we have one hazard, such as the mythical one Professor Sandman calls "dimethylmeatloaf," that kills twenty people each year. These victims die one at a time, and are scattered throughout the nation.

Now we have another hazard, perhaps dimethylmeatloaf plants, that operate safely year after year. Every ten years or so, there is a gigantic explosion, perhaps due to what the engineers whimsically call "valve heartburn," and 200 people are killed in the subsequent gas release and fire.

The risks of the two sources are the same—twenty deaths, on average, a year. But the dimethylmeatloaf plant explosion has extra baggage. It's the outrage felt by the public when they read the headlines. Those headlines do not accompany the solitary victims felled in obscure places.

Any siting system has to encourage people in a potential host community to consider the data on risks more dispassionately. Some will continue to say, "The risks are just too high; I do not want that here, no matter what." Others may be led to muse, "Maybe the risks they're talking about aren't quite as big as I first imagined."

Risk versus Benefit

Sidney Harris, the cartoonist of science, once had one in the *New Yorker*. It portrayed a diner looking at the prices posted on the wall of a small restaurant. She saw "Hamburger, $1.35; Cheeseburger, $2.95," and so on down the menu. Posted next to each of the items were two further columns. One was "Risks"; the other was "Benefits."

Whatever the risks are, if there is no commensurate benefit to the facility it will be rejected. We adopt the same approach in our daily activities. Skiing may appear highly risky to non-skiers. If skiers felt they were not getting a series of benefits—the thrill of hurtling in space, fresh air, vigorous exercise, camaraderie with fellow skiers, and so on—the sport would be abandoned.

The present siting system sometimes promises compensation and benefits. They are almost never certain. When the benefits *do* appear, they are often, in the old Southern expression, "a day late and a dollar short." That is, they do not fulfill the expectations of the host community.

The host community has to know *exactly* how much of a benefit they will derive from acceptance. If it's adequate to them, they will welcome it; if not, they should not be required to accept it.

Memorability of Hazards

Some accidents stick in our minds, whether we want them to or not. Love Canal, Chernobyl, Three Mile Island, and Bhopal all make disasters and events come alive in our consciousness. Has a hazardous waste facility been proposed in the last decade without the words "Love Canal" being mentioned at some point?

From the viewpoint of the risk analysts, this is unfair. These are systems that have failed, or caused harm, in the past. The new systems will be much better, in their estimation, and meet a host of strict environmental regulations.

From the viewpoint of the public, the television and newspaper images are all they have. They often do not understand the detailed studies, but they know what they have seen on the nightly news.

Do the media give a fair presentation of risks? Here the debate goes to the root of exactly what is news. As editors put it, "Dog bites man isn't news; man bites dog *is*."

Some of this was analyzed quantitatively by the Decision Research group in Oregon. They studied the reports of deaths by an Oregon and a Massachusetts newspaper (excluding the obituary columns). There was not much of a match between what was reported in these two sources and the major national causes of deaths.[8]

For example, at the time of the article, stomach cancer killed about 95,000 people annually. There was only one mention of it in the two newspapers. Lung cancer was only a bit behind in reality, with 75,000 deaths. It was mentioned only five times in total. I hope this omission is not because some newspapers run cigarette ads.

On the other hand, tornadoes killed about ninety people annually at the time. A considerable number—sixty-one in all—were mentioned in the news columns. Those who died from tornadoes usually had their name in the paper. Those who died from stomach cancer were all but invisible to the media, even though there were almost 100,000 of the latter.

What does this show? Some hazards receive more publicity than they deserve on an actuarial basis. Others are close to non-existent in the media. This lack of relationship with reality accounts for much risk misunderstanding.

An editor might take exception to this. "Look," she could say, "tornadoes, accidents, murders are interesting. My readers want more stories on them—our surveys back this up. They don't want to hear about stomach cancers and strokes, unless there's a magical new cure. Print your own newspaper filled with stories on diabetes and emphysema cases, and see how many copies you sell."

So we reach a tautology. Editors emphasize stories on certain hazards of life, and exclude most of the rest from their columns or TV stories. They do this because readers tell them that's what they want. Meanwhile, readers are told only of a few risks. They believe, as the song title has it, that's all there is. They are inevitably not interested in stories on other presumably boring sources of death, such as tuberculosis. The circle goes round and round, and nobody seems able to break it.

Are celebrities worthy of that status because their names appear on the front page of the *National Inquirer*, or do we see their names on scandal sheets just because they are celebrities? Are memorable disasters like Love Canal and Chernobyl unforgettable because they have appeared before our eyes, or would we remember them if terrible pictures had not been flashed in front of us?

Dread of Risks

Some aspects of risk just conjure up more dread than others. Exactly why this should be so is far from clear to psychologists.

Consider a few examples that have nothing to do with undesirable facilities. AIDS, for millions of people, is about as desirable as the black plague. Students who have contracted it or its predecessor, HIV, have been expelled from schools merely for that fact. Barbara Bush and Princess Diana made front pages around the world when they picked up babies with the disease.

While the AIDS epidemic is a terrible one, it still causes fewer deaths than diseases receiving much less publicity. I have already mentioned such "unknowns," as far as newspapers are concerned, illnesses such as stomach cancer, diabetes, and tuberculosis. We clearly have a greater dread of AIDS than these more obscure maladies.

The Decision Research group, mentioned in chapter 2, found that events most dreaded were nuclear weapons, terrorism, warfare, and nerve gas. The research was done before the onset of AIDS. Presumably that disease would not be far behind the others listed.

No known method of finding waste sites can eliminate dread. However, a fair siting system should allow people to put their dread into the context of other factors. They cannot be merely told, "You don't have the right to fear certain things."

Morality of Waste Sites

What does morality have to do with a landfill? As Professor Sandman notes, "American society has decided over the last two decades that pollution isn't just harmful—it's evil."[9] Questions that once only a minister or rabbi wrestled with now come from the audience in public information meetings.

If something is wicked, and not just undesirable, it falls into an entirely different mental category. This tends to upset risk analysts and other technical experts. I doubt that many have taken even one course in ethics and morals, let alone minored in them.

The scientists and engineers who evaluate risks are probably as moral as the rest of us. It's just that they have not thought of how their personal standards are applicable to a potential leak from a hazardous waste site.

If pollution is indeed sinful, by definition it is more than a matter of microrems and milligrams. *Any* emission is then a bad thing. As Sandman writes, imagine a police chief who said that one or two child molesters roaming the streets were "acceptable."

"Unreasonable," might respond the risk analysts. "We've been trained to evaluate and understand risks. Now you ask questions about morality, more suitable to a philosophy or religion course. We can't deal with this. Now if you'll just look at the next slide on the screen..."

That approach generally does not get far. At least some people in a potential community see things in terms of ethics, and will not be swayed by talk of obscure chemicals.

Loss of Control over Hazards

Loss of control is precisely what communities often feel when an unwanted facility is proposed. As Charles Wolf writes,

> On the local level, implementation of national policy comes down to a question of alternative sites, not whether a facility is wanted at all. It does no good to remind "locals" that their elected representatives participated in formulating the policy. Community people will contend *they* were not consulted, did not approve, and will not accept the proposed action.[10]

The scenario has been played out innumerable times. Technical experts from the state capitol check in at the local motel, setting up a meeting with community leaders or the public. They have good news: "You are the best site in the entire state or region. Aren't you pleased?"

Then the battle for control gets underway. Sometimes the locals win, sometimes the outsiders. Neither would deny that it is control that's at stake.

We see the same effect, on a smaller scale, getting into a car. Most people would rather drive than be a passenger. Back-seat drivers try to retain some control by instructing the driver on what to do and not to do.

In 1958, a famous psychological experiment was performed. Pairs of rhesus monkeys were given electrical shocks that could be avoided by pressing a control. Only one of the pair could operate the control. The other was a passive member of the team. So each team had an "executive" monkey who exerted control, and a submissive member who could do nothing to avoid shocks.

The executive monkey corresponds to the siting agency, which gets shocks but has some control over the situation. The passive monkey corresponds to the local community, which usually feels that it has no authority over what happens to it (although in reality it often does).

After the experiment was over, the animals were examined for internal ulcers. Which of the two monkeys had the most ulcers? As Gentile notes,

> If you chose [the passive monkey], you are most probably correct. Despite these earlier findings [that the executive monkey had more stress] and the popular consensus of opinion, it is not the stress of decision-making that causes ulcers, or other psychogenic disturbances; rather, it is the lack of predictability and control over the outcome that causes such problems. With lack of predictability comes fear, often helplessness and depression, and sometimes even death.[11]

Because local communities targeted for these facilities often feel a lack of control, many of their citizens do experience this helplessness and depression. Curiously enough, many of those in the siting agencies think that the local communities are the ones in control. The lawsuits trying to block the site originate from the towns and counties trying to keep the proposed facility away. The executive monkeys think they are the passive ones. In reality, it is the communities that almost invariably undergo the lengthy psychological distress. They correspond to the passive monkeys.

Any siting system, to be acceptable, has to have a fundamental rule: No community is forced to take a facility—a precise definition of control.

If one of the major psychological outrage factors is loss of control, who should control the facility *after* it is built? There are a number of possibilities—the community itself, the agency that planned it, a contractor, or yet another group.

Planning agencies do not want even the hint of local control because they think the locals would shut it down at the first opportunity. If it's been shoved down their throats, why wouldn't they?

If a community has willingly accepted the site, this tug-of-war does not take place. There is little reason for a community to shut down a facility they have agreed to, unless it leaks or is otherwise defective.

Since a Dutch auction will, by definition, produce a community that has voluntarily accepted the unwanted facility, there is little or no threat of a subsequent shut-down. It would be equivalent to a community's shooting itself in the foot.

Because people do occasionally, for various reasons, point a gun at their lower extremities, in chapter 11 I will discuss the unlikely possibility of a change of heart. For the vast majority of cases, the community should have as much control as it wants. This should definitely include the option of owning and operating it themselves. Whether or not it hires environmental engineers and other professionals, or contracts it out, will be completely up to them.

Paul Slovic, the noted risk psychologist to whom I have referred in chapter 2, published an invaluable poll in 1993. He asked respondents two types of questions. First, what actions by an agency would increase your trust in them? Second, what would decrease your trust? As well, he asked, for each of the questions, how much trust would be increased or decreased.[12]

Slovic asked about forty questions in all. The results confirmed some notions of social scientists, but contradicted others.

He found marked asymmetry of the results. Actions that produced a decrease in trust had a greater negative effect than positive actions. For example, if records of a facility were falsified—the action producing the greatest loss of trust—the level of trust went down by about 60 percent. If an evacuation plan exists—the second-most action generating the second-most increased trust—the level of trust rose by about 10 percent. Put another way, it is easier to reduce trust than it is to increase it.

What does all this have to do with who controls a waste facility? The action that would *most* increase trust is the ability for a local authority to close a plant or facility, that is, having complete control over its fate. This would increase trust by about 20 percent, about twice as much as the second-highest action, the aforementioned evacuation plan. Control over the facility is something the reverse Dutch auction offers, and other siting systems do not. The other siting systems allow for dialogue, negotiation, citizen's advisory boards and the like, but no ultimate control.

Over the past two decades, social scientists have worked on various proposals to make waste sites more acceptable to surrounding communities. Slovic's work shows that most of their proposals have little if any effect. Only the ability to control the closing of the plant is significant in increasing trust.

For example, if plant officials met with the public, it would increase trust by about 1 percent. If radioactive emissions were monitored (assuming the facility contained radioactivity), trust would go up by about 2 percent. A local advisory board would boost trust by perhaps 5 percent. Tours of the plant would do about the same. On and on the list goes, but only the ability to shut down the plant, or true local control, stands out in terms of trust generating.

Control is one of the key issues in any siting controversy. Only the reverse Dutch auction allows for it, since other siting systems are ultimately a form of coercion.

Loss of Community

Related to the loss of control that many people feel when a waste site is being considered is the potential loss of togetherness. Mary Douglas, the noted anthropologist, has called attention to the "loss of community" when a disliked facility is built. A siting agency may say, "look at the new jobs this facility will bring to your town." They may not realize that is just these phrases that turn some citizens away from the project. Some want their community to remain just the way it is and has been.[13]

Others may regard this as foolish. No place can remain in a time capsule forever. That's true enough, but some people want it that way. As Wolf says, "In building a [locally unwanted land use], regardless of attitudes towards its risks, residents perceive a threat to a settled way of life and a set of stable relations that constitute the sense of community and the satisfaction that provides. These social supports and informal services also sustain community viability by providing access to and control over local resources."

This is merely another way of saying, "there goes the neighborhood." While this phrase was once a quasijoke, it now forms fighting words when that unwanted land use is just over the horizon.

The loss of community factor extends even to facilities that almost everybody wants, such as a new college in town. There may be studious professors, but they are accompanied by loose living and noisy students. How much the town or county changing irrevocably impinges on the other outrage factors is not clear.

Fairness and Equity

Nevadans, who are asked under the Nuclear Waste Policy Act to accept high-level nuclear waste, have an enormous panoply of arguments why they should not accept it. Two of them cut to our sense of fair play. The first would be, approximately: "All this waste comes from nuclear power plants. No doubt the electricity derived from these plants has done some good for the people around those reactors. But none of these reactors are in Nevada. Why should we take wastes from plants that never benefitted us?"

The second would be, "Nevada is one of the least-populated states. We do have two Senators, but only two Representatives in Congress. The rest of the members are just ganging up on a small state."

The same principles apply when a rural community has to take the wastes, or prisoners, or mental health patients, from a big city. Large towns are generally resented in farm areas. When the documents proposing a hazardous waste site or a mental health facility arrive in the mail, it's like rubbing salt in a festering wound.

An example can bring the question closer to home. Each one of us generates some garbage. Suppose one week the garbage collection truck did not come around. The neighbors get together and decide that Mr. Jones' back yard, being the biggest one around, should be the place wastes should be dumped until the truck comes by. Regardless of how persuasive the neighbors are, chances are the unfortunate Jones will not be convinced that his back yard is the right place for the trash. "It's not fair," he will say, "I generate mine, and I'll take care of it. Why should I deal with yours?"

No community should have to take an undesirable facility unless it is convinced that it has struck a fair bargain. Only they can decide where the balance point lies. Nobody else, no matter how wise, can do it for them.

Low-Frequency versus High-Frequency Risks

Risk analysts sometimes joke about "the risk of the week." That is, we get so much information on risks—pesticides, cholesterol, Ebola disease—that we cannot keep up with them all.

One way we subconsciously cope with this is to screen out familiar, low-frequency risks. This may be the only way we can handle being bombarded with news about novel and sometimes frightening hazards.[14]

For example, we may assume a pose of personal invulnerability to risks—"it can't happen to me." This attitude was prevalent in the widespread resistance, lasting for decades, to using seat belts.

Another screening method is fatalism, most aptly described in the Doris Day song of the 1950s, "Que Sera, Sera"—what will be, will be.

In this view, small risks may affect us. Then again they may not. There is little we can do.

Finally, there is skepticism: "Joe smoked for 50 years, and never developed lung cancer. Don't talk to me about smoking."

How does our screening mechanism for familiar and low-frequency risks affect siting? By definition, unbuilt facilities are not known too well. They may or may not produce low-frequency risks, but a community does not know that. As far as they are concerned, the new installation is abnormal. The mechanisms it uses to screen out common risks just do not work. It looms as more frightening than it really is.

Distrust of Experts

Is there really distrust of experts in terms of waste facilities? In one survey, 77 percent of Tennessee respondents favored leaving siting decisions to "scientific experts" (in contrast to only 41 percent of state legislators who felt that way).[15]

This may be another example of the divergence between polling and reality. If these Tennesseeans had been asked, "Would you allow scientific experts to site wastes in your own town?" the responses would have been radically different.

The public siting meetings show clearly that the experts on the platform are not trusted. In a conference I once attended, the speaker, who had taken part in waste siting, explained what happened at these public meetings as part of a general phenomenon. According to him, *all* experts were not trusted, not merely the ones trying to explain siting decisions to an unbelieving audience.

"I don't understand it," he told me. "I've gone to all the right universities, taken all the right degrees. Yet I feel like Rodney Dangerfield: 'I don't get any respect.'"

Some experts get public trust. Consider doctors. Most people trust them. We generally go to physicians when something ails us.

In that sense, then, we trust physicians. They offer something valuable: relief from illness. Doctors cannot cure everything, but they help most of us.

Risk analysts offer little or nothing except hazard estimates. They produce no benefits. So when people do not trust them, it's not because of the platform presentation of these analysts. Rather, they have empty hands when it comes to benefits.

For example, consider a doctor instructing, "go down the hall and get your x-ray taken" and a risk analyst saying, "the hazards are fairly small for this hazardous waste site." Excessive x-rays can produce cancer. It can produce a benefit: knowledge about a medical condition such as a broken bone. The repellent facility rarely produces a benefit by itself.

Dentists are somewhere between doctors and risk analysts. Although we are supposed to visit the dentist every six months or a year, many do not. We often skip these visits even when they are covered by a dental plan at work. This implies a distrust of the benefits of a frequent check-up.

The reasons? Dentists often produce pain as well as saving decayed teeth and filling cavities. Doctors also inflict pain from time to time, but less than dentists. Doctors also usually work on parts of the body less sensitive than teeth.

So people intuitively perform a cost-benefit analysis when dealing with experts. Doctors produce, much of the time, large benefits with little pain or danger. Dentists produce benefits, but the good they do is often associated with pain. As a result, they are trusted less than doctors. Risk analysts rank lowest, generating few benefits but much psychic—not real—pain. No wonder they are not trusted.

While experts of any stripe do not like being distrusted, in the case of waste sites there is some rationale. As has been written, "It is rational to distrust the experts even without any expertise of one's own. People who are trying to sell a hazardous waste facility are no different from people who are trying to sell, say, insulation for a home. One does not have to understand what they are saying technically to suspect that they are not to be trusted."[16]

The public will trust experts in two situations. The first case is when they anticipate a benefit from the advice given. This condition applies to most medical advice.

The second case is when the information given by the expert does not really affect them. For example, the public may see a scientist on TV saying she has found the bones of the earliest ancestor of man. Most of the public will trust her statement, because it does not affect them strongly, except in a general, philosophical way. If that same trusted scientist advised the populace to accept something they do not want, she might be ignored.

Even in the best siting system, not *all* experts will be highly regarded. Believability is a function of personality and delivery as well as data. Nonetheless, if we had a rational siting system like the reverse Dutch auction, the overall level of distrust should decrease. This will be a great comfort to my risk analyst colleagues.

Luxury versus Necessity

Some things are luxuries; Donald Trump does not really need a yacht, although he obviously desires one. Food is a necessity.

Unwanted land uses have both these characteristics. The siting agency says, in effect, "This proposed new prison is a necessity for our state. A judge has ordered an end to the barbarous overcrowding of present prisons. If we don't build it, dangerous criminals will have to be set free to murder and rape."

The targeted community responds, "It may be a necessity for the state as a whole, but it's a luxury for us. We don't think too many of those freed criminals will come here. As you know, we're located just back of beyond. In fact, if some of these criminals escape from the new facility you're planning for us, we'll see a lot more of them that way. We can live without this luxury."

The Siting Process Can Be Just a Screen

The word "ham-handed" was invented long before the first dump was sited. It could be applied to most of the consultations since. Professor Sandman asked, "Does the agency come across as trustworthy or dishonest, concerned or arrogant? Does it tell the community what's going on before the real decisions are made? Does it listen and respond to community concerns?"[17]

The answers to the last two of these questions are usually "no," at least from the viewpoint of the public. The agencies do not often see it that way. That why David Evans, a Canadian consultant on siting, said that agencies often think, "the problem with public consultation is the public."[18] Just get rid of those pesky questioners, and all will be well.

This was echoed by Eleanor Winsor: "A member of the League of Women Voters...commented disparagingly to me, 'All the companies want to do is talk down to us. They never want to hear what we have to say. You know, sometimes our ideas work. The public is not as dumb as they think we are...I'm tired of being lectured 'at', but rarely listened 'to.'"[19]

Winsor goes on to tell the tale of a public meeting in which a citizen in the audience requested some air pollution data. She was told by the representative of the waste management firm on the platform, "You may have them. They are part of the regulatory record. Ask the [siting] agency to send them to you."

"Can't you just send them to me?" she asked.

No, she was told, you can get them from the siting agency under the Freedom of Information Act. As far as the questioner was concerned, the company may have had the data right in front of them, but was asking her to take legal action to get it.

The siting agency person saw the anger building up. He turned to the company spokesperson. "Is there any reason why you can't just send Mrs. X the information?"

"Well, no," was the answer.

"Then I suggest you send it to Mrs. X," the siting agency person said. As Dr. Winsor notes,

> The damage that the [waste management firm] sustained in this exchange was immediate and lasting. By making it so difficult for Mrs. X to obtain the informa- tion he infuriated her, the other people in the audience and the [siting] agency. The agency facilitator commented to [Winsor] afterwards, "That company is just so darn arrogant. They could have gotten their facility if they had just paid a little attention to the citizens. Not providing the information when Mrs. X requested it was just one more example of how difficult they can be."

In New Jersey, the Siting Commission chairperson complained that the siting hearings "have turned into political rallies. The last thing that was discussed was siting criteria. It was how many people you can get into an auditorium to boo the speakers you don't like and cheer for the ones you support."[20]

Mentioning the *process* of consultation with the public could give the impression that just a few of the kinks have to be just ironed out. Then siting would be as easy as getting a sunburn in the Mojave Desert. Just hire a velvety public relations firm. Get Mr. Smoothie in front of the assembled townspeople, the reasoning goes, and we are home free. But Mr. Smoothie has already appeared many times, and he gets about the same amount of booing and hissing as less polished scientists.

The problem lies not with the slickness—of lack thereof—of the speakers, but in the process itself. People have to *ask* for a community meeting, not have it thrust upon them. These meetings will be a lot more sedate and informative than those in the past, because attendees will really want the facts this time. Mr. Smoothie, there is the door.

Familiar versus the Unfamiliar

This outrage factor relates to the memorability discussed above, but is not exactly the same. We are naturally more concerned about the unfamiliar than that which is customary. As Aaron Wildavsky wrote,

Is it our environment or ourselves that have changed? Would people like us have had this sort of concern in the past? Imagine our reaction if most of modern technology were being introduced today. Anyone aware of the ambiance of our times must be sensitive to the strong possibility that many risks, such as endless automotive engine explosions, would be postulated that need never occur, or, if they did, would be found unbearable. Wouldn't airliners crash into skyscrapers that would fall on others, killing tens of thousands? Who could prove otherwise? Even today there are risks from numerous small dams far exceeding those from nuclear reactors. Why is the one feared and not the other? Is it just that we are used to the old or are some of us looking differently at essentially the same sorts of experience?"[21]

Familiarity can apply to facilities we turn up our nose at as well as more common events of life. V. Kerry Smith, professor at North Carolina State University, polled householders in the Boston area.[22]

Previous national studies had shown that a hazardous waste site would need to be 100 miles from respondents' homes before the majority would voluntarily accept it. Suburban Boston was different, but not because Bay Staters liked risks any more.

In Professor Smith's words,

Our results for suburban Boston households indicate a threshold of about 10 miles for a majority of our respondents to accept a hazardous waste site.... This difference may be explained by the set of current land uses in the suburban Boston area which had 11 hazardous waste disposal sites as of 1982. Since individuals in this area live relatively close to these facilities, they may have adjusted their distance responses to reflect their local experiences with them.

Familiarity in New Hampshire

A. L. Rydant, an associate professor of geography at Keene State College in New Hampshire, found a curious example of our longing for the familiar. He analyzed opinion about landfills in Chesterfield, New Hampshire.[23]

In the early 1980s, the state passed legislation that would close down most small-town landfills. The purpose of this law was environmentally sound—landfills of the time generally leaked, contaminating water supplies. Few if any of them had been designed to prevent leaks. The next question was, what would replace them?

In 1983, the state passed yet another law, encouraging regional waste-handling facilities. That is, rather than reconstruct all the small land-fills, towns and counties would get together to build a larger, presumably leak-proof, facility. It could be a bigger landfill, a trash-to-energy plant, or something else.

The problem arose with the creation of the agency charged with finding a site for these new, bigger facilities. The usual process was followed. Thirty-one sites were chosen using criteria that remained mysterious to most of the public. These thirty-one were narrowed down to ten, then to three. Chesterfield was one of the lucky ones.

Opposition groups formed in the three towns. The Chesterfield branch adopted an old New Deal acronym—CCC (Concerned Citizens of Chesterfield). Professor Rydant was called in to poll the townspeople on how they felt about the large regional site proposed for their back yard.

Rydant found contradictions in the minds of residents. Of the five possibilities they faced, by far the most popular was a regional trash-to-energy plant, with over 40 percent favoring it. However, 88 percent opposed it being in Chesterfield.

In terms of familiarity with the various waste facilities, Rydant found

> When asked if they were willing to see an individual town dump (i.c., similar to what they had in the past, only improved) half said no. An important minority (41 percent) said that were *in favor* of a town landfill; 9 percent were unsure. Perhaps the "acceptability" of a town landfill is best explained by the response of one long-time resident, who said, "We've always had a town dump. Why change?"...
>
> Interviewers noted that a number of the people replying negatively towards [a regional incinerator] were not sure what one was, or what its effects might be. More than one resident commented, "The idea scares me."

That so many people would favor a disposal facility of any type was greeted with joy by *Waste Age,* a leading trade magazine. It bannered the results in heavy type on the article's front page: "A poll of 112 of the 2,700 residents of a small town found a large minority (41 percent) favoring a small-town dump!"

The only problem with a local town landfill, that is, one that would not accept the wastes of other towns, is that it is precisely how the system started. The battles had produced untold arguments and legal disputes, but little had been accomplished. The desire for familiarity brought people, in the words of the old Al Jolson song, "California, Here I Come," "right back where [they] started from."

The solution that Rydant proposes for all this was the familiar one: more education. In the article's words, "Waste managers...must clearly dedicate greater resources to public education and its consequent public participation programs."

The people of Chesterfield already know quite a bit about the options, or at least think they do. For example, 70 percent claimed intimate knowledge of the proposed regional landfill. As I have noted previously, education is necessary, but from the viewpoint of building something that people do not want, it's not sufficient.

The question of familiarity with risks arose in the case of the Monitored Retrievable Storage proposal in Tennessee. This Department of Energy suggestion to temporarily store spent nuclear fuel rods from reactors was roundly denounced in the rest of Tennessee. The city of Oak Ridge, where the MRS would have been located if built, appointed a committee to look at the question.

Some of the task force members knew about matters nuclear, but others were unfamiliar with the technology. They could have adopted the approach of merely studying the voluminous literature on the subject, but they decided this would be too passive an approach. Rather, they traveled to many laboratories around the country where nuclear wastes were being analyzed and stored. They became knowledgeable about what was involved in setting up a waste site in Oak Ridge. Eventually, based in part on their recommendation, the Oak Ridge City Council unanimously approved the siting. As I have noted elsewhere, the project never was built due to other reasons, but the people most affected saw their representatives vote "yes."

As babies, the world is completely unknown to us. Gradually, we become familiar with both the good and bad in it. About the same can happen concerning the facilities we are nervous about, if the conditions are right.

The Rate of Change, not the Change Itself

As far as sociologists can determine, it is the rate of change of new risks being introduced that provokes our concerns. There has always been resistance to changes that might bring generate new hazards. A century ago in Britain, the "red flag" law required an auto to have a man carrying a small banner walking in front. Millions of cars whiz about today in Britain without benefit of a flagman.

We do accept hazards, but only so many at a time. Alvin Toffler, in *Future Shock* and other books, says that the overall pace of innovation has increased. Whether this is true is debatable, but there is little question that many people *think* that it has.

With innovation inevitably come risks and hazards of various types. The class of undesirable facilities I have been talking about seems to pose risks because, almost by definition, they are facilities to which we are not accustomed. After all, how many of us live next to a prison, mental illness half-way house or hazardous waste installation?

No siting system can do much about our *present* unfamiliarity. If the system works, more of us will gradually know about them. In the long run, they will become more of an everyday matter. The clouds of unfamiliarity will lift a bit.

Uncertainty of Risks

One of the major factors generating outrage by the public is the uncertainty of the risks associated with facilities. "We just don't know how big the hazards will be," is the refrain. "How can we be expected to accept something that is so inexact in its dangers?"

The scientists try to explain their calculations with probabilities and standard deviations, but without success. "How can we judge these estimates?" they are told. "There could be all sorts of hidden factors that we don't know about. They would appear when it's too late to do anything."

This opinion poses a fundamental question about practically anything new. We never know all the risks until some time has passed. The invention of the water closet by Joseph Bramah in 1778 was thought to be a great boon to humanity.[24] Yet a book reviewer wrote,

> [It] brought death to multitudes of people...the immediate causes of death were epidemics of cholera and typhoid, and it was not until a century later that the link between Bramah's device and these epidemics were fully confirmed.... The privy discharged into a sewer; the sewers discharged into rivers; private companies drew water from the rivers and returned it to the taps of private houses.[25]

This example shows that we will *never* be able to predict all risks, even for technologies, like the flush toilet, that seem to be much better compared to their predecessors.

Unloved facilities are no different. The community considering accepting it will have to weigh both what is and what is not known, and come to a conclusion that suits them. The water closet example shows that nobody venturing upon new ground can ever be completely certain of its risks.

Undetectability of Risks

An undetectable risk is less acceptable than a detectable risk.[26] This accounts in part for the dread shown about many nuclear facilities. Radiation cannot be seen. It cannot be detected without the use of scientific instruments that members of the public do not own. Even if they owned them, they would find difficulty in operating them. While radiation is not a *scientific* mystery, it remains one to the general public.

A community might prefer a facility that spews out easily seen plumes of air or water pollution. They would say, "At least we can keep an eye—or nose—on it."

The real problem is not so much the undetectability of radiation or other pollution, but the inaccessibility of the information. A radioactive waste site will have various counters and monitors around the perimeter to measure any radiation emitted. If the waste site leaks, radiation will be detected. However, the collected data will be buried in reports and scientific articles, mostly unreadable by the general public.

"You want last year's data on beta-radiation? No problem," the public will be told. "It's contained in *Report of the Conference on Ambient Water Radiation,* volume 232, issued by Los Alamos Scientific Publishers. Should be at your university library. The graph is on page A17. You can see the numbers—they're in picorads, of course. I'm sure you know how to translate that to microrems; just use the appropriate quality factor." Most people will have given up by this point.

If a community receives adequate compensation, some of it can be devoted to collecting environmental data, independently of the site operator. It can be put into a form that is understandable by the site's neighbors, since they—not a far-away and bureaucratic organization—will control the data collection.

This is what has been done in Japan.[27] For some waste-to-energy facilities, the instantaneous level of air pollution is displayed in big neon signs above the installation. It may also be published in scientific articles, but the latter do not much interest the local community. They can see for themselves, minute by minute, exactly what is happening. It is a little like the moving headlines over Times Square.

So the problem of undetectability is linked to the related question of inaccessibility. The buried data can be unearthed with enough funds for the local community.

Delayed versus Immediate Risks

Allied to the concern about undetectability is the dichotomy be-tween delayed and immediate effects. Cancer is almost never immedi-ate. Because it can appear many years after exposure, many people become much more concerned.

Asking people whether they want an immediate or delayed effect from pollution poses a cruel choice. Intuitively, we shrink from effects that appear decades later. We may have been carrying a destructive agent within us all that time.

High versus Low Informativeness

When I discussed the memorability of a hazard, it was primarily how the media covered it. There are aspects of how we get information that are not merely a measure of headline size.

One of them was described by the Decision Research group in Or-egon as "informativeness." Some accidents that take many lives "may have little or no impact on perceived risk if it occurs as part of a famil-iar and well-understood (although improbable) process. In contrast, a much smaller accident may greatly enhance perceived risk and trigger strong protective action because it signals a possible change in the system that may lead to further accidents."[28]

Informativeness is then the size of the signal we get from an acci-dent or disaster. Even if no newspaper or television station had carried news about Three Mile Island, the regulators at the Nuclear Regula-tory Commission would have changed many of their procedures. The accident gave them a strong signal that all was not well.

Informativeness is related to familiarity, although the two ideas are not exactly the same. The Decision Research group gives some ex-amples to illustrate the concept.

Two jumbo jets colliding on a runway, killing 600 (this actually happened in the 1970s) was regarded as giving low information on risks. However, botulism in a well-known brand of food, killing only two, was highly informative. This was even though the food itself was quite familiar. It gave information that steps had to be taken to prevent it from recurring. The jumbo jet accident could have been regarded as giving low information because it was "just one of those things," that is, something that happens from time to time. Little can be done about it (although in reality, many regulatory measures were later taken to prevent runway collisions of this type).

The example shows that we are not always governed by the number of total deaths in an accident or event. Its informativeness can affect how we perceive it.

A Summary of Outrage

The above outrage factors are only part of what makes up the sense of outrage, so evident at public meetings. Some are related to each other: undetectability is obviously akin to unfamiliarity. Others are more distinctive.

Each of us will react differently to each of these factors. Whatever the precise blend, terminology and relationship, they produce the strong emotions reflected in the NIMBY dragon.

Many of the above outrage factors come into play when the threat, explicit or implied, is made that the facility will be built using the powers of eminent domain.

Governments have the right to take land or build facilities if they pay "fair compensation" to those affected. For example, a new highway takes up land that otherwise would be employed for farming, houses, or other uses. Most landowners will sell chunks of property to the highway authority at a reasonable price. There often are a few hold-outs who want more money. If those who do not like the price offered continue to resist, the entire highway could be halted.

Laws of eminent domain come into play here. The government can expropriate the land of those who refuse to cooperate, and then let a court decide what is a fair price.

In the vast majority of cases, there is little outside sympathy for the resisters. The public says, "Two or three farmers are holding up a multi-million dollar highway just to make a few extra dollars. We can't face any more traffic jams." The farmers who have already agreed to compensation say, "I won't get my check for the property they're taking from me until old Harkness down the road gives in. I sure could use the money today."

Old Harkness soon finds he has few friends. He is abandoned by all those who would ordinarily support him in his battle against a vast government bureaucracy.

The system has worked well for projects like highways and hydro dams. As a result, siting agencies often think they can do the same, either by using the power of eminent domain or some variation on it.

Consider two examples. In New York, legislators who drew up the bill governing low-level radioactive wastes thought they had solved the problem with a variance on eminent domain. The law was drawn up so that objectors found it very difficult, if not impossible, to sue the state. The inability to have one's day in court is, of course, what fuels resentment over eminent domain proceedings. Not deterred by the inability to take legal action, protesters took to the roads to battle state troopers, and eventually brought the siting process to a halt.

The 1991 National Energy Strategy issued by the U.S. Department of Energy had a clause dealing with the state of Nevada. The Silver State had effectively blocked DOE from proceeding with the proposed high-level waste repository by declining to issue state permits for the necessary drilling and testing. DOE wanted to get around this, and exercise a type of eminent domain, by legally abrogating the need for these licenses. Then Nevada could not stop the Federal government from proceeding. Most Nevadans thought this was yet another example of Federal arrogance.

The history of most siting attempts using eminent domain, or some legal variation on it, is bleak. In almost all instances, the agency trying this legal device gets little or no public sympathy, in contrast to the support they receive when using eminent domain to build roads and dams. They almost invariably find that while they may have the legal power to build the uninvited facility, protest stops them. In the process, they have made many people extremely angry.

Tragedy of the Commons and Psychology

Garrett Hardin is one of the chief theorists of the environmental movement. In "Tragedy of the Commons," written almost three decades ago in 1968, he said that sometimes the minority has to be coerced for the benefit of the majority. In 17th century Britain, sheep were grazed on a commons within each town. From the viewpoint of each sheep owner, adding one more animal to his flock could profit its owner without much harming the shared grassland.[29]

If enough shepherds brought their extra sheep to the commons, it would be ruined. There would not be enough for all. Laws had to be passed infringing on the previously untrammeled rights of sheep owners, to save them from mutual destruction.

In a modern vein, "The construction of a dam benefits a large number of people by providing flood control and irrigation. A small number of people are hurt by the dam because their land is covered with water. The value of the submerged land is less than the value of the *improvement.* Similarly, we set aside wilderness areas, which theoretically benefit the entire population at the cost of the timber or minerals on the site."[30]

The effect of these measures is to restrict the legal rights of certain people—those living upstream of where a dam is to be built, sheep owners, and so on. Hardin argues that these measures are necessary for the preservation or creation of something worthwhile. Examples would be a commons that is not overgrazed by sheep or a hydro dam.

Now return to the raucous public siting meeting. Almost all of those speaking will identify themselves as environmentalists, if pressed. Some speakers will explicitly refer to their Sierra Club or National Audubon Society memberships. Yet the voices from the audience are clear— keep that facility away. We do not want any of our rights infringed or abrogated.

Why would Hardin's message, read by most environmentalists, be discarded in the heat of a siting battle? They probably would say that the examples that Hardin uses are of projects that do more good for more of the people than they do harm to some of them. Each sheepherder has to cut down somewhat on the size of his flock. If he does not, the commons will be overgrazed and all sheep will perish.

The argument about an unloved site is then, in the Hardin way of thinking, a debate about the relative good and harm deriving from the facility. The potential harm seems real and concrete, whereas the good seems nebulous and diffuse.

Take, for example, a proposed high-security prison. The loss is easily imagined—a hardened convict breaking into one's house and holding a family hostage. The good is more vague. The convicts may be overcrowded in their present facility, but they deserve it for their crimes against society, do they not? There may be some judge's order to relieve cramped quarters floating around the judicial system, but who knows exactly what it says or demands? Besides, most of the criminals are not from this area, so why bring them here? Put this way, the harm is clear, but the good, if any, would go to other communities. The case against it is then clear, in spite of Hardin's demonstration.

The siting arguments that have raged in this country are, in a sense, Hardin's "Tragedy of the Commons" writ large. We all live in a commons that require some type of restrictions. When those enforcing those restrictions knock on our door, we make a point of not being home.

Can Psychological Attitudes Change?

Attitudes toward undesirable facilities *do* change, although the precise mechanisms are not known.

Take, for example, trailers. For decades, people who lived in a trailer were not just regarded as from the wrong side of the tracks—they were not anywhere *near* the tracks. Having aluminum skirts around your dwelling was about as low as you could sink.

Popper writes that trailers were

> a classic American [local unwanted land use]. Localities have traditionally shunned trailer parks. But when soaring prices and interest rates for conventional housing sent the industry into decline, manufactured housing began to thrive; by 1982 it had a 36 percent share of the nation's entire market for new homes, and it was no longer ugly, flimsy, unsafe, or considered tacky-cheap. In most parts of the country, a two-section, energy-efficient manufactured home with three bedrooms, two bathrooms, a garage, and 1,200 square feet of floor space sold for under $40,000, including land, and was hard to distinguish—inside or outside—from a standard single-family house.... Many states and localities, particularly those with acute shortages of affordable housing, moved to revoke or loosen land-use laws that discriminated against trailers, trailer parks and manufactured housing generally.... Manufactured housing was not yet universally desirable, but in many places it was no longer a [local unwanted land use].[31]

So attitudes can shift. In the case of trailers, it was partly driven by economic factors as well as aesthetics. The earliest trailers were built as cheaply as possible, with tarpaper and odd bits of wood. Little wonder that they were despised by those who did not have to live in them.

Manufacturers eventually discovered an upscale market. They improved their product, making it closer in appearance to regular housing. At the same time, the costs of nonmanufactured houses were soaring. Many people thought, why pay $80,000 for a house when I can get something that looks almost the same for half that amount? The gradual improvement in trailers' appearance led to their aesthetic acceptance. What was once unappreciated became tolerated.

What seems terrible in one year or decade may be met with grudging acceptance the next. There are no trailer parks in Beverly Hills to this day, but they are now scattered in many middle-class communities throughout the land.

Some of the psychological factors that affect our attitudes are more important than others, but ultimately we each have our own personal mixture. The NIMBY dragon perches on each of our shoulders.

Notes

1. Jane Hansen, "Two States May Force Georgia to Seek Dump," *Atlanta Journal* (9 June 1985).
2. Stanley M. Nealey, Barbara D. Melber, and William L. Rankin, *Public Opinion and Nuclear Energy* (Lexington, Mass.: Lexington Books, 1981) 100.
3. Michael O'Hare, "'Not on *My* Block You Don't': Facility Siting and the Strategic Importance of Compensation," *Public Policy* 25 (4) (Fall 1977): 437.
4. Richard E. Schuler, "Let's Make a Deal!" *Waste Management Research Report* 2 (1) (Winter 1990): 1.
5. Quoted in Paul Slovic, Baruch Fischhoff, and Sarah Lichtenstein, "Facts vs. Fears: Understanding Perceived Risk," presented at Royal Society, London, 12 November 1980.
6. Frank J. Popper, "The Environmentalist and the LULU," *Environment* 27 (1985): 10.
7. Peter M. Sandman, "Risk Communication: Facing Public Outrage," *EPA Journal* (November 1987): 21–22.
8. B. Combs and P. Slovic, "Causes of Death: Biased Newspaper Coverage and Biased Judgments," *Journalism Quarterly* 56 (1979): 837–43.
9. Sandman, "Risk Communication," ibid.
10. C. P. Wolf, "The NIMBY Syndrome: Its Cause and Cure," *Annals of New York Academy of Medicine*, 216.
11. J. Ronald Gentile, *Educational Psychology* (Dubuque, Iowa: Kendall/Hunt Publishing, 1990), 89. The original experiments were described in J. V. Brady, "Ulcers in 'Executive' Monkeys," *Scientific American* 199 (1958): 95; J. V. Brady, R. W. Porter, D. G. Conrad, and J. W. Mason, "Avoidance Behavior and the Development of Gastroduodenal Ulcers," *Journal of the Experimental Analysis of Behavior* 1 (1958): 69; and R. W. Porter, J. V. Brady, D. Conrad, J. W. Mason, R. Galambos, and D. M. Rioch, "Some Experimental Observations on Gastrointestinal Lesions in Behaviorally Conditioned Monkeys," *Psychosomatic Medicine* 20 (1958): 379. However, as Gentile notes, "There was a serious design problem that inadvertently led Brady and his collaborators to the wrong conclusion. More carefully controlled research was done by Weiss who, in studies on rats, isolated the operative factors to be predictability and control—or rather, their absence—in producing ulcers and emotionality." See also M. E. P. Seligman, *Helplessness: On Depression, Development and Death* (San Francisco: Freeman, 1975): 116–21.
12. Paul Slovic, "Perceived Risk and Democracy," *Risk Analysis* 13 (6) (1993): 675.
13. Mary Douglas, *Risk Acceptability According to the Social Sciences* (New York: Russell Sage Foundation, 1985).
14. Daniel J. Fiorino, "Environmental Risk and Democratic Process: A Critical Review," *Columbia Journal of Environmental Law* 14 (2) (1989): 501.
15. W. Lyons, P. Freeman, and M. R. Fitzgerald, "Public Opinion and the Legislative Response to the Hazardous Waste Challenge," presented at American Political Science Association, Washington, 1986. Quoted in Wolf.
16. Peter M. Sandman, "Getting to Maybe: Some Communications Aspects of Siting Hazardous Waste Facilities," *Seton Hall Legislative Journal* 9 (1985): 437, especially 446.
17. Ibid.
18. David Evans, "Facing the Fallacy that the Problem with Public Consultation is the Public," presented at "Hazardous Materials/Wastes: Social Aspects of Facility Planning and Management," Toronto, Ontario, September 1990.

19. Eleanor W. Winsor, "Public Relations and Participation: A Trail of Frustration with a Chance for Improvement." In *Toxics and Hazardous Waste*, ed. Jeffrey Evans, (Lancaster, PA: Technomic Publishing, 1987) 377.
20. Goldensohn, "Opponents, Officials Charge Politicizing of Waste Site Debate," *Newark Star-Ledger* (2 December 1984): 12. Quoted in Sandman, "Getting to Maybe."
21. Aaron Wildavsky, *American Scientist* (1979). Quoted in Slovic et al., "Facts vs. Fears."
22. V. Kerry Smith and W. Desvousges, "Value of Avoiding a Lulu: Hazardous Waste Disposal Sites," *Review of Economics and Statistics* 68 (2) (May 1986): 293.
23. A. L. Rydant, "A Micro Study of NIMBYism," *Waste Age* (January 1990): 44.
24. Christopher Hamlin, *A Science of Impurity* (London: Hilger, 1990).
25. Eric Ashby, "Signature of Deadly Water," *Nature* 348 (6301) (December 6, 1990): 495.
26. Sandman, "Getting to Maybe," 451.
27. Constance Hornig, "How Japan Keeps NIMBY At Bay," *Waste Age* (January 1990): 56–57.
28. Slovic et al., "Facts vs. Fears."
29. Garrett Hardin, "The Tragedy of the Commons," *Science* 162 (1968): 1243–48.
30. Daniel E. Willard and Melinda M. Swenson, "Why Not in Your Backyard? Scientific Data and Nonrational Decisions about Risk," *Environmental Management* 8 (2) (1984): 93–100.
31. Popper, "The Environmentalist."

7

Economics of Auctions

A Story about Auctions

Consider how auctions worked in an unlikely setting, a university department. The tale has nothing to do with nuclear or toxic wastes. Rather, it illustrates how the auction mechanism can be used to solve a seemingly intractable problem. For this delightful yarn, I am indebted to William Boyes, Chair of the Department of Economics at Arizona State University.[1]

The problem was as follows: The entire College of Business was to be moved to a new building. Ordinarily, this would be a cause of celebration: Out of the dingy and musty old rooms, and into the new and sparkling offices.

However, there was an unseemly squabble over who should get which of the new offices. Some were interior and had no windows, clearly less desirable. Others had magnificent views of Phoenix. Who should get which?

The Management Department specified that the selection of rooms for *its* faculty would be solely by seniority. The longer you had been teaching at the school, the better your chances of getting a favored window office. The reason? "It had always been done that way."

Lowly assistant professors, few of them assigned a window office, pointed out that they usually spent long hours in their offices, doing research. Full professors with tenure would rarely use their window offices even if they had them, being occupied elsewhere.

Besides, some of those on the bottom of the pecking order pointed out, management, the subject of their academic department, had to be concerned with factors other than mere seniority. What type of example would they be setting to the world? Thus, in the view of those who got the interior offices, the process was unfair and unreasonable. Nonetheless, the decision stood.

The chair of the Finance Department noticed the argument in the adjoining hallways, and chose a different approach. The selection of offices would be done on a more rational and presumably fairer basis.

One fine morning, the Finance Chair posted a sign-up sheet outside his headquarters. The first professor to write his name would get his or her choice of offices; the second, the choice after that, and so on. What could be fairer?

It is true that seniority had been discarded, those unfortunates at the bottom of the list noted. But the advantage now went to those whose present offices were close to the chair's. They passed his bulletin board frequently. Those professors who, by luck, happened to be out of town or on sabbatical on the day the sheet was posted ended up with windowless offices, regardless of their seniority. While correcting one type of unfairness, the sign-up sheet created another one.

Let us be completely random, said the head of the Statistics Department. Give everyone an equal chance, by rolling dice or spinning a roulette wheel. That way, there would be no complaints about seniority ruling everything, or missing your opportunity on the sign-up sheet because you were in the washroom when it was posted.

Even this perfectly fair system was never tried. Those in the Statistics Department who already had good offices in the old building were afraid of getting a worse deal in the new. Why trust blind chance?

While Professor Boyes never mentioned it, there might well have been a Department of Rational Expectations with a different approach. In this mythical department, the chair might have said,

> This emphasis on rolling dice or sign-up sheets is foolish. Different professors have different needs, and we should take account of this. What is an office for, anyway? It's for doing research, talking with other faculty, making phone calls, storing books, among other things. We'll compile a list of all the purposes to which an office can be put, poll the professors on what is or could be most important, and develop an equation describing all these factors. Then we'll let a computer, not a mere human, assign the offices based on this equation.

These fine words would have proved unworkable in practice. The faculty in this imaginary department would spend so much time debating all the factors that should go into the equation, and the weights that should be attached to each factor, that no agreement could ever be reached. The computer would never flicker on.

The Economics Department Develops an Auction

Now it came down to the economics professors. They were fond of telling colleagues in other departments that they had found the key to how society works. But could they come up with a better system, based on that knowledge?

After some debate, they decided to hold an auction, or what economists call rationing by price. Before they got to that stage, they considered a variety of other proposals. The more senior faculty members said that there was really only one way to allocate offices. I need not specify what it was.

Other proposals were to base the allocation on research productivity, teaching effectiveness, height, weight, race, sex, and religion—the factors we often pretend to ignore. Since that complicated process could not be made to work by the Department of Rational Expectations, it was abandoned.

One burly professor pulled off the gloves and suggested a brawl for the right to the best offices, calling it office wrestlemania. This suggestion was thrown out of the ring, and the auction concept won.

The next question was, what type? There is more than one category of auction, as we will discuss below. The chair chose a single sealed-bid auction, similar to that used for bidding on government contracts.

This auction was as fair—or unfair—as other auctions. An assistant professor earns less money than a full professor. If the bids had gone to the thousands or tens of thousands of dollars level, that would have kept poverty-stricken junior faculty from ever looking out a window. However, the lowest successful bid was $75. All the faculty, even the poorest, could afford *that*.

The auction was different from government contract bidding in that the bid envelopes had to contain real money, which was not returned to the bidder. In an auction to perform services for the government, if I bid $100,000 and you bid $110,000, I get the contract.

The loser is not expected to pay the government $110,000, the amount of the losing bid. In the Economics Department auction, the bidders forfeited their bid money to a graduate student fund. This paid for student academic and travel scholarships.

In a government sealed-bid auction, the bidders are not supposed to know what their competitors are doing. There are severe legal penalties for collusion. Occasionally, in spite of these laws, passing of information on bids *does* take place, leading to bids that are suspiciously similar.

If there is collusion in government sealed-bid auctions, there has to be a kickback to the pre-arranged losing bid or bids. In other words, the losers have to be compensated for taking a fall. In the case of the office window auction, there would be no kickback. You either got a window in your office or you did not.

The Economics Department auction allowed bidders to ask others what their bids would be. Of course, questioners might not be told the truth. Someone might say that they were planning to offer $100 when their real bid was to be $200.

Consider how this relates to a community considering a bid to have an undesirable facility in its back yard. County X might really plan to enter the auction when the price to take the wastes reached $100 million. When other counties inquired about County X's price, they might be told, "We'll never enter the auction. We don't want those wastes at any price." Yet when the level reached $100 million, there would be County X, with its hand figuratively in the air.

Results of the Economics Department Auction

The results of the Economics Department auction? The highest bid was $500, and the next highest was $250. This is an example of the "winner's curse," well known in auction theory. The winner usually pays a much higher price than the runner-up.

Anyone who bid $75 or more got a window office, so the winner bid $425 too high. The $500 bidder could have gotten a window office for $75. Of course, if he had bid $70, he would have received an interior office. In effect, he bought himself a $425 insurance policy.

Faculty members are by nature prima donnas, as any university dean can attest. However, the auction worked well. The only complaint came from the winner, not the losers. He wished he had not paid the extra $425.

Counties, towns, and states are prima donnas, too. But if they used auction to site wastes, there would be few if any complaints from governors and county executives that they had been railroaded into something they did not want.

The Beginning of Auctions—in Babylon

Auctions go back to antiquity.[2] The first major historian in the Western World, Herodotus, describes a custom in Babylonian villages, 2,500 years ago, of auctioning maidens for marriage in an annual meeting.[3]

In every village once a year all the girls of marriageable age used to be collected together in one place, while the men stood round them in a circle; an auctioneer then called each one in turn to stand up and offered her for sale, beginning with the best-looking and going on to the second best as soon as the first had been sold for a good price. Marriage was the object of the transaction. The rich men who wanted wives bid against each other for the prettiest girls, while the humbler folk, who had no use for good looks in a wife, were actually paid to take the ugly ones, for when the auctioneer had got through all the pretty girls he would call upon the plainest, or even perhaps a crippled one, to stand up, and then ask who was willing to take the least money to marry her—and she was knocked down to whoever accepted the smallest sum. The money came from the sale of the beauties, who in this way provided dowries for their ugly or misshapen sisters.

It is not recorded whether these maidens were slaves—common at the time—or free. That would make a difference in how the auction was run, and the prices paid. Slave maidens presumably were not allowed to leave the auction block on their own; free young women could, for whatever reason.

Historical novels sometimes depict auctions of maidens, invariably beautiful. That was not true in Babylon. There were some that were attractive, but as Herodotus notes, others left a lot to be desired in terms of looks. I might add here that I am not endorsing the sexism or male chauvinism of these ancients, but merely describing what happened.

Now look at the situation for the viewpoint of the auctioneer. For the beautiful maidens, the bids rose rapidly. High prices were paid for the privilege of marrying them. The auctioneers had plenty of gold at the end of this phase.

If that is all there was to it, the system would not be of much historical interest. It would have been about the same as auctioning grain or fruit.

There *was* a difference. After all the beautiful or reasonable looking maidens left the auction block, there were some left standing. They may have been unattractive to Babylonian eyes, (although perhaps attractive to modern men), older, or both. For whatever reason, the auctioneers had some maidens remaining that no man would pay to wed.

Apparently they were under some legal obligation to make sure that *all* the maidens, not just the attractive ones, marched down the aisle. What to do? There was only one solution they could think of—pay the men in the audience to take the maidens off their hands.

Where did the money paid to the bidders on less attractive maidens derive? There was only one source—the bids that had been made for the attractive ones. This in turn highlights a potential problem for the auctioneers. If they had to pay out more money in dowries for the less attractive maidens than they gained in payments for the beauties, they would have gone out of business. Somehow they had to arrange matters so that most of their maidens were attractive. In that case, they did not have to pay out too much. Exactly how they did this is yet another tantalizing detail left out by Herodotus.

How Would a Babylonian Auction Work?

How did this ancient Babylonian auction work? While no transcripts of the auctioneer's patter have survived, it might have sounded something like this:

Now, gentlemen, gather round. *All* of these fair young ladies will be auctioned off today, without exception, from the most beautiful to the—well, less beautiful. And remember the rules: They are only for marriage, not for any other nefarious purpose you may have in mind. You will have to sign the marriage certificates on your way out, or no sale.

Since we all understand the ground rules, let the auction begin. Here is lovely Zelda, with long black hair. She's a hard worker, and will make a wonderful wife. She has already won three, count them, three beauty contests. What do I hear for Zelda? That gentleman in the back row—50 ulans? A pitifully low price. You can do better, I know. The gentleman in the front row, 100 ulans. And now I hear 200? Can we do better? 250? Now 300. Now 400. Sold to the gentleman with the plumed hat for 400 ulans.

Now on to Graecma. I admit that she isn't very good-looking, and maybe she walks with a bit of a limp. And you have undoubtedly read, in the ceramic brochures in front of you, that poor Graecma has been divorced three times. But this is all due to bad luck at these auctions. To make sure this doesn't happen this time, we're going to throw in, for free, a special charm to the god Zelibund.

Remember, we shouldn't get hung up on good looks, gentlemen. If you want a wife, you're looking for the long run. Good looks fade quickly, as we know. Are there are bids for Graecma? Can't we get at least 10 ulans? Nothing? Very well, gentlemen, we will now have the reverse part of this auction. Those of you who have attended this auction in the past know the rules. We will pay one of you gentlemen to take Graecma in marriage. As you know, this is part of our agreement with the Society of Unwed Maidens.

The gentleman over on my left in the yellow robe holds up ten fingers, so he wants 100 ulans to take Graecma from me. For newcomers to this auction, this money comes from the 400 ulans that the previous gentleman was kind enough to pay me for the lovely Zelda. In this section, we will pay one of *you*. Anybody else? The heavy-set gentleman on a camel raises nine fingers, so that's 90 ulans. We now have a lower bid, so the gentleman gets Graecma unless.... Now eight fingers. Now seven. Any other bidders? Going once, twice.... The bald gentleman with the long white beard will receive 70 ulans and Graecma. Sign the marriage certificate on your way out.

What does this historical tale have to do with installations that people do not want nearby? It may sound cruel, but the unattractive maidens correspond to undesirable land uses such as mental health facilities, landfills, and the like. Apparently it was Babylonian public policy that *all* marriageable maidens be wed, not just the lookers. So there had to be a provision to take account of those who avoided mirrors. That is how the negative auction happened.

In the same way, it is public policy that we find a site for wastes and mentally ill people. We cannot just dump them out over the countryside or stuff them into attics, as we once did. Some type of reverse auction is the solution, just as it was for those long-ago Babylonian maidens.

History repeats itself in curious ways. In recent times, Richard Stroup of the Political Economy Research Center in Montana has proposed an auction remarkably similar to the Babylonian one. His plan deals with *existing* waste sites, such as those to be cleaned up under the Superfund law. It would eliminate them faster than the present ponderous system and I discuss it further in chapter 12. Stroup's ideas deal with past problems. The reverse Dutch auction copes with future waste sites.

Most ancient auctions were of relatively small items, excluding the human auctions noted previously. However, at one point in the Roman Empire, the Praetorian Guard took power after the murder of Pertinax.[4] They were more interested in money than in domination, so the entire Roman world was auctioned. Julian won this competition. It is unlikely that anything of that importance will ever be sold to the highest bidder again.

Four General Types of Auctions

There is a vast economic literature on auctions. McAfee and McMillan list scores of articles published in the 1980s alone. [5] There are at least four types of auctions.[6] The first two are public, in the sense that all bidders at one time used to assemble in one room. In modern times, telecommunication has allowed bidders for certain valuable objects, like French Impressionist paintings, to call in bids from around the world. The level of bidding is known to all the bidders, regardless where they are. A Japanese bidder on a Monet in Sotheby's knows the rising price as well as if he were in London.

These first two "open" auctions are the familiar English auction, the best-known of all, and the Dutch auction. I have previously described both in chapter 4.

Economists have shown that the price for an object auctioned by the Dutch or English methods will be about the same. However, there is little analysis on whether the Dutch system is *faster* than the English.

Sealed-Bid Auctions

The other two auction types are sealed-bid systems, divided into first- and second-bid auctions. Items auctioned by the government are often handled in this way.

In the first-price auction, a bidder who submits the highest bid is awarded the objective. The price he pays is his submitted bid. In the second-price auction, a participant submits a bid. If his is the highest one, he is awarded the merchandise, but at a price equal to the *second-highest* bid. For example, suppose A bids $1000, B $900, C $800 and so on. A wins the objective, but he does not pay $1000, as he would under the first-price system. He pays $900, the second-highest bid.

The second-price auction is what the economists call "truth-revealing." In a first-price auction, the bidder will tend to bid lower than his estimation of the true value of the merchandise, because he does not want to waste money. For example, a bidder might value an object at $1000, but would bid only $800 in the hopes of getting a bargain.

In the second price auction, a bidder who hopes to be successful does not know what the second highest bid will be. He will then tend to make his bid close to his true evaluation of the object. In the preceding example, the bidder might bid $950 for an object worth $1000 to him, in the hope that the second-highest bid would be substantially less.

The above description of the four auction types assumes that they will run forward, in the mode described. Auctions can also be run in *reverse*. This takes place when the objective is regarded as undesirable, rather than desirable.

For example, suppose a city wanted some trash hauled away. They could run a *reverse* sealed-bid auction. The government would be paying the successful bidder, rather than the other way around. In this case, the *lowest* bidder would win.

The reverse Dutch auction works in this way. Hazardous, radioactive, and toxic wastes, prisons, and mental health facilities are regarded as undesirable by most. The government, one way or another, will have to pay a state or community to accept them. So any auction would have to be run in reverse, not forward.

Why have an auction at all? Cassady, who wrote the major book on auctions, summarizes it as well as anyone:

> One answer is, perhaps, that some products have no standard value. For example, the price of any catch of fish (at least of fish destined for the fresh fish market) depends on the demand and supply conditions at a specific moment of time, influ-

enced possibly by prospective market developments. For manuscripts and antiques, too, prices must be remade for each transaction. For example, how can one discover the worth of an original copy of Lincoln's Gettysburg Address except by auction method?[7]

Cassady's second reason, the uniqueness of an object, fits a hazardous waste site almost perfectly. There have been few if any of them built in the U.S. in recent years, so by definition, they are rare. There have been *no* sites built for high-level nuclear wastes.

It is true that both an original of the Gettysburg Address and a hazardous or radioactive waste site have vastly different properties, besides that of uniqueness. But in both cases, their value, one to acquire and the other to avoid, can be determined by auction.

Negative and Positive Auctions

The types of auctions we have described are examples of broader classes, named "negative" and "positive." Consider the types of facilities or industries that towns generally want—computer companies that employ childless Ph.D.s in highly taxable, smokeless, silent factories that look like single-family homes. If these Ph.D.s are also independently wealthy, so much the better.[8]

Very few industries have all these qualities. So when a real-life, as opposed to a mythical, industry wants to build in a specific town, we often have a negative auction. The town may say, "You are allowed to spew only 200 tons of goo into the air instead of the 400 tons that you, Mr. Industrialist, were proposing. And you have to cut the amount of water pollution by at least 60 percent."

This is a *negative* auction, similar in principle to the second half of the Babylonian auction I described earlier in this chapter. The town (or county) is trying to reduce the "pollution price" of this new industry. The process is public, since details of the negotiations are often leaked to the media. We have all seen the headlines: "City Council Puts Strict Rules on New Plant Discharges."

If the owners of the proposed plant feel that the town-imposed rules are *too* tough, they can pick up their marbles and walk away. We have all seen the other headlines: "Firm Breaks Off Talks with Town Board."

Now consider a *positive* auction between towns for that computer laboratory through whose portals only Ph.D.s walk. A facility of this type is highly prized, since it brings in much tax money without requiring the town to lay out much revenue. Towns—or even states if the stakes are high enough—will bid upward, not downwards, as in the case of the "ordinary" factory.

A prime example of this was the Superconducting Supercollider, proposed in the late 1980s and canceled in 1993. While not everyone who was to work there had a doctorate, the facility was planned to employ the largest number of Ph.D.s of any new American installation for decades.

Because of the rules imposed by the Federal government, which was to fund the facility, states could not bid directly, as in an English auction. Instead, they resorted to indirect bidding. They did not say to the Federal government, "We will give you $X million if you site it in our state." Instead, they pointed out, "We will build roads, construct apartments, provide utilities, and so on, all out of our own money. This all will be worth $X million. We'd be glad to provide these free goods and services, if you locate the facility in our state."

Some of these indirect bids did not take too much imagination to dream up: cheap land (bought with state funds) and free engineering studies. Others were more ingenious—low-cost electricity (the collider would have been a prodigious user of electricity), new professors of physics at state universities, and day care centers.

Those who think there is no justice in this world were astonished. The highest bidder, Texas, with a bid of $1 billion, won the later-cancelled prize.

What are the Requirements of a Successful Auction?

What are the minimum requirements for success of an auction system? Michael O'Hare has reduced them to four:[9]

1. A description of the project and its consequences. This could be an environmental impact statement, a series of risk analyses, or something analogous. Without studies of this type, the potential hosts of an unwelcome installation will not know what they are entering. Admittedly, very few of the potential neighbors will read the often voluminous documents.

2. A mechanism for compensating citizens. This can be by direct payments, or a collective allocation to state or local governments.

3. Legal authority so that the host community can bind itself to build the facility. Because sentiment can change over time, there could also be a mechanism to have the host community pay back the compensation, with interest, in case it alters its decision.

FIGURE 7.1

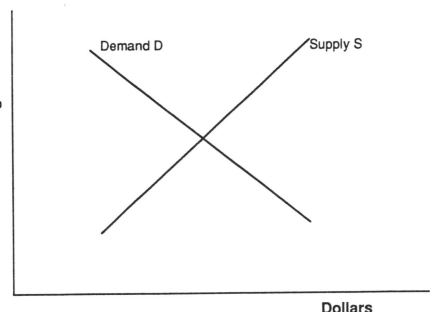

A typical demand-supply curve in economics. In this case, we are considering the production of widgets, a mythical commodity. As the price (horizontal axis) increases, the demand curve D falls. At the same time, supply rises as the price offered rises.

4. A procedure whereby the residents of the affected areas can "bid" for compensation. Who speaks for the citizens has to be made clear. Ordinarily, this is done using the collective wisdom of the state legislature, the governor or county officials, all elected.

In all four categories, an auction system relies on standard political mechanisms. No new system, fraught with bugs, has to be set up, unless the people in the affected area want it.

Some areas may want referenda. Others may wish to organize public or town meetings to gauge public sentiment. Because something like a mental illness half-way house has a long history of controversy, mere voting may not be enough. The voice of the people may have to be heard in a variety of channels.

With these four requirements in place, an auction system will work. The auctioneers will be successful in finding a site.

We can begin understanding the economic aspects of a reverse Dutch auction by means of a demand-supply diagram, as shown in figure 7.1. This illustration will be familiar to everyone who has taken Economics 101, as well as to many others.

The diagram, at first glance, appears to have nothing to do with waste sites or a reverse Dutch auction. The vertical axis is in widgets, that mythical commodity well-beloved of economists, and the horizontal axis is in dollars.

Consider the demand curve (or line) D. When the price is low (i.e., when the line is in the upper-left-hand corner), the demand for widgets is high. We know this because the line at that point is near the top of the vertical axis.

This line is then realistic. If BMWs—or most any other commodity—were cheaper, there would be a lot more demand for them.

Now consider widgets from another viewpoint, that of the manufacturer. She is represented by the supply curve (or line) marked S. When the price being offered for widgets is low—corresponding to the lower left-hand corner—few of them are produced. We know this because the line S is at the lower part of the vertical widget axis.

As the price being offered for widgets rises, the line S moves to the right. Because the manufacturer is getting much more money for her widgets than before, she produces more of them. The supply curve S rises.

Demand-Supply Curves in Terms of Auctions

Figure 7.1 may dredge up memories of a half-forgotten course. Does it have anything to do with finding waste sites?

Consider the next graph, figure 7.2. This looks similar to the previous one. The demand curve D slopes downward, and the supply curve S rises. There is a difference, though. We are not talking about widgets any more, but how the reverse Dutch auction changes attitudes while producing a viable site.

The vertical axis is no longer denominated in widgets, but percentages of people within a given county who oppose making a bid. It could be called the "disapproval axis." If it is read from the bottom to the top, it could just as well be called the "approval axis." To be neutral on this, and for simplicity, I will call it the "opinion line."

FIGURE 7.2

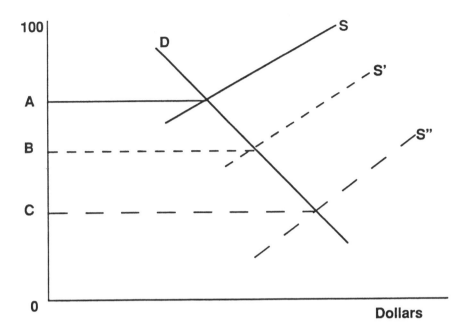

Demand-supply curves for finding sites using a reverse Dutch auction. Here the vertical axis is an "opinion line," ranging from 100 percent disapproval at the top to O percent disapproval, or complete approval, at the bottom. As the bonus level increases, the supply curve, S, moves to the right. It becomes S', S", and so on.

At the top, 100 percent are in opposition, probably not too far from the truth when a controversial site is first proposed. At the bottom of the opinion line, nobody is opposed. This is highly unlikely ever to happen. In any case, we do not need unanimity to get a viable site.

The demand curve D again slopes downward. As the bonus level, represented by the horizontal axis, increases, the opposition to the site drops. This accords with experience. Offer a few dollars to citizens to site a high-security prison, and there will be looks of disdain. Offer millions, and earnest consideration will ensue.

The demand curve sloping downward to the right then corresponds to the well-known "spectrum of risk aversion," in which some people are highly risk-averse and others are less so.[10]

The Rising Bonus Changes Opinions

Returning to figure 7.2, the supply line S again slopes upward. It now represents the rising value of the bonus offered to volunteers, rather than the going price for widgets.

The demand curve D is for a particular county. As the supply curve S rises, it intersects line D. A horizontal line drawn from the intersection cuts the vertical axis at point A. This represents the proportion of people still opposed to the installation within their county—in this diagram, about 70 percent.

What we have shown so far is a static situation, with supply curve (or bonus line) S. What would happen if a greater bonus were offered? Consider dotted supply curve S'. A horizontal line drawn from a point on demand curve D will cut the new supply curve S' farther to the right of the intersection of D and S. This implies more money is being offered as a bonus.

The horizontal line drawn from the intersection of line D and the new supply curve S' meets the vertical opinion line at point B. This point, at about 50 percent approval, is lower than point A. Some people have swung over to the "pro-siting" camp.

Now the supply of bonus funds rises to S". This supply curve cuts demand line D even lower. The horizontal line extended from the intersection cuts the opinion line at point C, lower than A or B. By this point, perhaps only a third is opposed. Chances are this county will make a bid around this stage, although that event will depend on what proportion of approval they want.

A reverse Dutch auction is applicable only to a multi-locality situation. If there was only one possible site, the citizens around it could extort what they wanted from the siting authority.

Figure 7.3 shows what happens in this case. For simplicity, I have shown only three localities or counties, A, B, and C. The demand curve or lines will vary from one county to the next. For example, the demand curve D_A for county A has a small slope downward to the right. As the bonus level rises, on supply curve S, a comparatively small number of people will move from the anti-site to the pro-site camp.

On the other hand, county C has a demand line D_C that drops rapidly. A relatively small change in bonus level will send many from the anti camp to the pros.

The rising supply curve S cuts the demand curves D_A, D_B, and D_C for each of the three counties. The extensions of the intersections meet

FIGURE 7.3

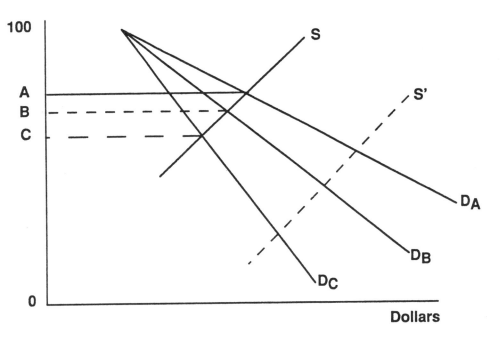

Demand-supply curves for three counties A, B, and C. The slope of the demand curves will naturally vary from one community to the next. As a result, the effect of an increasing bonus will produce different effects.

the vertical opinion line at points A, B, and C. Because the demand curve for county A slopes only gradually, more people disapprove the site than for county C. Point A on the approval axis is closer to 100 percent disapproval than point C. County B is somewhere in between these two extremes.

As the bonus supply increases, line S moves to the right. It now becomes supply line S'. It will meet demand lines D_A, D_B, and D_C closer to the bottom of the diagram, that is, where there is greater approval of the site. To avoid cluttering the diagram, I have not shown the horizontal lines extending from the intersection of the supply curve S' with the demand curves D_A, D_B, and D_C. However, in each case, the points where they meet the vertical opinion line are lower than points A, B, and C.

None of this tells us which specific county will bid. On the face of it, county C should make a bid, since its demand curve drops much more steeply than that of the other two counties.

However, it is possible that some counties may have stricter approval requirements than others. For example, county C may require a referendum with 90 percent approval before they submit a bid. If the requirements for the other two counties are not as stringent, A and B will likely make a bid first.

The Implication of Non-Straight Lines

Up to this point, we have been assuming that the demand curves are perfectly straight. This means that each time the bonus rises by $1 million, say, exactly the same proportion of people go from the anti-siting camp into the pro group. While this makes the resulting diagrams a little neater, it does not always accord with reality.

Examples of what could well happen to the demand curves are shown in figures 7.4 and 7.5. In figure 7.4, the demand curve D, starting at the upper left-hand corner, is straight for a while.

As it descends to point D_1, something happens. The owner of the local newspaper or TV station may decide that his county should receive the bonus, so he bombards his fellow citizens with pro-bid information. Chances are that the demand curve will drop more steeply, that is, more citizens will move from the anti camp to the pro camp than would have before the barrage of advice. If the publisher had stayed neutral, chances are the demand curve would have continued in a straight line from point D_1 to D_2. Instead, it curves downward from D_1 to D_3, ending up at point D_4. This last point is much closer to the bottom of the vertical opinion line, indicating that many fewer people disapprove of the site.

How does all this affect the level of approval or disapproval? As we go down the straight demand curve to point D_1, it is intersected by supply curve S. The intersection meets the opinion vertical axis at point A, with perhaps 75 percent disapproving the site, and 25 percent approving. If the publisher had remained silent, the demand curve would have continued to point D_2, where it is intersected by supply curve S'. As discussed in figures 7.2 and 7.3, the new supply curve S' represents an increase in the bonus offered. The horizontal extension of the intersection at point D_2 meets the opinion axis at point B, with perhaps 50 percent disapproval (or 50 percent approval).

FIGURE 7.4

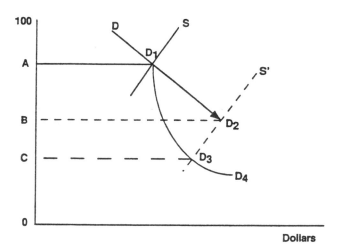

Changing slopes of demand curves. The demand curve is not always a straight line. In this figure, it drops much more than it was expected to under the influence of a rising bonus, due to the change of mind of an opinion leader.

FIGURE 7.5

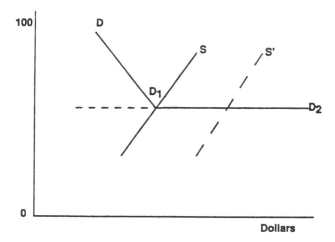

A constant demand curve. In this case, after a period of dropping—that is, becoming more favorable to the site—the demand curve stays level. This particular community will not be swayed by an increasing bonus after it gets to point D_1.

When the publisher decides to speak up, the demand line is now curved. The increased bonus supply curve S' meets it at point D_3. The extension of that intersection to the left meets the opinion axis at point C, substantially below point B. The level of disapproval is now perhaps only 33 percent (67 percent approval). The publisher has greatly increased the approval level in his county.

The opposite can also occur, as shown in figure 7.5. The publisher issues a barrage of anti-site statements. The demand curve D again slopes downward in the usual way. But at point D_1, the curve levels off and becomes horizontal. No matter how the bonus supply curve increases (from S to S' in the diagram), the disapproval level of about 50 percent never falls. The intersection of the demand and supply curves, when extended to the opinion axis, stays at point A, no matter what.

Some might be tempted to call the people in this county "stubborn," but I would not. They have just decided to refuse to budge. If this were the only county in the reverse Dutch auction, the site would never be built. However, other counties will have downward-sloping demand curves, in contrast to the one depicted in figure 7.5, which remains horizontal after point D_1. In consequence, the reverse Dutch auction will work, although the county that makes a bid may not be the one we expected from initial polling results.

What Approval Levels Should be Required?

Because of the controversies accompanying siting of noxious facilities in the past, some counties will want to achieve more than 50 percent approval.

In votes on nuclear waste siting, approval levels of substantially more than 50 percent have, on occasion, been given. For example, in March 1995, Mescalero Indians in New Mexico voted almost 60 percent positively to store nuclear fuel rods from utilities on their reservation.[11]

A certain county may want to have two-thirds, three-quarters, or even 90 percent approval before making a bid. However, there is a good chance that a second county may bid before the approval level in the first one gets high enough. In that case, the "hesitant" county will receive nothing. This is the consequence of taking too long to decide.

Should a community wait until there is 51 percent in favor, two-thirds, 90 percent or any other fraction? There is no way that any outsider can tell the people of the potential volunteer community what level of consensus to choose. Their elected officials know their people, and what constitutes a consensus. Let *them* decide when to bid, not an outside siting authority.

What can we make of this brief excursion into the economics of finding sites? First, the demand curve will slope downward in most cases, corresponding to an increase in the pro-site group. Second, the supply curve can always be moved to the right in the diagram, as the bonus level rises. Third, as the supply or bonus curve moves to the right, the proportion of "pros" will increase. Fourth, trying to determine the shape and slope of the demand curves in advance is probably an exercise in futility. The citizens and their leaders will always make up their minds in unpredictable ways.

Finally, none of this has to be done with the slightest bit of coercion and arm twisting. The reverse Dutch auction thus avoids the high-pressure tactics that have marked previous attempts at siting undesirable facilities. Yet it retains environmental standards. It is the best of both worlds.

Almost all the examples used in the preceding sections were of specific objects being auctioned—marriageable maidens, fish, widgets, and the Gettysburg Address. When a hazardous or radioactive waste site becomes part of an auction, it will be more than an object. It will be a reflection of public policy on wastes. It is more than auctioning old furniture.

In the nineteenth century, in an early American example of public policy auctions, the capital of Georgia was auctioned among towns in that state. In 1970, Yandle proposed that highway corridors be located in response to an auction among landowners.[12] Locations of highways, while not as controversial as the siting of potentially dangerous wastes, have still provoked heated debates.

We think of a highway as a pleasant structure to ride over, but it can destroy neighborhoods it traverses. The homes and land of the few are sacrificed for the convenience of the many. In the same way, the wastes that all of us generate must be handled in a small number of spots. A highway is a positive structure, and a waste facility is negative. Yet the way that we have to deal with a small number of citizens is not too different in the two cases.

Zoning Auctions

Where we live is, for most people, the most important aspect of their environment. In most communities, the types and uses of buildings and land is governed by zoning. In that sense, the rules affecting zoning are the public policy regulations affecting the most people.

Zoning auctions were proposed by Wiseman in the mid-1970s. They were suggested to eliminate the often violent battles that rage over zoning of land, and the corruption that often accompanies these clashes.[13]

Consider a typical confrontation. A company proposes to build a possibly disruptive facility—call it an apartment building—in a neighborhood zoned for single-family homes. The firm applies to the city or town council to have the zoning for the land in question changed to "high density."

Those living in single-family homes around the site are naturally upset. They bought their homes on the understanding that the neighborhood would remain about the same. Now it seems likely that there will be drastic alterations. They troop down to the town council, demanding that the zoning remain undisturbed.

Sound familiar? The situation is analogous to a search for a hazardous waste site. In the minds of many prospective neighbors, that dump would change their community irrevocably. It is not a question of whether it would *really* do this, but that a large proportion *thinks* it would.

In the analogy, the siting commission corresponds to the apartment developer, "invading" what was previously a bucolic existence. The future residents around a possible waste site correspond to the unhappy homeowners.

Every zoning confrontation is different. In our mythical scenario, the developer might offer to set aside some of the apartments for low-income families. This impresses a few members of the town council, who believe strongly in social justice. The homeowners promise to defeat, in the next election, any town councilor who votes "yes." Perhaps some money changes hands behind closed doors.

The way the battle proceeds is highly inefficient. Charges and counter-charges of bad faith, oppression of the poor and money-grubbing fly back and forth. The political system may be subverted. "Change has to occur in our town," the homeowners admit, "But why does it have to be in our neighborhood?" The outlines of the NIMBY dragon can be seen.

On the other hand, the developer has raised his "bid" by setting aside some apartments for the poor. The analogy to an auction is clear. However, this zoning "auction" is crude and partly conducted in secret. The flow of information between all parties—the developer, the homeowners, other citizens, and the town and the town council—is confused and irregular. Without adequate and accurate information understood by all, the process is economically inefficient.

Wiseman proposed a radically different way of handling zoning changes, one that balances the interests of the *total* community, not just the battling developer and homeowners. Briefly, interested parties would be allowed to vote for or against any zoning or rezoning proposal by stating the dollars they are willing to pay for or against the change. The amount would be in a sealed bid to the political body that has the legal right to make the change.

The Zoning Auction Begins

Suppose developer Albert, hoping to make money from the apartment building, bids $1,000 *for* the zoning change. (All amounts in this example are hypothetical.) Consider two homeowners, Benedict and Charlie, as representative of the group. Benedict, who is highly sensitive to noise and traffic, bids $900 *against* the change. Charlie, who drives a truck for a living and who is out of town most of the time, is not particularly concerned about loud sounds and crowding. He is against the apartments, but only mildly so. He bids $200 *against* it.

If these amounts corresponded to the depth of feeling and financial resources in this section of the community, the proposal would be defeated. There would be $1,000 for, and $1,100 opposed. One of the advantages of zoning auctions is that the *entire* town can vote, not just homeowners in the affected neighborhood.

Now suppose that homeowners in other parts of the town get together. They reason that if the apartment is not built where the developer first proposed, it might be constructed in *their* neighborhood. Since this is only a guess on their part, they are not inclined to bid very much. Ten voters in other parts of the town each vote $20 *for* the construction (on the original site), for a total of $200 (= 10 × $20). This makes the total bid *for* the apartment $1,200; the amount *against* is $1,100. The apartment is built.

What happens to the bids? In an ordinary sealed-bid auction for a government contract, the losers do not have to pay anything to anybody. Their bids end up in the waste basket.

In a zoning auction, the money has to be real. Otherwise, both opponents and proponents would bid millions or billions, far beyond the worth or detriment of the project.

Return now to our example. The apartment was approved, $1,200 to $1,100. The losers get their money back, so noise-sensitive Benedict gets his $900 and Charlie, the noise-resistant truck driver, gets his $200. Since the apartment will be built in a location that these two individuals do not like, they should not have to pay out funds for something they did not want.

If there was true equity, the results should be just the *opposite*. The losers should get some recompense for the trouble they think the apartment will cause them.

Recall that in a present-day zoning change, the homeowners who claim they will suffer get nothing. The law says, "like it or lump it." If they cannot tolerate the nearby apartment, they can move out of the neighborhood.

How much compensation should the losers in a zoning auction get? The answer is simple—precisely the amount that they bid. When Benedict bid $900 against the project, he was saying that would be his loss, financial, psychological or both, if the apartment went forward. Benedict then receives $900 of the money that was bid *for* the apartment. Similarly, Charlie, who thought he would be affected only about $200 worth, gets that amount. The positive bids, from which Benedict and Charlie are compensated, were made by the developer and the people in the other side of town. The latter avoided having the apartment built in *their* neighborhood.

One advantage of this zoning auction is that it forces both opponents and proponents to be precise about how much detriment or worth the project will produce to them. Any local politician can tell stories of people opposed to a change in zoning coming to them and saying, "If that new factory goes up in our section of town, I will be completely ruined. My total investment in my house will be worthless. Those are my life savings. Please help me by voting no."

Wise politicians know how to discount statements like this. A year or two later, they may find formerly distressed homeowners co-existing quite happily with the new building. The value of the properties in the neighborhood may even have risen.

The zoning auction does not allow exaggeration of this type without consequences. Bidders have to be accurate in estimating how much they will lose or gain as a result of the zoning changes. If they are not precise, they pay for it in real dollars.

If the Apartment Building is Defeated in a Zoning Auction

What happens if the project loses, that is, gets more dollars bid against than for? In the above example, suppose that the ten voters in the other part of town, after some reflection, washed their hands of the whole affair. They decide not to bid after all. In that case, the sole bid *for* the project is $1,000 (from developer Albert). The two bids *against,* from Benedict and Charlie, total $1,100. The project loses. In that case, $1,000 is paid to the developer, the only positive bidder. If there were more than one positive bidder, the bids of the winners—those against in this case—would be pro-rated among them.

It might seem unfair that Benedict has to spend $900 for the privilege of not having an apartment building in his neighborhood. By making his bid, he said, "It's worth $900 to me not to have that building be erected." What could be fairer?

The zoning auction reflects how much people are willing to pay to keep a detrimental facility far away. Consider the analogy to high-level nuclear wastes, for which a state would bid in a reverse Dutch auction system. If the bonus for the repository rises to $5 billion and Montana (or any other state) declines to bid, it means that it is worth at least $5 billion to Montanans to have the repository built elsewhere.

The major difference between the two types of auctions is that a waste site auction is a continuing process. It goes on until a state, county or town comes forward.

The zoning auction is a one-shot affair. Bidders have to get the size of their bid correct the first time. In the first example described above, the opponents of the apartment won by $100. The developer is not allowed to come back and say, "Maybe when I bid $1,000, it was too low. It's really worth $1,200 to me to build this building. So I win." It is easy to see that if that were allowed, the process might stretch out forever, causing even more acrimony than now exists in zoning.

While zoning and unwanted installation auctions differ in some ways, they have a mutual purpose: To strike a balance between environmental concerns, taken in the broad sense, and economics. Both are reasonable approaches to equalize the interests of small and large groups.

Poverty, Equity, and Auctions

Will any auction system always be unfair to the poor? Will they be the inevitable recipients of everything that nobody else wants? I discuss this in detail in chapter 10. In the auction context, Howard Kunreuther at the University of Pennsylvania Wharton Business School has suggested a *two-stage* auction. It holds out the possibility that the poorest communities or blocks have a chance to escape.[14]

In the first of the two stages, all communities are *required* to submit a sealed bid for the bonus they would want in order to accept the wastes. This is different from the reverse Dutch auction, in which the majority of the communities would not participate.

To make Kunreuther's proposal more specific, consider an example. We have five communities that submit sealed bids, A through E. A is the poorest and E is the richest. Community A, being the worst-off, would want a payment of only $10 million to take the unwelcome installation. Community E, being well-to-do and thus not really needing the money, would want $50 million. The other communities, B, C, and D, are between A and E. Note that this assumes that communities make their bids in inverse proportion to their average income or wealth. Jeffrey Himmelberger, then a graduate student at Clark University, found that, at least for Wisconsin, this was not true.[15] I discuss this in chapter 10. We are thus operating with conventional wisdom here.

If this were a reverse Dutch auction, community A, with the lowest bid, would receive the wastes at this stage. Some observers might then claim that this shows that the system is inequitable, that is, the wastes are palmed off on the poorest community.

Now we go on to the second round. One of the five bids is chosen randomly. This choice does not necessarily mean that the chosen community gets the wastes. All that happens is that its price is announced publicly. Before this happened, recall that no community knew what the others had bid. They had submitted sealed bids.

Suppose that community C, with a bid of $30 million, has its envelope opened. In the second stage, the remaining four communities bid again, this time with knowledge of community C's bid. They now know that community C's bid was higher or lower than theirs, but not how it compares to everyone else's. For example, community B, which bid $20 million, now has learned that community C bid $10 million more than it did.

In the *second* stage, sealed bids are again used, but they are all open to the public after they are submitted. If one or more of the bids from the four remaining communities is below $30 million (C's bid), that community receives the wastes. If no bids are below $30 million, then community C gets the wastes.

In this two-stage process, a poor community might bid low in the first stage. Community A, with a bid of $10 million, was an example of this. Since they were not chosen in the random drawing between the first and second stages, they can now raise their bid above the community selected by chance.

For example, community A now has learned of community C's $30 million bid. If, on further reflection, community A thinks it does not want the wastes, all it has to do is raise its bid to $30 million and one dollar. Then a community other than A would get the wastes. It could be community C, or it could be another community whose bid in the second round was less than $30 million. Of course, community A will not get the $10 million it would have received if its first-round bid had been successful. However, that is a matter for the residents of community A to decide.

The two-stage process might remove some potential inequity in the process. It allows a poor community, with a low bid, to revise that bid based on further knowledge of another community's bid. However, to do this, a random drawing among the communities has to be introduced.

Siting hazardous and radioactive wastes is such a contentious issue that anything smacking in any way of chance and luck would undoubtedly sink the process. Imagine what would happen if, through luck of the draw, Beverly Hills got a radioactive waste site. Even if the two-stage auction had been carefully explained beforehand, the yowls would ascend to the very heavens.

For political reasons, a lottery among communities or states would almost certainly fail. As a result, although the two-stage auction has attractive features, it could be unworkable.

Collusion, Rewarding Neighbors, and Free Riders

Economists have pondered how and why auctions work.[16] What are some of the potential booby traps in an auction?

In any auction, there is always a chance of collusion. The possibility depends on the type.

In the English or "normal" auction, it is not uncommon for some of the bidders, in collusion with the auctioneer, to escalate the price higher than the worth of the object. They need the help of the auctioneer, who is assigned the task of ensuring that the final bid is from someone outside the group of plotters. Otherwise, one of the group would be stuck with the object.

In an auction for unwelcome facilities, such collusion is close to impossible. First, there is no auctioneer in on the plot. The increase of the bonus is governed by the calendar, not by a corruptible auctioneer.

Second, even if two, five, or fifteen counties or states jointly said, "We'll hold out until the price rises to $X million or billion," there is no way that every state or county could agree on a bonus price. Under the American political system, states and counties are independent. There has never been a case where every American state colluded on *anything*.

There might be a mild form of collusion in which County A said to adjoining County B, "We're planning to submit a bid at the $1 billion level. We know that most of the wastes will be passing through your county on its way to us, if our bid is successful. Citizens of A don't want citizens of B to feel uncomfortable. After all, we're neighbors. So when we get the bonus—if some other county doesn't bid first—we plan to give 10 percent to you, County B. You can use it to make your transportation system safer, or for any other purpose."

There has to be some form of recompense to adjoining counties or states for their psychological damage.[17] One way of handling it would be to require at least a small percentage of the bonus to go to these adjoining political entities, as described further in chapter 8. A region that was planning to bid could also give more than the required amounts to its neighbors.

This is not collusion, but simply good neighborliness. If states and counties take care of the concerns of others, so much the better. It does not happen all that often.

An auction in which a government body participates, as opposed to one in which only individuals take part, will always have free riders.

Suppose a reverse Dutch auction is held, and a county makes a bid when the bonus rises to $20 million. Suppose further this is after a referendum in which 51 percent of the voters approve the amount. Considering the supply-demand curves we showed earlier, this means that many voters would have accepted substantially less—perhaps $5 or $10 million. For these citizens, the $20 million is a bonus on top of a bonus.

There is no theoretical way to eliminate these free riders, who get even more than they expect. It is in the nature of many economic transactions. I may have my eye on a $20,000 car, for example, and be willing to pay that price. When I am ready to buy it, due to rebates it is marked down to $18,000. In that sense, I would be a free rider due to lucky timing.

The problem is endemic to an auction in which groups of people, as opposed to individuals, bid. As has been written, "It is in the nature of goods that must be consumed collectively that no one gets exactly the right amount."[18]

Willingness to Pay and to Accept in the Northwest

One of the major controversies in waste site compensation is the divergence between willingness to pay and willingness to accept. If we ask people how much they would take in compensation to have a hazardous waste site near them, they might say, millions, billions, or "there is no price high enough."

On the other hand, if we asked the very same people how much they would be willing to pay, out of their own pockets, to have it sited away from them, the amount will be much lower—often of the order of a few dollars.

This is shown by an article by Hubbard in *Scientific American*. He discusses a poll taken among residents in the Bonneville Power Administration (BPA), a publicly owned utility in the Northwest with about 3.6 million rate payers. We can use the numbers he quoted to estimate what would be a possible bonus level to a community where the unwanted establishment is located.[19]

On average, they were willing to pay $13.30 annually to avoid having a nuclear power plant sited near them. This corresponded to $48 million extra each year over the total population served by this utility. Corresponding figures for a coal plant were $12.80 per person, or $46 million in total. For a hydro dam, the numbers were $5.50 per person, or $20 million in total.

Hydroelectricity is a renewable resource. According to some, renewable energy sources have no known drawbacks. In principle then, people should be willing to pay to have them nearby, rather than pay to have them far away. At least in the Pacific Northwest, this does not hold.

Almost all comparative risk analyses have suggested that nuclear has a substantially lower risk, on average, than a fossil-fuel plant.[20] They come out about even in terms of how much those polled are willing to pay to keep them away. That nuclear did not have a significantly higher value should give at least some comfort to nuclear proponents.

Now consider how these numbers could be used to estimate a potential bonus level. Suppose that a community with a population of 50,000 was considering accepting a site. Not all communities would think about bidding. Parts of the Pacific Northwest are flat, and they would never have a hydro dam nearby, even if they wanted one.

To make this more specific, suppose the establishment was a nuclear plant. According to Hubbard's figures, BPA rate payers would be willing to pay $48 million annually to keep that nuclear plant away from *them*. Now divide that amount by the 50,000 people in that hypothetical community. Each of them would receive, as a bonus from other customers, $960 annually. If each of the families in this community had the mythical 3.2 people, this would be a payment of about $3100 per family.

The typical license for a nuclear power plant is 40 years, according to the Nuclear Regulatory Commission. Some have been shut down earlier than that. Yet others will apply to have their license extended at the end of four decades, according to nuclear industry experts. For simplicity, take the forty-year period as standard.

One alternative method of allocating the bonus would be to give the affected community all the money up front, when the installation is built. This would assure these people that the money promised them is really there. Very few government programs survive unchanged for four decades.

In this case, rather than their community getting payments of $48 million annually for forty years, they would get a lump-sum payment of 40 × $48 million, or $1.9 billion. This seems like a large amount, but the nuclear plant would be producing electricity worth vastly more than this value over its lifetime. Its operators would at last have a place to put it, with the acceptance of the host community.

The $1.9 billion is almost certainly a maximum amount. The actual compensation would be a tiny fraction of $1.9 billion, because of the auction mechanism.

The Reverse Dutch Auction is a Self-Adjusting Mechanism

The amount each person within the affected community receives will depend on the population of that community. A bigger town or county will have smaller checks *per capita* than a larger one.

A conurbation like Seattle is the biggest in the Pacific Northwest. With a population of around 2.5 million, it would be about fifty times the size of the hypothetical county of 50,000 we have been describing. The payments per family would then be 1/50 that of the mythical county, or about $62 annually. For residents of Seattle, that small payment for a nearby nuclear reactor probably would not be worth the trouble.

To which a proponent of the reverse Dutch auction would reply, "The auction is self-adjusting. First, the Nuclear Regulatory Commission would never allow a reactor in the heart of a major urban area. Second, even if they did, the bonus per person would obviously be smaller for a large town than a smaller one. All other factors being equal, residents of the bigger town would be less favorable to the site than those in the less-populated community, because the size of their bonus would be inferior. Then residents of the larger town will wait much longer to bid than those of the smaller one. This would hold even if average sentiment towards the facility was about the same in the two communities. Experts in risk have usually suggested that waste sites be sited away from highly populated areas. For example, the New York State Low-Level Radioactive Waste Siting Commission suggested sites in the two least-populated counties in the state. The reverse Dutch auction will also almost certainly yield a relatively small community. The difference is that it will be a volunteer, not a draftee."

The willingness-to-pay figures are not completely firm. Someone being polled might say she was willing to pay $13.30 annually—about $1.10 a month—to have a nuclear reactor far from her hack yard. When her electric bill says at the bottom, "$1.10 NIMBY charge," she might not be so enthusiastic.

In spite of this, the values estimated by the polls at least give us an estimate of how much people are willing to pay for the privilege of summoning up the NIMBY dragon. It is more than a few cents annually, and much less than a few hundred dollars.

Willingness to Pay and to Accept—The Clarke Auction

The Clarke auction takes account of willingness to pay and willingness to accept. The concept applies to towns or counties within a state, as well as states. Clarke's analysis is based on the assumption that each region would rather have a waste site or other undesirable facility located outside, rather than inside, its boundaries.[21]

The willingness to pay and willingness to accept values will usually be different. For example, suppose we have three counties, Q, R and S. County Q might be willing to accept $8 million to have the hazardous wastes of R and S buried within its boundaries. This county might, at the same time, be willing to pay each of Counties R and S $5 million to have the latter two accept its wastes. Presumably, if County R, rather than County S, accepts the wastes, it would collect $10 million (= $5 million + $5 million), including the payment that would otherwise have gone to County S.

Each county will have its own values of willingness to pay and willingness to accept. How do we find out what they are? The simplest way is a sealed-bid procedure, in which every county says, at the same time, what it is willing to pay other counties to take the wastes, and what it is willing to pay to accept them itself.

For example, suppose we have a hypothetical state with thirty counties. County T might say, through its sealed bid,

"We are willing to accept everyone's wastes if we are paid at least $20 million. We are also willing to pay each of the other twenty-nine counties $1 million if they take ours."

These bids have to represent real money. County T would be committed to pay $1 million to any other county that took its wastes.

Now that we have these thirty sealed envelopes, what should be done? According to the Clarke analysis, add up the willingness to pay and the willingness to accept values for each county. The willingness to pay numbers are counted as *negative* in this system. The willingness to accept values are counted as *positive*. The county with the highest total sum is then the "winner"; it gets the wastes.

To return to the County T example, the first number in its column would be minus $20 million. County U might be willing to pay every other county $2 million to send its wastes out of its territory. We then add $2 million to the County T column, bringing it up to minus $18 million. The procedure continues until all counties have a final sum.

The way that this auction operates gives the illusion—it *is* only an appearance—that the other counties are ganging up on the "winner," the one that gets the wastes.

For example, suppose as a result of the Clarke auction County T is slated to get the wastes. Even if all the ground rules had been agreed on in advance, it is almost certain that this county will claim that the bids of the other counties were rigged in such a way to leave it holding the bag—of wastes.

Ganging up is precisely the claim made by the Congressional delegation from Nevada when the 1987 amendments to the Federal Nuclear Waste Policy Act were passed. Many observers agree that the Silver State was targeted by the revised law. In the Clarke system, the envelopes are opened and lo and behold, one county (or state) is chosen.

Differences between the Reverse Dutch and Clarke Auctions

There are at least three fundamental differences between the reverse Dutch and the Clarke auction. First, the reverse Dutch auction is analogous to a volunteer army. The Clarke auction is similar to a draft. All must make bids, or the auction cannot be held.

The reverse Dutch auction works on the self-selection principle. No community is forced to bid. Most will not even consider bidding.

Second, there is always the possibility of at least partial collusion among some counties in the Clarke auction to foist the wastes on another. It would be unlikely that all except one county within a state would conspire to award the wastes to the odd one out. But there could be cabals or groups of counties coordinating the numbers they submit in their envelopes. For example, suppose the counties in the north of the state do not want the wastes anywhere near them. They might juggle the numbers in their envelopes to make sure that it goes to the south. That would destroy the entire ethical basis of the Clarke auction.

Any site auction should make it impossible to have collusion. Nobody should be made to volunteer by others forcing them.

Third, the Clarke auction depends on each county (or state) being willing to spend its own money to get the wastes put elsewhere. In most states, the number of counties that generate hazardous wastes is not great. If the money to pay for the bonus in the Clarke auction is to come from waste generators, counties that generated absolutely no hazardous wastes would be forced to spend money from their general funds. This would in essence set up a two-category auction, one for those counties that generated hazardous wastes, and one for those which did not. This would lead to enormous complications, and would almost certainly be politically unworkable.

In a fair auction, whether a county generates wastes itself is of no consequence. It can bid or not bid without worrying about how much it does or does not produce itself.

In summary, the Clarke-type auction has a number of deficiencies. It resembles a draft more than a system designed to encourage a volunteer.

The Problems of Sealed-Bid Auctions

Initially, a sealed-bid auction, like the Clarke version, holds certain attractions. Its advocates might say, "Why go to all the trouble of consulting people? All you really have to do is to get each of the mayors of potential host communities to send in their sealed bids—the minimum bonuses they would each accept to take the establishment. Then you just open up the envelopes. The lowest bid gets the undesirable facility. No fuss, no muss."

It sounds simple, but it is a recipe for disaster. First, few if any mayors will submit bids if they think that there is a chance that theirs might be the lowest.

Second, claims of "ganging up" will crop up, regardless of which community submits the lowest bid. Citizens of that community who are unhappy with the site coming to their town will accuse other communities of rigging their bids to produce a pre-determined winner. These accusations will be made whether there is any evidence to back up the charges.

Third, and most important, the sealed bid-system is based on secrecy. Clandestine activities are precisely what have sunk hundreds of past siting attempts. Why continue an action that has ruined previous siting efforts?

The sealed-bid system *requires* secrecy. It is not an option.

For example, suppose the mayor and the city council are considering a sealed bid. After locking the doors to city hall carefully behind them and checking for electronic bugs, they make a bid of $10 million.

There is no way that they can tell the citizens of their town about their decision. If they did, the news would inevitably spread to other towns participating in the auction. These other towns would all bid $10 million plus one dollar, ensuring that the blabbermouth town got the site. A better recipe for recrimination and agitation could hardly be devised.

The sealed-bid system would indeed avoid the finger-pointing of the present siting arrangement. But the other communities could maneuver to foist the facility on the town that did not keep its lips shut.

Contrast this with a system where the people take part, and where secrecy has been abolished. All the residents of a community know the level of the rising bonus. It is in their newspapers and on the TV news. As the bonus increases, a consensus to submit a bid will build. The mayor and the city council will not have to hide away to make a decision on the bid. They will be urged to submit a bid by citizens who do not want the bonus to go to another community.

For all these reasons, but especially the one on secrecy, the sealed bid auction founders before it sets sail. This is yet another example of a compensation mechanism that looks reasonable on paper, yet turns out to have more holes than Swiss cheese.

Unusual Auctions

Auctions appear in unusual places. Another example was held in a field which most people would think is unlikely—prize-fighting. Arranging prize fights is one of the shadiest legal activities. All sorts of double-crossings and disreputable deals take place before the boxers get in the ring.

According to a news story in June 1990, the Buster Douglas-Evander Holyfield heavyweight title bout slated for that September was auctioned. The Mirage Hotel in Las Vegas bid $32 million; Main Events Promotions bid $29 million. The auction was ordered by the World Boxing Association after the two boxers were unable to agree between themselves on when and where their bout was to be held. The procedure, open to all, undoubtedly removed much of the stench that precedes these bouts. This apparently was the first auction for a heavyweight title bout in history.[22]

The bout was eventually held in October, 1990, and Douglas lost. However, he probably made more money than he would have if he had relied on the standard method of secret negotiations between crooked promoters.

Alan Blinder is a former professor of economics at Princeton, columnist for *Business Week*, and later member of the U.S. Council of Economic Advisors and Federal Reserve Board of Governors. He came up with a scheme to auction import quotas. This may seem a long way from waste sites, but it neatly illustrates the advantages of auctions.

Allotments for such items as Japanese cars and steel became standard for many products in the 1980s. Quotas for these autos entering the U.S. are valuable to car manufacturers in that island nation. They can get more money for their cars in the U.S. than they can in the world market.[23]

The U.S. government gave these quotas away for free, in effect saying, "first come, first served." Blinder advocated auctioning them to the firms wanting to use these quotas. The money raised from these auctions could be applied to reduce the trade deficit. Best of all, there would be no U.S. losers in this transaction.

For example, Uncle Sam might figuratively stand on a platform and say to Toyota, Nissan, Mitsubishi, and the others, "What am I bid for the right to import 1,000 Japanese cars into the U.S. this year? I hear a bid from Nissan of $100 per car. Can anyone top this? Toyota bids $150 per car. Any other bids? Going once, going twice, sold to Toyota. Pay at the window, gentlemen, and make your checks payable to 'U.S. Treasury.' Now for the second batch of cars."

I bring up this example not to discuss abstruse questions of foreign trade, but to show how auctions can be used to break policy logjams in other areas. The figurative logs in finding sites for hazardous and radioactive wastes have been piling up for decades.

Summary

Auctions are simple. We have all participated in one, so they are not difficult to understand.

We have been so accustomed to thinking of them in this way that we might not realize they can be a part of public policy questions like siting hazardous and radioactive wastes. Yet the same principles that make them easy to use on a Saturday morning allow them to be employed to solve tough societal questions.

Notes

1. W. J. Boyes and S. K. Happel, "Auctions as an Allocation Mechanism in Academia: The Case of Faculty Offices," *Journal of Economic Perspectives* 3 (Summer 1989): 37.
2. "Auctions and Auctioneering." In *Encyclopedia Britannica* 11th edition, 2 (Cambridge, England: 1910), 895.
3. Herodotus, *The Histories*, Aubrey de Selincourt, translator, (Harmondsworth, England: Penguin Books, 1972).
4. "Auctions and Auctioneering," ibid.
5. R. Preston McAfee and John McMillan, "Auctions and Bidding," *Journal of Economic Literature* 25 (June 1987): 699.
6. Ronald L. Lehr and Robert Touslee, "What Are We Bid? Stimulating Electric Generation Resources Through the Auction Method," *Public Utilities Fortnightly* (12 November 1987): 11.
7. Ralph Cassady, *Auctions and Auctioneering* (Berkeley, Calif.: University of California Press, 1967), 20.
8. Michael O'Hare, "'Not in *My* Block You Don't!'—Facilities Siting and the Strategic Importance of Compensation," *Public Policy* 25 (Fall 1977): 407, especially 440.
9. Ibid.
10. Council on Environmental Quality et al., *Public Opinion on Environmental Issues: Results of a National Opinion Survey* (Washington, D.C.: The Council, 1980), 13.
11. Eduardo Montes, "Mescaleros-Nuclear," Associated Press, 10 March 1995, story 1917.
12. Bruce Yandle, Jr., "Externalities and Highway Location," *Traffic Quarterly* 24 (4) (1970): 583.
13. C. Wiseman, "Land Zoning and Zoning Changes: An Economic Perspective," *Rocky Mountain Social Science Journal* 12 (1975): 59.
14. Howard Kunreuther, Paul Kleindorfer, Peter J. Knez, and Rudy Yaksick, "A Compensation Mechanism for Siting Noxious Facilities: Theory and Experimental Design," *Journal of Environmental Economics and Management* 14 (1987): 371.
15. Jeffery J. Himmelberger, *The Practice of Compensation and Facilities Siting: A Case Study of Wisconsin's Recent Experience*, master's thesis submitted to the

Department of Environment, Technology and Society, Clark University, Worcester, Mass., 1990.

16. McAfee and McMillan, ibid.
17. Letter from Peter B. Myers, Staff Director, Board on Radioactive Waste Management, National Research Council, Washington, D.C., to Herbert Inhaber, 8 August 1990.
18. O'Hare, ibid., 444.
19. Harold M. Hubbard, "The Real Cost of Energy," *Scientific American* 264 (4) (April 1991): 36–42.
20. See, for example, Herbert Inhaber, *Energy Risk Assessment* (New York: Gordon & Breach, 1982) for a detailed discussion.
21. E. H. Clarke, "Multipart Pricing of Public Goods: An Example." In *Public Prices for Public Products,* ed. S. Mushkin (Washington, D.C.: The Urban Institute, 1972), 125. Quoted in Kunreuther et al., "A Compensation Mechanism."
22. "Douglas-Holyfield Fight Scheduled for Sept. 20," *Buffalo News* (June 11, 1990): D2.
23. Alan S. Blinder, "U. S. Import Rights: Going Once, Going Twice...," *Business Week* (9 March 1987).

8

Compensation and Its Relation to Auctions

Can environmental questions and incentives, compensation, and other aspects of money really blend? Or are they like oil and water, fundamentally incompatible? This chapter will deal with compensation and incentives generally. The next will give a number of examples of how the environment—taken in the broad sense of the word—and compensation have formed a happy marriage.

Is Compensation Equivalent to Payoffs?

Whenever an undesirable facility is built, there is compensation of some type. The only questions are, to whom? When? And how much?

The fundamental issue is sometimes summarized as, "Everything can't be measured in money. Damaging a town's (or state's) social structure, its physical environment or the health of its citizens can't be mitigated by cash."

In a comprehensive outline of the theory behind compensation, incentives and auctions, O'Hare evaluates this crucial issue.[1]

First, there is a spectrum of feelings within any town or state on whether an undesirable facility, such as a hazardous waste site, should be built there. A small number will favor it.

One reason might be patriotic. There are still those who want to do something for their country, even if it involves personal sacrifice. John Kennedy's brave inaugural words in January 1961, "Ask not what your country can do for you, but what you can do for your country," have not been completely forgotten.

Others might have a more selfish motive. They see the opportunity for better jobs than they now have.

Most citizens will be indifferent, as with most public policy issues. Others will oppose the site with varying degrees of intensity.

This last-named group has the right to persuade their fellow citizens to demand a high degree of compensation. Here by "compensation" we mean not only money, but all the other ways in which a community could have control, such as the ability to shut down the facility.

The first group, the patriots, might say, "While we're not enthusiastic about taking these wastes or a prison, this is what we will do for our state or nation. We don't want any money for it." The degree of compensation will depend on the relative strengths of these various groups. If the compensation requested is high enough, the project will be located elsewhere.

The introduction of compensation into the discussion does not prevent citizens opposed to the project from speaking. As would be the case even if compensation were not involved, they still have to persuade other voters.

Second, suppose that those who oppose the facility do not succeed in swaying most other citizens. Then there really is no alternative to compensation of some kind. It has to go somewhere, and at some time. Nobody disagrees with that statement. In that sense, there can be no "uncompensatable cost."

Third, if we accept the two preceding propositions, we would have to show that for some people, being forced to accept the unwanted facility and getting some money in the process is *worse* than being forced to accept it and not getting a dime. Does this make sense?

So using some fairly simple logic, we can demonstrate that environment—in the broad sense—and compensation are *not* incompatible.

Auctions Act as a Mixer for Environment and Compensation

Consider an analogy—a bottle of salad dressing. Oil and vinegar do not mix. But the addition of a few simple ingredients to the two fluids—ingredients that are safe for humans—*does* allow them to blend. We see this every day where we shake the bottle and combine the two liquids.

In the same way, an auction system acts as a mixer, allowing the otherwise dissimilar environment and compensation to combine. It also leaves a good taste in the mouth.

The Science Advisory Board of the Environmental Protection Agency has endorsed the use of incentives. Composed of eminent scientists who advise on long-term questions, the board is the highest scientific authority in the agency.

They said,

> The forces of the marketplace can be a powerful tool for changing individual and institutional behavior and thus reducing some kinds of environmental risks. Whenever appropriate and feasible, [the agency] should use and/or support them. Marketable permits, deposit-refund systems, and pollution charges are types of market incentives that could—and should—play much larger roles in this nation's efforts to reduce environmental risk.... [The agency] should take the lead in fostering more widespread use of market forces to reduce environmental risk.[2]

An auction system for siting wastes is nowhere mentioned in this excerpt. Yet the committee, composed of some of the top environmentalists and administrators in the nation, agreed that market forces have to be a major part of environmental strategy. The auction system works with these market forces to solve siting problems.

The Requirements for Compensation to Work

What should be the general requirements for compensation, with or without an auction? A first answer might be unlimited funds, but that would miss the point. Human beings are only partly economic animals. If we forget the second part, any compensation scheme will not work.

Sam Carnes, a researcher at Oak Ridge National Laboratory, lists a number of requirements for successful compensation. They are not in any particular order of importance. They *all* should be fulfilled if compensation is to work.[3]

First, the compensation has to be *certain*. Vagueness and unfulfilled promises will kill off a compensation system before it begins.

For example, both the Federal and state governments have frequently changed radioactive and hazardous waste policies over the years. This does not inspire confidence among citizens trying to deal with the issues in a fair-minded way. If governments can change general policies on these issues, they can change compensation policies as well. Will citizens be left holding the bag?

Consider a specific example, from the field of high-level nuclear wastes. The emphasis to date on state-Federal relations in this field has been to get a state to sign on the dotted line that they would accept a final repository. If such a signing takes place, presumably the years of argument would end. The Federal government would be obligated to pay whatever compensation had been agreed.

Yet Washington can get out of obligations in certain cases. Suppose the President declares a budget crisis, and says he has to impound the annual bonus set aside for the repository state. If he does this, the compensation process would be a lot less certain. Citizens of the repository state would feel cheated if this happened, and rightly so.

The present Nuclear Waste Policy Act (NWPA), dealing with high-level nuclear wastes, gives the impression of certainty in compensation. It says clearly that $10 million annually will be paid to the repository state until the facility is completed, and $20 million annually afterwards.

States that might be considering accepting the high-level nuclear wastes might not be quite as certain. They might point out that Department of Energy speeches rarely, if ever, mention the payment schedule. In the few cases they do, it's buried in verbiage. If Federal officials are trying to emphasize the certainty of payments, they have a peculiar way of doing so.

Besides, the states that might conceivably be interested in accepting these wastes might say, there are many clauses of the Waste Policy Act that have been dead letters for many years. Look, for example, at the Nuclear Waste Negotiator. It took three years after the amendments to the Act that were passed in 1987 for him to be nominated by the President.

Many other clauses have been essentially inoperative since NWPA was passed in 1982. Anybody knowledgeable about Congress understands that this is common to all Federal laws, not just this one. How will any state volunteering for the repository know that the payment schedule is not just another inert paragraph?

This difficulty is avoided neatly in the auction siting system. Much of the bonus, say two-thirds, would go immediately to the state or county volunteering for wastes. They would not have to depend on Congress or a state appropriating funds. What could be more certain?

With an immediate payment, the constituency that has developed to make a bid would stay in place. Every day of delay in paying the bonus would start to unravel the pro-facility consensus.

Constancy of Compensation

A second criterion that Carnes mentions is *constancy*. This implies a steady stream of benefits over time. The problem here is reconciling constancy with certainty, the previous requirement. Under the auction system, one alternative is to have most or almost all the bonus payment in the hands of the volunteer county or state at the time the ribbon is cut to open the facility. This implies that there would *not* be a constant stream of financial benefits, stretching into the future. Of course, there would be long-term jobs at the waste facility, but in some cases they may not be plentiful.

Is this a drawback to paying most of the bonus immediately? Not really. Any financial adviser would say that it's better to get most of a payment up front, rather than have it strung out over time. With the large amount of cash on hand, interest can be drawn from a bank or it can be invested. Retaining all the funds under the control of the county or state is better, from their viewpoint, than having to go, hat in hand, to the legislature every year for the annual payment. So what looks like a drawback in the auction system from the aspect of constant compensation really is not.

In many state lotteries, the big winners do not get all the cash immediately. The payments are made over a specified time, twenty years in the case of Georgia. While undoubtedly some winners would prefer to have all the cash up front, there have been few public complaints about the lengthy payment time.

Having a long payout time avoids having different benefits paid to the project's beneficiaries (those alive today) and those who will be living around the site in the future. Economics and sociology clash on whether the instant cash or long payout time is preferable.

The third requirement for compensation that Carnes specifies is *adequacy*. The incentive has to be large or comprehensive enough to make it acceptable to the county or state taking the wastes.

Nobody can measure in advance how adequate a given level of compensation will be. Gallup and other types of polls can be taken, but they will not reveal the whole truth of what people want. That basis is only disclosed when the auction or negotiation begins. That's why the *process* of choosing a compensation level may be as important as the level itself.

Consider how the payment schedule for high-level nuclear waste was written. A committee of Congress met, and the amounts were agreed. If there was any consultation with potential volunteer states, it escaped public notice. The process, such as it was, became completely one-sided. No state is on record as believing that compensation for taking high-level wastes was adequate, because no state was asked for its opinion.

About the same thing happened in New York State, one of many states where counties were asked to take low-level nuclear wastes. A total of $1 million annually was to be paid to the county selected.[4] Again, there is no record of the counties being asked if that sum was adequate.

Now contrast this with an auction. The system does not start out with a pre-conceived notion of what an adequate level of compensation would or should be. That level is chosen by the state or county that eventually volunteers, not officials of a siting commission. By definition, the level of compensation is adequate. If it were not, a state or county simply would not come forward. The contrast with the present system is almost complete.

Ease of Compensation Administration

The fourth Carnes requirement for a workable compensation system is *ease of administration*. Every student of government has come across programs that looked good on paper, but proved to be such an administrative mess that they were abandoned.

If a compensation system requires elaborate boards, commissions and other official bodies, as well as the filling in of complicated forms and petitions, it may collapse from the paperwork. Any state that has tried to get money owed to it from the Federal government knows the complexities that result. The situation is probably little better on the state-county front.

On the face of it, the payment schedule for taking high-level nuclear wastes, as outlined in the Nuclear Waste Policy Act, seems easy to administer. A state agrees to take the repository, and then is paid $10 or $20 million annually, depending on the state of construction. What could be easier?

But any payment by the Federal government is subject to a whole gaggle of laws and regulations, not mentioned in the Act. When a state edges up to the payment window, it will be confronted by the Administrative Procedures Act and many other ordinances. Ease of administration is not one of the qualities for which the Federal government is famous.

The problem could arise in the auction system as well, unless special steps were taken to prevent it. That's why the bonus should be placed in a special temporary trust fund. If the rules of the trust fund were set up carefully, it would not be subject to many of the complications of ordinary Federal and state administration.

Even better, if the trust fund was handled by the waste generators themselves, from whom the money would have to be raised in any case, life would be much less complex. Either way would be an improvement over cumbersome Federal and state administrative machinery.

The last of the Carnes requirements with which I will deal is *local perception of incentives.* How much do voters and their representatives know about a compensation system?

Nevada, being the proposed site of a high-level nuclear waste repository, will be the beneficiary of compensation if that facility is ever built. While no polls have been taken in the Silver State on what knowledge people have about the compensation scheme proposed by Congress, I would wager that it is close to zero. Department of Energy officials have downplayed the subject for years. Some news reports have mentioned the payment schedule, but they have not sunk into the public consciousness. Carnes says that if the compensation system is not known and understood by the people who will be affected, it will be useless.

Contrast this with the auction system. Because of its novelty and the large amounts of money that will be at stake, there will be great interest. The attention will naturally be greatest in the states (or counties) that are considering volunteering.

Not all voters will know the amounts involved or how an auction works. After all, years after the Moon landing and the enormous publicity it generated, millions of American still do not believe that it happened.

However, it is certain that the vast majority of citizens will be aware of the bonus. It is entirely possible that the rising amount will be listed in the newspapers and TV day by day, much as Walter Cronkite in 1980 daily intoned the time that American hostages had been held in Iran.

That most citizens in a county or state considering taking an undesirable facility will know about the auction and the level of the bonus does not, of course, mean that all will agree. There will be many who do not want their community to participate at any price. Yet others will want to wait until the price goes higher.

The auction system will generate a broad understanding of the compensation system by almost all people who could be affected. Social scientists, such as Carnes, say that this knowledge is necessary before a consensus among citizens can be reached.

In summary, in most of the areas that Carnes says are required for a compensation system to work—certainty, constancy, adequacy, ease of administration and local awareness—the auction method stands heads and shoulders above the present system. In one or two areas the two procedures are comparable.

Overall, the auction system, in terms of the requirements to make *any* compensation system work, is an enormous improvement over what we have now.

Types of Equity and Fairness

Any decision to build an undesirable project will please some people and infuriate others. Those who will not ever have it in *their* back yard will be happy. Some of those who have it near them will regard it as unfair. Does an auction system violate fundamental societal rules on fairness and equity, or does it help them be achieved?

To answer that question fully, we would have to define exactly what we mean by those troublesome three little words, fairness, equity and justice. Although the subject has been debated by philosophers for centuries, if not millennia, it has yet to be resolved.

Part of the problem is that there is more than one kind of fairness, as Ervin and Fitch have suggested.[5]

For example, consider *procedural* equity. This is concerned with due process and equal access to political and regulatory procedures. In the South before the mid-1960s, black people were treated inequitably in many ways. One of them was procedural in nature: They generally could not vote or serve on juries.

Now one of the claimed strengths of the present siting system is procedural equity. The regulations to carry it out are published at great length—and expense—in the *Federal Register* and similar state publications. Comments on the proposed regulations are invited from states, interested organizations and the general public. Each of the comments is considered carefully by civil servants and other officials, so it is claimed.

Any valid points raised by the public become part of the final regulations, again published openly in the *Federal Register*. All the steps are also public. What procedures could be fairer?

For high-level wastes, probably the longest-running waste show in town, Nevadans do not see it that way at all. Their state is the only one slated for "site characterization," that is, detailed evaluation, under the Nuclear Waste Policy Act amendments of 1987. They might, if pressed, admit that the methods by which the regulations were written have a certain degree of procedural fairness. That is, they have been checked for legal and bureaucratic requirements, and all the rules and regulations have apparently been met.

But, they would say, "The law on which these regulations are based was inherently unfair. Why worry about the color of the wallpaper if the walls rest on rotten foundations? Just as you can't make a silk purse from a sow's ear, you can't make a fair regulation from an unfair law."

They claim that, because Nevada had only a tiny representation in Congress, the rest of that body ganged up on an underpopulated state. Nevadans often used the term "steam-roller" in their Congressional outcries. As far as the rules of Congress were concerned, none were apparently broken in passing this law. But in the opinions of Nevadans, they received no procedural fairness.

Return again to the way that Southern blacks were excluded from voting before the mid-1960s. The regulations requiring detailed knowledge of State constitutions (one of the ways in which blacks were kept off the voting rolls) had been duly passed by various Southern legislatures. They might allow a voting registrar to say to a black person approaching the polls,

"Now Ebenezer, according to the law, I can ask you the following question before you're allowed to vote. In our constitution, each of our counties is allotted a certain number of representatives. Tell me the number of the clause that contains that provision, and the number of representatives for each of our forty-seven counties."

The laws from which these regulations derived were drawn up by state legislatures in which few if any blacks served. They had almost no voice in these laws. Blacks and others said, with justification, that no electoral regulation drawn up using unfair voting laws could itself be fair. Procedural fairness has to extend to the *entire* process, not just part. If one aspect is inequitable, it contaminates the whole.

Contrast this with the site auction. The entire procedure is open and public, so there is no procedural unfairness in singling out one state or county. Since nobody is required to enter the auction, it is impossible to have procedural inequity of this type.

Could there be Residual Procedural Unfairness in a Site Auction?

This does not mean, of course, that procedural unfairness can be excluded in every aspect. Given that humans have to run the system, there is always the chance of this happening.

For example, suppose that polls within State X showed that 80 percent of its citizens favored a high-level nuclear waste site when an auction reached the $5 billion level. Suppose further that 80 percent of state legislators are willing to approve a bid at that point.

Now, for some reason, the governor refuses to sign the state bid to the siting authority. There could be all sorts of reasons for that refusal—a grudge against the legislature, or a half-forgotten run-in with his high-school physics teacher that prejudiced the future governor against all aspects of radiation. All we know is that he refuses to sign. Those in State X who favor the repository within their state, with the accompanying large bonus, will then claim procedural inequity. In their opinion, the governor is not listening to the voice of the people.

This is a potential problem in any democracy. At least the auction system does not make it any worse. On any decision made by elected representatives, from tax levels to finding a waste site, opponents can always say that democratic procedures were not completely followed. In the case of the recalcitrant governor, there are rules for impeaching a Chief Executive. If the people felt strongly enough about his refusal to sign the bid document, they could try to get him out of office.

Of course, by the time the voters got around to removing him, another state may have made a successful bid. These are the inefficiencies that are part of any democratic system.

Individual and Categorical Equity

There are also individual and categorical views of equity. In the former type, what happens to a specific person in paramount. In the latter, what happens to groups—for example, people living above or below the poverty line, minorities, residents near a potential waste site— is of more importance.

Society is always torn between these two types of equity. Let us take an extreme example of how the two ideas might clash in siting a high-level radioactive waste repository. Return to State X. The bonus level has now risen so high that the state legislature and the governor are unanimous in saying the state should make a bid. If they wait another day, another state may jump in ahead of them. Then State X will lose billions.

The landowner nearest the proposed repository site declines to get on the bandwagon. "I'm concerned about the radiation," he says. "The rest of the state may have its opinion, but why should mine be trampled on? I've lived here for fifty years, and I don't want this land changed. I don't believe that the state should make a bid."

Most of us would say, "One person can't hold up the decision of an entire state." We would be right, according to the laws of democracy. But suppose it were two people. Or 2,000. What would be the rule then?

The conflict between individual and categorical equity can be described in a simple question: Where does the approval process end? This point was brought out to me by Peter Myers. He noted that when the Monitored Retrievable Storage system was proposed for Oak Ridge, Tennessee, the City Council of that town approved the Department of Energy high-level waste project unanimously. But the State of Tennessee blocked the project.[6]

If Tennessee had approved it, no doubt some of its neighbors would have objected. (Tennessee has the most adjoining neighbors of any state). They never did, because Tennessee was so vehemently against the project. If Tennessee had the right to veto what Oak Ridge did, did Tennessee's neighbors have the right to veto what *it* did? As we move out from the immediate neighbors of a waste site to the town, to the county, to the state, to adjoining states, where does the veto or approval process end? This question is clearly tied to individual *versus* categorical views of equity.

It's not a simple question to answer philosophically. Laws usually have a list of who has the right to veto or approve. In the case of unwanted land uses, neighboring counties do not have the legal right to disapprove, but they can exert political pressure. There is no reason for an auction system to change that procedure. If every legal entity had the right to block action, we would have a *de facto* rule of unanimity.

Finally, there is a distinction between *vertical* (between categories) and *horizontal* (within a category) equity. Within the context of an auction, we would have vertical equity if both rich and poor states and counties were treated equally. Horizontal equity would result if equally rich (or poor) states and counties were administered in the same way. The auction system does precisely that.

What Are the Types of Compensation?

Carnes' work described the *qualities* of a successful compensation system. Now we consider the *types* of compensation available.

Legislated compensation has been part of many attempts to site wastes. The Nuclear Waste Policy Act, when it was first passed in 1982, proposed giving a limited type of compensation to any state that was being considered for a repository.

The payments were solely for the states to study the implications of the repository on their territory. There were to be no payments for any real or psychological damage done to its citizens if the repository were built there. Most people would not dignify this type of payment with the word "compensation."

Not surprisingly, all the states that took these payments used them to show that they were completely unsuitable for the repository. This was eminently logical from their viewpoint. Since they had no assurance that they would ever receive another penny after the repository was opened, why should they bother accepting the wastes?

In 1987, after the Act was amended, extra payments were specified. A state would get $10 million annually after construction of the repository got underway, and $20 million annually after it was completed. Payments to the only state mentioned in the 1987 revisions, Nevada, for studying it would still continue.

The changes in this legislated compensation are then a form of auction, although at a glacial pace. The price rose from zero in 1982 to $10-$20 million five years later. Any auction in which the bids were separated by five years would be called off for lack of interest.

The process also differs from an ordinary auction in that the price is set by only one party, the Federal government. In a *real* auction, the final price is a compromise between the seller and the buyer.

The Nuclear Waste Policy Act is not alone in legislative compensation. A Massachusetts law specifies a payment of $1 a ton of waste processed in solid-waste recovery facilities. Other states have similar systems.[7]

Any legislative compensation is highly rigid. The state that accepts the repository would get $10 or $20 million annually, not a dollar more, not a penny less. Differences between a potential host state in terms of its size, public feeling within the state, its financial needs, and other factors are ignored.

Members of Congress who drew up the 1987 amendments might say that it was aimed at only one state, Nevada. There was no reason to consider factors relating to other states.

However, there is no indication in its legislative history that Nevada conditions were considered in the bonus amounts. No legislature, not even Congress with its gigantic staff, can anticipate all the possible impacts in a host county or state. Legislatures simply cannot determine, in a way regarded as fair by the potential hosts, how much compensation could or should be paid.

Administrative Compensation

Administrative compensation implies that an agency—state, federal, or possibly some combination of the two—would set a "fair" amount to be paid. State or federal courts might also be used in the process.

Many of us have in the back of our minds the idea that somewhere there is an organization that is completely even-handed and knowledgeable. That agency is clearly the one to set compensation, if a bonus has to be used. If only we could find it!

That approach has already been found wanting in site hunting. Experts in risk, chemistry, radiation and other scientific specialties have assured the public that the dangers of these sites would be very small. If the dangers are as tiny as they are claimed to be, then any compensation should be zero, or close to zero.

Unfortunately for the experts, their testimony has been hooted down by many citizens, as I described in my encounters with Tennessee public meetings. Now suppose that a special board made up of experts on compensation were to meet and set the amount that neighbors of the waste site should get. Is there any reason to believe that this new set of experts will be believed, when the old set were not?

When we think of administrative compensation we also recall the payments that are specified by juries in the case of wrongful death. If someone is killed due to negligent action, juries in some cases can set damages, based on their estimate of how much survivors have suffered economically as a result of the death. Note that it is juries (and sometimes judges) that do this. If a board tried to set the value of a human life, they would be adrift in a storm of controversy.

As someone who has occasionally been called an "expert" himself, I do not like to see the work of these people thrown out the window. Yet the whole issue of siting has become so inflamed with arguments that the voices of experts are drowned out by the din. If experts on risk cannot make themselves heard, then experts on compensation will have exactly the same problem.

Negotiated Compensation

Negotiated compensation works when there are only two parties to a dispute. "Lock 'em in a room and don't let them out till they agree" is the common attitude. Labor-management contracts are a classic example of this type of compensation method. In principle, this should work in finding a waste site. It has not.

The Nuclear Waste Negotiator identified in the Nuclear Waste Policy Act should have been the very model of a modern negotiator. (His office was closed in early 1995). According to the law, he could not be. He was given almost no leeway to do his job. There is no way he could spend a cent more than was specified in the statute.

Suppose Lee Iacocca, former head of Chrysler and known as a tough negotiator, went into a room with union representatives to hammer out a contract. If he had been told by his board of directors that he could not budge a millimeter from the conditions they had set down, he never would have achieved his reputation as a master wheeler dealer. The cigar-smoking executive would never have gone into the room under those conditions.

Perhaps the worst aspect of negotiated compensation, as it presently stands, is that it is *secret*. Woodrow Wilson may have asked for "open covenants, openly arrived at" during World War I, but these noble sentiments have not found their way to siting compensation. One of the main complaints by citizens around potential sites is the blackout in the selection process. That concealment would only be increased with negotiated compensation, with discussions taking place behind closed doors.

If elected officials keep out reporters to talk privately with a compensation commission, there undoubtedly will be an enormous outcry. It will blast the doors open.

The auction method has the advantages of negotiated compensation, without the disadvantages. The rising bonus is a form of negotiation with all parties. The difference is that it is completely in the open. Nobody has to enter the auction if they do not want to, or make calls to the siting authorities from pay phones so the originator cannot be traced.

The auction system will also move faster than traditional negotiated settlements, because the siting authority will not have to wrangle with states and counties. Its prime function will be to set the clock ticking. After that, it is up to the states and counties that might be interested.

Negotiated compensation might work if one and only one site was viable, i.e., there was a universally agreed-on "best site." If the risks are as small as the experts tell us, there is no "best" site. Thus negotiation, while it has its advantages in other fields, seems doomed to failure when it comes to picking sites.

Is Compensation Disguised Bribery?

Is the whole idea of compensation just out-and-out bribery, or is it a higher concept, like a reward? Some people do indeed equate a reward with a bribe.

According to a strict definition, a *bribe* is an illegitimate use of money or favors to influence someone, usually with the goal of financial profit.[8] A *reward* is a legitimate benefit received for some worthy behavior or special service. There is a vast distinction between the two, both ethically and morally.

While there are many aspects of bribery, three relate to what is proposed here. First, bribes are illegal. Second, they are secret. Third, they target a specific person, group, or agency.

Consider illegality. Everyone supports burying hazardous or nuclear wastes safely, finding group homes for mental patients, and building new penitentiaries. These tasks are, by definition, legal. Taking bribes to construct these facilities is obviously illegal, but the facilities themselves are legal.

Bribes are secret. Nobody thinking of bribing a legislator would dream of doing it on television or on the floor of the legislature. In the Abscam bribery case of the 1970s, some members of Congress took bribes. They thought they were doing it in private. They were not, as it later turned out; it had been video-recorded. If they had known that, they would not have accepted a nickel from the fake Arab "sheiks" who propositioned them.

Bribes always have a specific target. Suppose someone wanted to get a contract from government Department X and was willing to bribe someone to obtain it. He would not wander through the halls of Departments Y and Z, handing out money. He would try to find the official in Department X who handled the contracts. He would then attempt to bribe him and *only* him. Any other bribe would be a waste of money.

If compensation is the equivalent of bribery, why would the State Planning Council on Radioactive Waste Management, an organization of states concerned about the subject, advocate compensation for any damage done as a result of nuclear waste facilities?[9] Granted, the states are usually looking for new sources of money, but they do not usually allow themselves to be publicly bribed.

The point was once made succinctly in a letter to a Seattle newspaper: "Coating such bitter pills [nuisance facilities] with a bit of sugar would undoubtedly remove much opposition. It is when the undesirable is rammed down the throat without compensation that people feel unfairly treated."[10]

Mary Poppins said it as well as anyone: "A Spoonful of Sugar Makes the Medicine Go Down." This beloved movie character was not a briber.

Could Compensation Ever be a Bribe?

Compensation *could* be a bribe if it were done in hidden ways, and if its purpose was to save money for the person or organization doing the bribing.

For example, suppose that siting authorities decided that County A was a logical waste site, and they wanted to spend the least amount of money to get the county's signature on the dotted line. They know that using an auction system would cost more than a bribe. By definition, a bribe costs less than the legal way of doing something. Nobody would pay $1 million to obtain a $100,000 contract.

In this hypothetical scenario, the officials would pass checks to the county's officials, all the while wining and dining them. None of this would be made public, of course. Now *that* would be a bribe, and all of us could recognize it.

Contrast that sleazy situation with an auction system. There can be no secrecy—quite the opposite. There can be no back-door "deals" between state and local legislators because of massive publicity. Each state or county legislator will get exactly the same amount of cash as any other citizen if they see fit to make a bid, and not a penny more. There will have been no bribery of the elected representatives in the ordinary sense.

As well, there is no targeting of counties or states, as with the present system. Without a target lined up in the cross-hairs, there can be no real bribe.

Are the people being bought off with their own money? This was one of the main objections raised to the New Deal measures of the 1930s. Welfare or unemployment compensation recipients would always vote for Roosevelt, critics claimed, since he was the one who sent them their checks.

In the case of unwanted facilities, this claim fails. The money for the bonus—or any other compensation, for that matter—ultimately must come from waste generators. For example, in the case of high-level nuclear wastes, all the funding comes from a levy, imposed by Congress in 1982, on nuclear generated electricity.

Money for the bonus will probably pass through the hands of the government at some point, although that is not a fundamental requirement of the auction system. But no government will be printing new money for the bonus. There is no element of self-bribery here.

Ultimately, the extra charge levied on the waste generators comes from our own pockets. Every time that we have a medical test performed at the doctor's office that uses a radioactive tracer, every time we use a plastic product that produces chemical wastes at the factory or refinery, we will have to pay a little toward the bonus.

"Not In My Back Yard" Has to Have an Associated Cost

We can look at the question of compensation and bribery another way. When we cry "NIMBY! NIMBY!" we are saying that we don't want facilities in our own back yard. We haven't had to pay much for the privilege of that complaint. When we compensate the areas that agree to accept the wastes, we bear the expense of the opportunity of shouting "NIMBY!"

Siting arguments have already suffered too much from loaded words—cancer, poisoning, pristine neighborhood. We do not need another one—bribery—ruining the atmosphere.

If some sort of compensation is paid for dealing with environmental problems, how should the bonus be divided? If Ronald Reagan had done the cutting, he probably would have suggested a check to each of a state's or county's citizens. "Let each person decide for himself how to spend it," he might have said.

If Jesse Jackson were in charge, he probably would have proposed, "Let the government spend the bonus on improved and expanded services."

Rather than set down my personal and political views on how the money should be allocated, I leave that weighty question to the citizens of the volunteer state or county. Undoubtedly, some will want a check in the next day's mail. Others will want lower taxes.

Yet others will demand improved state and local services, such as education, health care and police. Nobody outside the affected area should dictate how the money should be divided. If their citizens are wise enough to cut through the claims and counter claims, they certainly are intelligent enough to handle the bonus.

How Much Should be Spent on Monitoring?

Nonetheless, it seems almost certain that any area winning the bonus will set aside some of the money for environmental monitoring, testing and checking for health effects.

The Environmental Protection Agency and the Nuclear Regulatory Commission, and their state counterparts, will undoubtedly perform monitoring of their own. However, the climate of suspicion is such that local bodies will want to have their own instruments and technicians in place.

Under the auction method, the localities will have enough money to do their own monitoring. They will not have to rely on handouts from federal or state agencies, or complicated inter-agency agreements. The technicians will be paid by and under the control of local bodies, and their paychecks will be assured.

How much should be spent on this monitoring? Here we return to the question of local *versus* centralized control. Again, it would be unreasonable for an outsider to say, "You are to spend 5 percent (or any other fraction) of the bonus on environmental safety and monitoring." The host community can make the decision for itself. The auction system ensures enough money is on hand so the host community or state *can* make that decision.

In spite of these general *caveats* that should apply to all allocation schemes, O'Hare and his colleagues in Massachusetts drew up some general guidelines on how incentives could be spent.[11] One of them deals with trust funds.

The auction system I have outlined already has a trust fund, but it is only temporary. Most of the bonus is put into this temporary fund when a state or county bids. If it passes the environmental hurdles, it gets full use of the total bonus. The trust fund is dissolved. However, it may wish to set up another trust fund.

I can mention the experience of Alberta, in Western Canada. In the 1970s, the price of oil shot skyward, thereby enriching that petroleum-soaked province. Some of the extra oil revenue was used to lower taxes, but a substantial portion was set aside in a special heritage fund. The money was to be used to prepare for the day when the oil dwindled. The Albertans were wise enough to recognize that day would come.

Drawing on the Alberta experience, the volunteer county or state may wish to put part of its bonus money in trust for a rainy day. The money would not be idle, since it would be drawing interest until it was needed. It is unlikely that the volunteer community will ever get a check of that size again.

The Bonus Can be Used for Conditional Payments

Parts of the bonus could be used for "conditional payments." For examples, site neighbors might claim that their homes will lose value when they are sold. There is no way to estimate this loss until the homes are put on the market. Some studies have found that homes around places where severe industrial accidents have occurred, like the reactor at Three Mile Island, have eventually *increased* in value. However, in the weeks and months following the accident, most home-owners near Three Mile Island would not have believed that could happen.

Part of the bonus might be allocated to pay any losses of this type. If, as in the case of Three Mile Island, homes increased in value, that aspect of the bonus would not be used.

There can be in-kind compensation. For example, suppose that a site took up part of an existing park. This would be highly unlikely, because this would be yet another strike against the facility.

If some park land had to be expropriated, new park land could be added as a requirement. The new land might even be better than the old.

Finally, part of the bonus could be allocated to extra health, safety and environmental protection. Any new waste facility will be better engineered and designed than those that have gone before. One risk analyst has told me that the new generation of facilities could be called "gold plated." In other words, he thought that excessive measures were being taken to reduce an already small risk.

In spite of this, it is possible that local officials may demand certain improvements, such as more leak-proof enclosures, than are neces-sary. Some of the bonus could be allocated, by local people, to these measures.

Can the People Deal with an Auction System?

There are many possible objections to an auction system. Many of them relate to the nature of auctions, compensation and incentives, and how they work. I have discussed almost all of them. One objection is more fundamental. To put it succinctly, it's that "people can't handle it."

In other words, "ordinary people" cannot deal with difficult choices like pricing the effects of a waste site on their neighborhood, town or state. If they cannot do it, then there is only one group that can: the professionals.

This objection is more a matter of belief than proof. The people's representatives in Congress attempted twice to decide the fate of the high-level nuclear waste repository, in 1982 and 1987. They did the same for low-level nuclear wastes in 1980 and 1985. State legislatures have, on innumerable occasions, debated the locations of a host of other unwanted projects, from prisons to AIDS treatment centers. So have town and county legislators. If members of Congress, the President, state legislators, and town and county representatives do not speak for the people, who does?

Those who believe that the public is not equipped to handle the subject might respond, "Members of Congress can work on these complicated areas. They have staffs with science doctorates, even if they themselves aren't all that knowledgeable. Even members of state legislatures have some inputs from scientists and engineers. What does an ordinary citizen know?"

This contradicts the basic principles of democracy. Our ideas are ultimately founded on the vibrant New England town meetings of the 17th century, which still continue in Vermont to this day. The nation has changed greatly since that long-ago time, but the democratic foundations show remarkably few cracks. Whenever possible, we should place decision-making on the level closest to the people. They are wiser than some imagine.

The Usefulness of a LULU

For many years, it was thought that chemical waste sites had such a terrible image that few would accept them, whether or not compensation was involved. There is some indication that is changing. An article in *Chemecology,* put out by the Chemical Manufacturers' Association, notes:

> [F]or the first time ever, more people actually would not object to a waste-to-energy plant in their community than would oppose it, 55 percent to 37 percent (8 percent were not sure). A little over one year ago, 48 percent were opposed to such a plant versus 39 percent who would have been in favor (13 percent were undecided). Landfills are still far from welcome in most communities. Fifty-five percent of individuals would object to a new landfill being built in their town, while a little over one-third would be unopposed.[12]

The reason there is an apparent shift of public opinion on waste-to-energy facilities is not difficult to explain. We are bombarded with messages to conserve energy and use less from hostile countries like Iraq. If we can produce some of it in a local incinerator, we are lessening our dependence on mustachioed dictators.

Landfills also are a form of waste-handling. But waste-to-energy facilities produce something positive, (i.e., energy of some type). Landfills produce nothing positive, unless we count the chance to deposit garbage. As a result, waste-to-energy facilities will be favored over landfills.

Roger Kasperson, professor of geography at Clark University in Worcester, Massachusetts, has pointed out for years that nuclear power plants are generally regarded more favorably by the public than low-level nuclear waste facilities. This is even though the former contain much more radioactivity than the latter. Objectors to low-level waste sites often formulate their objections on how much radioactivity the facilities contain. If they were being completely logical, there would be many more complaints about nuclear plants as opposed to nuclear waste sites.

Kasperson notes that nuclear power plants, regardless of their problems and risks, produce something of value, namely electricity. The waste sites produce nothing, and can *never* produce anything of value.

A Vote on a Bonus Should Not Require Unanimity

Some people will always regard a site in their town or county as uncompensatable, that is, beyond money. The claim of "uncompensatable costs" is merely another way of saying, "Give me a veto on the waste location—I will decide for everyone if they are acceptable." Once that is conceded, then we have given everyone a veto. Then no facility to which anyone could possibly object will ever be built, anywhere.

There have been historical examples when efforts were made to enforce a rule of unanimity. The cases may seem strange to modern ears, accustomed as we are to majority rule. For example, in the Middle Ages, the Polish Parliament could not take action if even one of its nobles objected. Historians often credit the resulting paralysis for the division of that unhappy land by its rapacious neighbors.

Unanimity in a region will never be achieved. If it could be attained easily, we as a nation would have built toxic and radioactive waste facilities many years ago.

In reality, some people accept compensation for environmental hazards or problems that we think that *nobody* can tolerate. We rarely see discussion of this compensation in newspapers or on TV, so we think it does not exist.

It *does* exist. It's often indirect, so we generally do not see it. In chapter 9, when we discuss such topics as airport noise and Love Canal, the "hidden environmental compensation" will become evident.

Entering or Leaving a Volunteer Community

People can move in or out of the region that receives a bonus. Americans are probably the most mobile society on earth, apart from the Gypsies. How does this relate to compensation for environmental problems?[13]

At first glance, the two conditions do not seem to have any relationship. However, consider this: State A accepts a site, and receives a large bonus. It distributes checks for $1,000 to each of its citizens. The day after the checks arrive, Mr. and Mrs. Jones arrive to take up residence. Of course, not having been there when the checks were delivered, they get nothing. Is this fair?

If, for example, the volunteer county builds a chain of community centers with part of the bonus money, newcomers would get the benefit. On the other hand, they will be exposed to whatever dangers the site generates.

Conversely, consider those people who flee the county or state in fear of the facility. There will undoubtedly be a few, although much less than the number that would be estimated from polls. Remember the divergence between willingness-to-pay and willingness-to-accept revealed by these questions. We get the same difference between the number who say they will flee and those who do. As well, some of those who depart the affected region would have left anyway for other reasons, such as better jobs.

If most of the bonus goes to the community's government, which in turn builds capital-intensive facilities and buys new high school band uniforms, those who move out will get little compensation for their decision. If, as has sometimes been claimed by those who have fought siting, thousands would bolt any community that accepted LULUs, those who take flight should get some recompense.

Only the permanent residents of a community that accepts an unwanted project can decide which proportion of the bonus should go to government, and which to individuals. As the above examples show, they should look beyond their personal philosophy. Those who leave and those who enter should also be considered.

Environmental Impact Statements and Economics

It seems unreasonable to talk about environmental impact statements in a chapter on compensation and incentives. After all, an impact statement is science, economics is money, and never the twain shall meet. Or will they?

In the context of auctions, impact statements or similar compilations of fact serve as information sources to potential bidders. Without that information, they are operating in the dark. They will not be able to determine what would be a fair level to make their bid, a bid that balances risk and economics.

Consider a prospective buyer of a Van Gogh painting. Attached to it is a "provenance." This traces the history of the work from the time it was completed to auction day.

For example, a provenance for the Van Gogh work might say, "Allegedly painted in 1883 in Arles, according to Prof. Jones of Cambridge. First seen in 1897, exhibited at the Paris Museum, according to its catalog, available from the Library of Congress. Owned by John Smith of New York from 1901 to 1920."

Without such a provenance, the painting would fetch much less. The art world, especially at the top levels, is full of beautiful fakes. Some artists have earned a good living turning out nothing but these hoaxes. Shorn of the provenance, the unwary buyer could be buying something that Van Gogh never saw.

The impact statement, when done properly, should fulfill the function of a provenance to tell people what they are getting. However, impact statements, as generally written, may not be adequate for the concerns some people have.

For example, reports dealing with nuclear waste sites will have detailed calculations on radioactive waste leakage into ground water, and the effects of this leakage on neighbors of the facility. They will not say that the state in which the site will be built may be called the "Glowworm State" on a late-night TV talk show. No impact statement ever written can predict that. Yet far more people in the affected state, if polled, would be concerned about that rather than some abstruse mathematical calculation on leakage rates.

People in other parts of the state in which a waste site is built will want to know how their *entire* state, not just the small area around the site itself, will be affected. This probably will not be in the impact statement either.

An impact statement on waste siting is more complex than the simple document implied by the National Environmental Policy Act of 1970. It implies the entire body of research. Readers may yet go blind to understand.

The sheer weight of the statement, usually in several bulky volumes, will prevent all but a handful of experts from probing all aspects of the waste site. Thus it has been ever since the first statement was written.

The picture is not quite as bleak and data-overloaded as is painted. Some information *does* filter down to the general public. In recent siting tussles, citizens were probably better-informed that those who took part in previous environmental battles. In future siting developments, the media is likely be full of facts gleaned from these statements.

Having a well-done impact statement cannot ensure that all citizens around a potential site will become miniscientists overnight. However, if the facts are written in a way that many can understand, it will allow a better-informed auction system.

Will the Auction System add Even More Uncertainty to Siting?

The success or failure of any incentive system will depend on what people think of the size of the compensation. The nature of any auction, whether sealed-bid, English or Dutch, precludes knowing its level in advance. A painting may be valued at $1,000 by its sellers and experts who appraise it, but may raise $500 or $2,000 at auction.

This might seem like an insuperable drawback to any auction system. We do not know how high the bonus will rise until a volunteer comes forward. Policymakers generally detest this uncertainty. However, there are simple techniques for overcoming this problem.

The history of finding waste sites has been the illusion of certainty followed by the realization that matters were uncertain after all. An auction, or any other compensation scheme, would not increase the uncertainty of an already erratic system.

For example, in 1982 Congress thought that it had forever solved the high-level nuclear radioactive waste problem. This came after decades of delay and dallying, itself a major source of uncertainty about whether the wastes would *ever* be buried.

Five years later, after strenuous objections from the states that were possible repository sites, Congress found that the problem had not been solved after all. It had to re-write the 1982 law, now focusing on Nevada. Yet today, few observers of the nuclear industry would be willing to bet the ranch that the wastes would land up in the Silver State. The uncertainty had not diminished much after the passage of the "final" law on the subject.

About the same thing happened in Congress with its laws on low-level nuclear wastes. In 1980, the solution was proclaimed. By 1985, it was obvious to all that the law had flopped. As Timothy Peckinpaugh wrote,

> Given the dismal failure of the original 1980 act and the haphazard process in which the 1985 amendments were passed, one must wonder if Congress won't find itself, perhaps when the interim access period ends in late 1992, trying to legislate yet another 'solution' to the low-level radioactive waste 'crisis'. Many thought that the 1980 act, with its regional approach and its "reasonable" exclusionary date [which allowed the three states accepting their wastes to keep out wastes from other states], would settle the equity complaints of Washington, South Carolina and Nevada and result in more disposal sites. But a series of political and logistical factors doomed the 1980 act and necessitated the 1985 amendments. Has anything changed to prevent another failure?[14]

There is already tremendous uncertainty about almost all aspects of finding sites. If it did not exist, neither would this book.

Compensation cannot make it much worse, and can reduce it. The auction system cuts down on financial uncertainty, by ensuring that no money changes hands until a site acceptable to its future neighbors is found.

The American Propensity for Lawsuits

If there is one characteristic that has marked the string of siting defeats throughout the nation, it is the series of lawsuits that have accompanied them, like fleas on a dog. Cynics have labeled the Nuclear Waste Policy Act—the source of many of these suits—and the National Environmental Policy Act, one of its predecessors, as the "Lawyers Permanent Employment Acts."

Some of the suits have been filed by towns, counties and states, others by environmental groups, and yet others by individuals. Some of the suits have had merit, and others have been thrown out by the courts at the first opportunity. Regardless of who filed them and what validity they had, they have swarmed around the process like a horde of hungry mosquitoes.

It would be pleasant to claim that if an auction system were employed, no lawsuits would be filed on either side of the issues. Lawyers would spend their days looking out windows and counting clouds. Nobody can give that assurance. On the other hand, the vast majority of lawsuits referred to above dealt with situations where little or no compensation was to be paid. They cannot be blamed on any incentive system, past, present or future.

Would an auction system reduce the spate of lawsuits? There is reason to believe that it would.

Consider a likely scenario, in which an auction is held among many counties. There will be no lawsuits from counties that have no interest in joining the auction. Why file papers if you have taken yourself out of the running?

Within a county considering a bid, there could indeed be lawsuits by individuals who oppose making an offer. However, there should be no lawsuits from the county itself against the siting authority holding the auction. By definition, if a state or county is considering making a bid, opinion there is either split or generally in favor of the offer. If a state or county makes a bid, how can it, at the very same time, sue to prevent the site from being built?

In the past, suits by a county or state against a siting authority have been filed only when public opinion was generally hostile. For example, consider the Monitored Retrievable Storage site proposed for Tennessee in the mid-1980s.

Its Attorney General knew that the Governor and most of the legislature, as well as most Tennesseeans outside the Oak Ridge area, were against the Department of Energy proposal. He filed suit against DOE, and was ultimately successful.

If an auction system had been used for siting, and Tennessee had not been interested, the Attorney General would never have bothered to get out his law books. He simply would have sat on his hands.

In the states that had some interest, their Attorneys General would also file no lawsuits. The auction would have built up a constituency within those states, one that the state's legal officer would not want to alienate. The constituency is those who want the bonus in their state. They do not want legal maneuvers designed to stop the process.

Lawsuits from Adjoining States or Counties

Lawsuits could still come from adjoining states or counties, who do not want the site anywhere near them.[15] In this case, the auction system would be no better or worse than the present system.

However, it can be modified easily. Suppose that at least 10 percent of the bonus had to be donated to adjacent counties or states for the psychological damage they may feel due to the undesirable material passing through their territories. The winning town or state could raise that percentage, but not lower it.

If such a modification were in place, there would be less reason for adjoining towns, counties or states to sue. Since they could lose substantial funds if their neighbor forfeited the bonus, they would have less incentive to go to court. Nonetheless, no conceivable siting system can guarantee lawsuits would disappear completely.

Private groups can also file lawsuits. However, one observer has said, "[I]t may be necessary to accompany an auction with limitations on individuals' standing to sue in order that the compensation program itself not furnish another procedural forum for delay on the part of still unsatisfied parties."[16]

How would these limitations work? One possibility, as suggested by Michael Gerrard, would be to require that lawsuits be filed within a reasonably short time after the auction is announced. One reason why many siting projects drag on for years is that lawsuits are often filed at all stages of the proceedings. Just as the first shovel is to hit the ground, opponents file for an injunction.

Another limitation would be to give preference to hearing these lawsuits in the courts over other types of trials. Many courts are overburdened with suits, and siting arguments now have to take their place in line. A Federal statute, the Speedy Trial Act, gives precedence to criminal cases in federal courts. The same can be done for siting questions.

"We're filing a lawsuit tomorrow" has been the key phrase of siting battles. While the auction system for finding these sites cannot guarantee that lawyers will collect unemployment benefits, it will develop constituencies strongly opposed to a strong of endless lawsuits.

These constituencies do not exist today, and the opposite is true. In Nevada and elsewhere, there are major segments of the population who are willing to devote enormous legal fees to keep wastes out of their back yard.

The salad dressing analogy showed that oil and water, corresponding to economics and environment, *did* mix. They will not combine by themselves. They need extra added ingredients. To find sites, those ingredients are an understanding of equity and compensation, reliance on volunteers and, most important of all, an auction system that requires no coercion.

Notes

1. Michael O'Hare, "'Not in *My* Block You Don't!'—Facilities Siting and the Strategic Importance of Compensation," *Public Policy* 25 (Fall 1977): 407, especially 454.
2. Science Advisory Board, *Reducing Risk, Setting Priorities and Strategies for Environmental Protection* (Washington, D.C.: U.S. Environmental Protection Agency, September 1990) report SAB-EC-90-021.

3. Sam A. Carnes, Emily Copenhaver, Jon H. Sorensen, E.J. Soderstrom, John Reed, D. J. Bjornstad, and Elizabeth Peelle, "Incentives and Waste Siting: Prospects and Constraints," *Energy Systems and Policy* 7 (4) (1983): 323.
4. "State Must Impose Waste Site, but with Payback to 'Host,'" *Buffalo News* (13 September 1990): B-2.
5. David E. Ervin and James B. Fitch, "Evaluating Alternative Compensation and Recapture Techniques for Expanded Public Control of Land Use," *Natural Resources Journal* 19 (January 1979): 21, especially 36.
6. Letter from Peter B. Myers, Staff Director, Board on Radioactive Waste Management, National Research Council, Washington, D.C., to Herbert Inhaber, 8 August 1990.
7. 16 Massachusetts General Laws, para. 24A. Quoted in Michael O'Hare, Lawrence Bacow and Debra Sanderson, *Facility Siting and Public Opposition* (New York: Van Nostrand Reinhold, 1983).
8. Carnes et al., "Incentives and Waste Siting," 334.
9. State Planning Council on Radioactive Waste Management, *Interim Report to President* (24 January 1981).
10. Quoted in David Morell and Christopher Magorian, *Siting Hazardous Waste Facilities: Local Opposition and the Myth of Pre-Emption* (Cambridge, Mass.: Ballinger, 1982), chap. 5, "Who Pays? Compensation and Siting," 167.
11. O'Hare et al., *Facility Siting*, chap. 5, "Compensation and Strategy," 67ff., especially 72.
12. "Americans Rally Behind Recycling," *Chemecology* 19 (July/August 1990): 4.
13. O'Hare, "Not on *My* Block!," ibid., 451.
14. Timothy L. Peckinpaugh, "The Politics of Low-Level Radioactive Waste Disposal." In *Low-Level Radioactive Waste Regulation: Science, Politics and Fear*, ed. Michael L. Burns (Chelsea, Mich.: Lewis Publishers, 1988): 45.
15. Letter from Peter Myers.
16. O'Hare, "Not in *My* Block!," 441.

9

Some Examples of How Dollars and the Environment Can be Compatible

There are innumerable examples of compensation for environmental harm, either real or perceived. Some of these ideas and plans have been warmly endorsed by environmentalists.

Market incentives are also used to handle other tough societal problems, not directly related to the environment. Finally, the last part of this chapter is devoted to what the man and the woman in the street have said about compensation issues. Evidence from three states suggests that it could be useful for solving NIMBY problems.

The Science Advisory Board

The Science Advisory Board (SAB), a prestigious part of the Environmental Protection Agency (EPA), has recommended using marketplace incentives to achieve environmental goals. I mentioned this in chapter 8. It is one thing to make a lofty statement, another to back it up with specific examples. Here are some of the SAB illustrations.[1]

Acid rain is one of the great environmental problems of our time. To date, it has been attacked mostly by means of regulations: You, Ms. Utility Executive, are allowed to emit X tons of oxides of sulfur and Y tons of particulates per year. While these regulations seem simple on their face, they often become embroiled in lengthy and expensive lawsuits, requesting exemptions and delays. The result has been that the regulations have not accomplished nearly as much as had been hoped when they went on the books.

The SAB says that "marketable permits" for emissions could be used as a solution. This takes advantage of the fact that some electrical utilities can reduce their sulfur dioxide emissions at lower costs than other utilities. For example, they may nave access to low-sulfur coal.

Using marketable permits, utilities that could reduce their sulfur oxide emissions at low cost would reduce them *more* than is required by the law. They would sell their credits for having overcontrolled to utilities facing high costs to achieve the same goal.

The SAB estimates that a 10 million ton per year reduction of sulfur dioxide would cost the nation $4 billion annually under the marketable permit system. It would cost about $8 billion annually to achieve the same objective through standard regulations. The extra $4 billion could remain in the pockets of electricity users, namely, you and me.

Environmental groups like the Environmental Defense Fund have endorsed the idea. They have seen it as a way out of the protracted and fruitless court battles over tiny details of the regulations. It was their advocacy that made it part of the 1990 Clean Air Act.

Some of the major sources of hazardous air pollution are volatile organic compounds (VOCs) such as pentane, propellants for spray cans and certain other chemicals. Can market incentives be used to reduce their level in the atmosphere?

The SAB proposes a deposit-refund system or tax on the VOC components in solvents, where they are often found. For example, there could be a deposit of 10¢ per gram of these solvents, much like the deposit on beer cans. If the manufacturers could demonstrate that the solvents had been recycled, then they would get their deposit back.[2]

Imposing a front-end charge of this type would create strong incentives for manufacturers and users of solvents to find substitutes, to reduce use, and to increase recycling. Right now, I, as well as others, do not have any reason not to chuck the waste into the garbage. To increase recycling, no tax would be imposed on recycled, as opposed to newly made, solvents.

In the last few years, radon gas in homes has been estimated to be the greatest source of radiation to most Americans. No riots have taken place over radon, even though its effects are much greater than any low-level radioactive waste site.

How can market incentives work to reduce radon levels? The SAB says that a rule could be passed that federally sponsored mortgages, such as those of the Veterans Administration, could require radon testing before a house was sold. This would be a market incentive, rather than a regulation, because it would be up to the house seller and buyer to decide what to do with this information. Some buyers and sellers might decide that the environmental harm was small, and do nothing.

Others might decide it was great, and try to reduce radon levels. It would be up them, not a government bureaucracy.[3]

Deforestation

Global warming on a scale that would have been thought impossible a century ago now is a possibility. As one of many strategies for coping with this, the SAB recommends a debt-for-forest swap.[4] Many of the Third World countries that are so busily engaged in cutting down their trees are the very same ones that have massive debts to Western banks. If some of the debt could be replaced by commitments to expand Third World national parks, two problems could be shot down by one financial stone.

Environmental groups have been in the forefront of advocating a debt-for-nature swap. Some organizations have worked out swaps of this type. The struggling Third World countries then have a major economic incentive to decrease deforestation, since some of their crushing debt burden would be reduced. Their response to mere exhortations by the West to "do the right thing" has been close to zero.

As examples of this trend, a private utility company in New England is planting 52,000,000 trees in Guatemala, somewhat out of character for a private American company. Their goal is to compensate for their stepped-up production of electricity by fossil fuel burning in Connecticut. As MacLeish writes, "The Nature Conservancy [a major environmental group] is brokering debt-for-nature swaps, valued at $9.2 million, between private companies such as American Express Bank and various Third World countries; they will benefit conservation in the Amazon, the Ecuadorian Andes, the Galapagos Islands and Costa Rica's rain forests."[5]

Sometimes an inventive program works not by increasing compensation, but by *reducing* it. So it is with the case of wetlands.

The SAB notes that there are tremendous financial advantages to developers to drain and build on wetlands.[6] It says, "subsidies on construction of Federal flood-control and drainage projects could be reduced or eliminated." The Tax Reform Act of 1986 already has removed several provisions that had provided an incentive for wetland development. As well, the Food Security Act of 1985 says that a farmer is ineligible for price-support payments, storage loans, crop insurance, and disaster payments for any year in which annual crops were produced on converted wetlands. The number of reverse-compensation measures that have been or could be taken to preserve wetlands is clearly large.

Bottles and "Product Stewardship"

When bottle laws were first passed, the beverage industry fought them tooth and nail. Now they are reconciled to them.

These laws, usually requiring a deposit of 5¢ or 10¢ on a container, are a perfect example of incentives promoting the environment. Anyone who drove down a highway in the 1960s or 1970s knows how much tidier they are now. Yet we have not hired a mammoth army of cleaners and sweepers.

The change is mostly due to these bottle laws. It is now in people's interest to save and collect used bottles and cans. Before, it was not. The proportion of bottles collected will depend on the size of the deposit. In California in 1989, it was only 1¢. Remarkably, redemption rates in the Golden State for aluminum cans were 57 percent, and 33 percent for glass bottles. It sank to 5 percent for plastic containers. The *Los Angeles Times* noted that the rate approaches 90 percent for states that require deposits of nickels and dimes.[7]

I was reminded of this when visiting a grocery store in Ottawa, Canada. The deposit on a bottle was 40¢, not the much lower value found in the U.S. You can be sure that I remembered not to throw *that* bottle in the trash.

A broader concept promoted by the SAB is "product stewardship." Under this strategy, responsibility for a product would not end when cash hits the seller's palm.[8]

Producers of goods with environmental impacts, like bottles or chemicals, would then have a reason to engender responsible use and disposal. One way of accomplishing this is a front-end tax like the bottle deposit. If it were big enough, we might *never* see a bottle on a city street or highway.

The SAB says that we do not have to stop with bottles. We have problems in disposing of lead-acid batteries, tires, car hulks, and a host of other wastes. Deposits could be charged for them.[9]

We usually have to return a dead battery when we buy a new one. I have always done this, so I do not know what the penalty would be if I showed up without the old one. I suspect I might get a cocked eyebrow from the mechanic, but that's all. If the penalty were large, we would see very few leaking and corroded batteries behind the gas-station garage. Incentives would have worked again.

The SAB also deals with waste disposal incentives, besides the broader environmental problems noted above. They say that

> a basic flaw in current waste management is that in most localities, disposal costs are paid out of property tax revenues rather than in proportion to the amounts of waste discarded. This system provides no incentive for those who dispose of wastes to reduce [its amount] or recycle; waste disposal seems "free." Correcting this disincentive, by charging for both the human and the environmental costs of waste management in proportion to wastes generated, is a fundamentally important principle for solid waste management. One form of such a charge is already being imposed locally in some communities, such as Seattle (and in many cities in Europe), where residents are being charged by the container for the amounts of waste generated.[10]

If I put out ten bags of trash a week and you put out one, in most jurisdictions we both pay the same amount. There is obviously little incentive for me to reduce the trash I generate. In Gloucester, Massachusetts, I would pay ten times as much as you.[11]

Many environmental problems cannot be solved solely in the laboratory. The SAB study shows that incentives and compensation can be used to tackle many ecological problems, from wetlands to old batteries, from air pollution to radon.

Chlorofluorocarbons and the Ozone Layer

Many of the SAB recommendations concern what could be called "global" problems, those which involve national policy as opposed to specific locations. Even before it passed the 1990 Clean Air Act, which enshrined emissions trading, Congress had also devoted some thought to incentives to solve other intractable environmental problems.

Excess chlorofluorocarbons (CFCs) can deplete the stratospheric ozone layer. There are two approaches to this problem: One is a simple ban, as enshrined in international treaties on the subject. However, the spate of CFC smuggling into the United States in the mid-1990s shows the difficulties in legislative fiats. Another approach is financial.

In an article entitled "A Clever Solution for Pollution: Taxes," Michael Weisskopf outlined a law buried in a 1989 Congressional budget reconciliation. It imposed a tax of as much as $1.37 per pound of CFCs manufactured. As Weisskopf writes, "it was designed to price CFCs out of the market by making them as costly as alternatives less destructive to the veil of ozone."[12]

There would have been at least two benefits from this tax. First, the ozone would have been protected, without cumbersome regulations.

Second, the Treasury would have pocketed about $5.6 billion over the next five years.

The bill, sponsored by Rep. Pete Stark of California, apparently marked the first use of the tax code to discourage pollution. Said a Stark aide, "We were looking for the easiest way to run industry out of CFCs and into producing environmentally benign alternatives." Dave Doniger, an environmentalist with the Natural Resources Defense Council, said, "It's helpful if it costs companies to pollute."

Incentives to Reduce Automobile Use

We all use our cars too much. Everyone has felt a twinge of guilt when we hear that statement. Then it evaporates in about a microsecond as we fumble for the car keys for the next trip.

In California, compensation for avoided car trips replaced guilt trips. In an article entitled "California Car Pools Can Mean Fast Cash," Jay Mathews outlined the efforts of the South Coast Air Quality Management District to change the almost immutable habits of Los Angeles-area drivers. He writes,

> Like most Southern Californians, Bruce Collins thought that car pools were not for him.... He had listened to public service announcements and noted the convenience of reading the paper on the way to work, but one new incentive won him over. It was cold cash.
>
> After years of largely fruitless attempts to change California commuters' habits with computerized ride-matching, highway billboards, and car-pool lanes, local business and government agencies threatened with huge fines for failure to encourage ride-sharing are offering monetary rewards—in some cases as much as $80 a month—to employees willing to leave their cars at home.[13]

According to Mathews, 80 percent of employers filing annual trip-reduction plans said they were giving money to employees that car-pool. Under California law, most major companies have to file these plans with the state.

Cindy Johnson, a vice president at Bank of America, said, "I think it is going to have a substantial long-term effect." At one of their 900-employee buildings, car pools increased from 20 to 70 in six months.

Los Angeles has been long known as a region where nobody rides in a car with anybody else. That's a bit of an exaggeration, of course; the average number of occupants per vehicle is 1.1. The agency managing the compensation program says their goal for the region is 1.5. By raising average vehicle ridership to this number, they could reduce daily emissions of hydrocarbons by 24 tons, nitrogen oxides by 34 tons, and carbon monoxide by 216 tons.

The idea of compensating employees who either car pool or take public transportation is spreading. In suburban Washington, DC, Montgomery County allows companies to buy $20 Metrorail farecards for $15, and sell them to their employees for $10.

This is a classic example of compensation working the way it is supposed to, helping the environment. Nobody is required to car pool or take the subway. Yet as the level of compensation increases, more and more will do so. Telling people to save the environment has had only limited success. Making it in their interests to do so works much better. Car pooling in Southern California, a land where almost all human activities seem to take place in a vehicle, is a major case in point.

Preserving a Neighborhood

In most big cities, keeping a neighborhood viable is a challenging task. Neighbors come and go, and new businesses can upset a carefully planned balance.

So it is in Washington, D.C. But that city is different from many in that neighbors around a prospective new business can, in certain cases, decide whether it opens. In that sense, they have the veto right that many potential neighbors of a hazardous or radioactive waste site would like to have.

Not every type of business, of course. More specifically, Washington allows a liquor license to be denied if a majority of registered voters living within 600 feet of the site sign a petition against it to the city.

The $40 million Embassy Suites Hotel in the Friendship Heights section of Washington was about to open. However, its neighbors were unhappy. One of them, Ethan S. Burger, said, "You're building something in our neighborhood we don't like. You have to award us for our suffering."[14]

The huge hotel was clearly going to change the neighborhood's character. Ordinarily, there would have been little that residents could do. The law gave them some clout. Incentives were the solution.

As part of the eventual agreement between the hotel builders and the neighbors, all the 150 people living within 600 feet of the hotel were given health club memberships. As well, liquor serving hours were drastically reduced from the legal limit, to cut down noise and congestion around the hotel.

In two words, problem solved. Incentives made the neighbors feel better about the new hotel, which was going to be built in any case. The *Washington Post* did not approve of the settlement, calling it "Spamail."[15] However, if they had tried to build a new printing plant near where people lived, they might have tried something along these lines themselves.

In the summer of 1989, Dorla Simmins, the town supervisor of Friendship, in Allegany County, saw an announcement that New York State wanted to build new prisons. She wrote for more information. In May 1990, a $65 million prison was announced for the town of 2,100.

Peter Simon wrote, "The prison issue presents a dramatic contrast to Allegany County's bitter, continuing battle with a state commission considering a low-level radioactive waste facility.[16] The degree of incentives was not specified. However, John Doran, head of the Friendship Chamber of Commerce, said, "The economy will pick up a lot. It will make the school system stronger, it will make the tax base stronger, and it will attract some businesses to the area."

The people of Friendship did not think potential escapes were much of a problem, voting 393–149 to accept the prison. In two words, it's because *they* chose, not officials in the state capital.

Personally, I would rather have practically any type of waste site in my back yard rather than a prison. The people of Friendship saw it differently. They thought that the influx of money would compensate them for any danger. Who am I to argue with them? By definition, the level of compensation is adequate. If it had not been, they would not have voted for a prison in their town.

Prisons are a classic case of LULUs, fought about long before hazardous and radioactive waste sites attracted attention. Yet they get built, primarily because of the direct or indirect incentives that attracted Friendship.

A Wall Around a Mall

You would not ordinarily think of a mall as an environmental hazard. To those living in a neighborhood where a mega-mall is about to go up, that's exactly what it is. Healy and Popper write,

> Consider the builder of a large new shopping mall [White Flint] in the Maryland suburbs of Washington DC, who faced a formidable opposition from residents of an adjoining residential neighborhood. Eventually he won them over by agreeing to build a large earthen buffer between his stores and their houses. He also offered

to reimburse the occupants if their property values were to fall. More prosaically, owners of liquor stores, taverns and other "nuisance businesses" are often among the most public contributors to local charities, voluntary associations and local politicians.[17]

I had once walked near this mall, and wondered how this earth berm came to be. Now I know. While building this wall did not put cash into the pockets of nearby residents, it was a form of compensation. The guarantee against loss was yet another form. I do not know if the mall builder ever had to pay out money for property losses. But the sky-rocketing house prices in the Washington area practically insured him against having to pay.

Love Canal; if ever there was a name to strike fear, that's it. Why would anyone ever want to go within ten miles of that despoiled community? What possible compensation could induce anyone to do so?

Suppose the Environmental Protection Agency and the New York State Department of Environmental Conservation (Love Canal is in Niagara Falls, New York) said that as far as they were concerned, at least part of the Love Canal area had soil about as safe as soil elsewhere. Would you move to that suburb?

Philip Palmisano would. The retired north Tonawanda (near Buffalo) bar owner said, "I really and truly want to buy one. As far as I'm concerned, the homes are well built, they're safe and they're fairly priced."[18] He, his wife and son lived in an apartment above his former business.

Having visited there myself, I can testify that Love Canal was never Mansion Row. The houses are single-family dwellings with small lawns, yet better than the apartment in which Palmisano lived.

Almost everyone has left Love Canal. The impression I got from my tour was truly haunting. It's as if Levittown had been suddenly deserted.

What does all this have to do with compensation? The original owners of the houses that had to be vacated had been paid off long ago.

Palmisano, and others who may buy homes in the Love Canal area, *would* get some compensation for any perceived risk. The homes were to be sold in the $50,000–$60,000 range, about 10 to 15 percent, below what they would cost nearby, according to James Carr, one of the officials of the Love Canal Revitalization Agency. Buyers like Palmisano would pay $5,000 to $9,000 less than they would for a comparable house far away from Love Canal. This "compensation" is not offered as a check from a government agency, but simply in lower mortgage payments.

Was this a fair deal for Palmisano and other prospective buyers? To answer this, remember that the houses that were most contaminated, those very close to the polluted canal itself, will never be offered for sale. Many of them have been demolished in any case. Palmisano could not buy one of them, even if he were willing to expose himself to the risk.

Second, as I noted above, any risk in the soil around the house that Palmisano wants to buy would be about the same as soil under your or my house. The EPA will never certify soil as "safe"; all it can do is compare it to that in areas in which no contamination is expected.

Ultimately, Palmisano had to make up his own mind about the level of compensation. If the Love Canal prices were exactly the same as comparable houses elsewhere in town, he and others would probably say that it was not worth the trouble. Since prices are indeed lower— and Niagara Falls, New York is a poor community—he had to balance the reputation of Love Canal versus the savings he and his family would make. There is no way that a government agency, or you and I, could do this for him.

Recycle—But Not Here

Recycling is one of those subjects on which almost everyone agrees. We should not just throw out our garbage, but find a way to reuse some of it.

That is, as long as the recycling is done far away from us. NIMBY applies to the desirable activity of recycling, as well as the undesirable activity of just heaving garbage into a landfill and letting it stay there forever. That's because to run a recycling plant, garbage of one type or another has to be brought to it, hence, NIMBY. Recycling is wonderful, helping to conserve resources—somewhere else.

This suggests the need for incentives to get a recycling plant built. That's what happened near Buffalo.[19]

Erie County, in Western New York, was having difficulty getting a community to accept a 100,000-ton-a-year recycling plant within its boundaries, although almost everyone said the idea was a good one. Having trucks carry 300 tons a day into their towns did not seem quite so desirable to elected officials.

Finally, they found Depew, a small town to the west of Buffalo. Why would Depewites take the garbage when everyone else held their nose? There was an incentive: Depew would get all its recycling done for free. Other towns contributing their garbage would have to pay.

In a flash, the problem was solved. The plant is built, residents of Depew are satisfied, and other towns avoid their recycling dilemma. And all because of incentives.

With landfills—formerly called town dumps—so much in the news, one might think that their number is ever increasing. Not so. Most of the old ones are being closed. In the 1970s there were about 20,000 in the U.S.; now there are about 6,000. Old landfills cannot meet new regulations—they leak too much into water supplies.

The difficulties of finding new ones are what propels the subject to the front page. One of the most successful hunts was in Gilliam County, Oregon.[20]

For a fee, residents of that county near Portland allow that city's trash into their landfill. When Gilliam Countians attended public meetings on the subject, their buttons read, "Portland's Trash is Gilliam County's Cash." It was very different from the buttons usually found adorning chests in other public meetings on landfills. The buttons often read, "Don't Dump on Me," or other phrases not fit for printing in a book on policy.

Environmentalists are sometimes the main NIMBY proponents. Not true in Gilliam County. The local chapter of the Sierra Club endorsed the landfill, saying only that they prefer the trash to be hauled by rail rather than by truck.

Marvin Katz, writing on the Gilliam County situation and advocating "YIMBY/FAP" (Yes, In My Back Yard—For A Price), says, "I see a reversal [of attitudes toward NIMBY] coming. Even residents that used to be NIMBY, when they see benefits going to the landfill host communities, will be saying, 'How come our dumb politicians aren't letting us get any of that money?'"[21]

How much is all this worth to the county? One estimate is that the workforce will increase by 100, to a total of 1,000. The landfill should add a total of about $4 million annually to a county economy estimated at $14.3 million, or about a third.

As Michael Parrish writes: "[E]ach arriving load brings its share of new life to a county that was economically dying. Before the landfill, some Portlanders probably felt some sympathy for their neighbor, dwindling Gilliam County. But there was nothing they could do concretely. The landfill allows them to solve their trash problem and, at the same time, aid their neighbor."[22]

Rhode Island Incinerator

Central Falls, Rhode Island, was described by the *Wall Street Journal* as "small and beleaguered."[23] Its report said that it wanted a trash incinerator built to produce energy, for the revenue it would provide. While most proponents of unwanted sites are hesitant about ever letting the matter get to a vote, Central Falls actually voted *for* the plant.

Charles City County is near Richmond in Virginia. A developer built a 289-acre landfill that will produce at least $1.1 million annually for the county.[24] That may not seem like much, until it is noted that total tax revenue for the county before the landfill was built was about $1.5 million. The total amount received by the county could range up to $2.3 million. If the county wanted to have the same level of services as before the landfill, it could have abolished virtually all taxes it levies.

As Fred Darden, county administrator said, "We're going from a poor county to one that's at least comfortable." He went on to say, "There's money in garbage. If we can gain an advantage by using our resources, that is certainly an option to be considered."

One of the complaints made against cash-for-trash deals is that the environment might deteriorate. In Charles County, that was unlikely to happen. The reason? Besides the payments to the county, the developer was to pay for a special fund to monitor the nearby Chickahominy river, with an engineer paid for by the fund. As well, a second fund was to monitor the landfill itself, regardless of the actions of the developer. Charles County residents were better protected from environmental degradation than the residents of many other counties with existing landfills, who cannot afford *any* monitoring.

The former U.S. trust territory of the Marshall Islands evaluated whether to accept ordinary trash from the West Coast.[25] According to the proposal, the 13,000 residents would get $56 million annually, or about $1,200 per man, woman and child. President Amata Kabua said, "We are alarmed by the rate of our [population] growth. And I certainly want to leave this government with enough money to go on. I don't want to leave it broke."

Under the proposal, the process of removing cans and toxic items from the trash would be monitored by the EPA. No U.S. environmental regulations would be broken.

The company making the proposal figured it could ship waste to the Marshalls for $22 per ton, about one-third or a quarter the cost of trucking city trash to rural landfills.

Why would Marshall Islanders want this trash, other than for the money? Their islands are gradually being washed away by the sea. As well, if the greenhouse effect is real, much of their land will be underwater. The trash could help build up their islands. This suggests that when it comes to siting an undesirable facility, it is very difficult for an outsider to determine all the reasons that citizens of the affected community might have to accept—or reject—it. In this case, the Marshall Islanders have considerations that the rest of us have not considered.

They will have to make up their own minds on whether $1,200 annually per person is enough. If it is, and the environmental rules are in place, they will go ahead. If it is not, the proposal will die.

Compensation Can be Reasonable

One of the major objections to compensation for siting LULUs is that the costs could skyrocket. "There's just no control on the payments," objectors might contend. "You're talking about millions, even billions."

Reality is considerably different. In an article entitled "'Bribes' Work in Wisconsin," (note the first word is in quotation marks) Richard Shuff, an official of a waste management firm, gives some numbers.[28] They are astonishingly low, considering the arguments that often rage over landfill siting.[26]

For example, Fond Du Lac County will receive $35,000 annually plus 1 percent of gross income from its landfill. A paper mill landfill will pay 45¢ per ton or $600 per month, whichever is higher. The Wisconsin Tissue Mills landfill will receive $6,000 annually, plus an inflation adjustment.

Many of the agreements contain compensation for negotiation expenses, such as lawyers' fees. These are also tiny. Manitowoc County will receive up to $2,500. Rusk County will get up to $62,500, and so on.

Shuff notes that the key to the twenty-one landfill siting successes in Wisconsin has been compensation, immediate or conditional, to governments and citizens. The compensation paid has hardly caused any bankruptcies. The largest amount awarded in all twenty-one landfills was $218,000 to twenty-one property owners by Wisconsin Tissue Mills. This worked out to about 15¢ per ton of the landfill's capacity, a tiny amount.

The results show conclusively that whatever the defects of compensation for environmental ills, it will never bankrupt the waste-generating firms and municipalities that have to pay the bill.

Not every proposed compensation system gets off the ground, of course. Some of the most interesting are those that might have been, but were not.

Every state that was even remotely considered for the proposed high-level nuclear waste repository ran the other way when they saw it coming. That's the conventional wisdom. At least one hesitated a bit.

The Nuclear Waste Policy Act was supposed to guide the selection of a site for the repository. One of its clauses says that whichever state got the facility would receive preferential treatment when new Federal research installations, such as the later-cancelled superconducting supercollider, were built. If such treatment was accorded Nevada, the proposed site of the repository, there never was any evidence of it.

Any preference given would have been a form of compensation for the dreaded repository. As Joseph Davis puts it, "Think of it as a nuclear combo-plate: Your state orders the multi-billion dollar 'supercollider' and gets the permanent repository for the nation's nuclear waste on the side."[27]

At least one state thought seriously about this Chinese menu. In 1987, Garrey Carruthers, then governor of New Mexico, came to Washington. According to one report, he explored with members of his Congressional delegation whether New Mexico could get the supercollider if it took the repository.

Why New Mexico? The state already has one major nuclear waste program, the Waste Isolation Pilot Project. It also is the recipient of much federal largesse through giant laboratories at Sandia and Los Alamos. Two committees of the state legislature backed the super-collider-repository swap. A poll by the *Albuquerque Tribune* did find that most people were against the proposed deal, but not strongly so. This was in contrast to the situation in most other states, where mention of a repository sets off alarm bells.

The deal never passed. Carruthers was unable to get enough support from his Congressional delegation, and the idea died. If it had gone forward, it would have been one of the shining examples of appropriate compensation .

Airport Noise

Consider airport noise. Most people cannot stand the roar of aircraft a few feet above their roofs, and try to live far away from flight paths. This depresses the cost of houses near airports.

These houses are never empty. Some people can always be found to move into them. They accept compensation like lower mortgage or rent payments than their fellow noise-sensitive citizens. The compensation is indirect, rather than a check from the government. It is still there, though.[28]

Consider how compensation for this admittedly serious environmental problem would be set following the "scientific" procedures used to site unwanted facilities. Everyone would have to be tested for hearing ability. Then more tests, to determine sensitivity to noise, would have to be performed. Next, a massive sorting system, designed to find locations near airports for those with poor hearing ability and low sensitivity, would have to be instituted.

That would be the easy part. The next step would be to "educate" those people who have been designated to move that living around the airport would be just the thing for them. The final procedure would be to allocate compensation by a board of experts, who would base their numbers on hearing ability, psychological testing, and other factors. The victims of the noise would have no say in how much money they would get.

Ridiculous, you say? It's not much stranger than the present system for finding sites. Environmental burdens are placed on a neighborhood, town or county by outsiders. Potential neighbors have little power in the matter, until they rise in righteous wrath. Any compensation, in the few instances it occurs, is also set by outsiders.

Contrast this with living around airports. No agency decides who should or should not live near them. A natural sorting-out takes place. The compensation levels, like lower rent, are also set naturally. Those who do not mind noise gravitate to airports. Those who are bothered, stay far away. No laws or regulations have to be imposed.

Paying Reactor Neighbors

Polls in this country show that most people are at least mildly in favor of nuclear power—as long as they cannot see the reactor from their back yard.

This may not pose much of a problem to U.S. energy planners, since we have much fossil fuel with which to generate electricity. In many other countries, they do not have that luxury of choice.

France, for a number of years, provided cheap electricity to neighbors of its many nuclear reactors. The French government felt it could not rely on expensive and unreliable fossil fuels such as oil, and undertook a massive nuclear power program. Many of the citizens around nuclear sites were hesitant about the whole deal—until they opened their electricity bills and found them substantially lower than before.[29]

Now that has also been done in Taiwan. Its electric utility, Taipower, offered residents around its new reactor $6 million a year during the ten-year construction period and $4.6 million annually thereafter.[30]

This may start a worldwide trend for nuclear power. If a nation wants to encourage this, it might skip the exhortations to be good citizens and the detailed explanations of low risks. If people around a potential reactor site find it worth their while, they might not spend too much time on picket lines.

The Japanese have been successful in finding waste incineration sites in the middle of cities, although, as Hornig writes, "NIMBY is a Japanese phenomenon, too. Japanese citizens despise and resist the siting of incineration plants in their neighborhoods as vehemently and vocally as do their American counterparts."[31]

The emphasis on incineration is a result of national policy. With a tiny, crowded land mass, the Japanese cannot set aside thousands of acres for landfills. As well, almost all their energy comes from abroad. One way of reducing this dependence is to burn the garbage to make heat and electricity.

All of this makes sense to the Japanese as a nation. At some point, however, this policy has to be translated into a specific location.

How do the Japanese overcome NIMBY? First, information sessions are held. The municipalities that want to build a waste-to-energy plant have something more to offer their citizens than scientific papers and pamphlets. They have real compensation, like facilities with hot baths, gymnasiums, meeting rooms, swimming pools, baseball fields, gardens, and goldfish ponds, as I pointed out in chapter 4.

How the citizens and the municipality arrive at the exact level remains a mystery. Nonetheless, its existence is well known to all.

The compensation comes from the central government, not the municipality that wants to build the plant. As a result, the mayor does not have to levy a tax to pay for all these goodies; they arrive from Tokyo.

Of course, there is really no free lunch. The central government collects municipal taxes on behalf of the cities and towns, and then returns it, partly by these goldfish ponds. Because of this, there is no obvious tax to pay for the compensation.

The Form of Compensation May be Most Important

The *form* in which compensation is made can be more important than the amount itself.

In the example of Charles City County and its landfill that I discussed above, two extra trust funds, for monitoring of the nearby river and the landfill itself, were set up by the developer. The trust funds could have been funded out of the main payment to the county itself. Apparently residents wanted the separate payments so they could keep track of the moneys—and their intended results—more easily.

One of the more unusual examples of how people react to the form, not merely the substance, of compensation was an attempt to site a solid waste incinerator in Connecticut:

> The firm seeking to site the incinerator was initially rebuffed despite offering the town $1 million in annual compensation. An anti-incinerator Planning and Zoning Commission had outlawed incinerators. The developer rephrased the compensation, offering to pay all current property taxes in the town for 25 years—a sum which came to the same $1 million annual figure. A subsequent non-binding referendum favoring the incinerator passed with 54 percent of the vote.[32]

Is there room for incentives in dealing with wildlife preservation? Preservationists would say that incentives, like bounties, have destroyed much wildlife. Why use a corrupt tool, one that has destroyed millions of wild animals?

Tell that to Defenders of Wildlife, a Washington-based group with over 80,000 members. They planned to introduce wolves back into Yellowstone National Park, where they once existed before they were wiped out by humans.[33]

Wolves don't respect national park boundaries. Even if most were confined to the park, a few would escape, to eat the easiest prey— helpless cattle. Ranchers do not appreciate this.

What to do? Defenders of Wildlife proposed paying for the few cattle and other livestock that would be eaten by the wolves. They have already started a program of this type, paying ranchers in the northern Rockies for losses caused by wolves that have migrated in from Canada. In the summer of 1987, the Defenders raised $3,000 in damages within forty-eight hours. In the fall of 1989, after another incident, they paid out $1,700. As has been written, "That doesn't make stockmen any less peeved, but it does disincline them to go out and shoot wolves—or hire lawyers."

It might be conjectured that environmental groups would despise any type of compensation program. Yet one of the major wildlife organizations paid compensation out of their own funds, not depending on some government agency raising the money out of taxes.

In the last twenty years, arguments of this type were liable to end up in court, where virtually the only satisfied parties were the lawyers. In the next twenty years, with the spread of compensation for environmental harm, the lawyers might be little hungrier, but both parties to the conflict will be more satisfied.

Compensation systems have been used to solve other seemingly insoluble societal problems, not always connected with the environment. I now give some examples.

Desegregation

Public housing is often more segregated by race than planners want. How can incentives work?[34]

Housing and Urban Development Department investigators found that segregation had taken place in the Buffalo, New York, Municipal Housing Authority. It was not the kind that had once existed in the South, enforced with bullwhips and snarling dogs.

Rather, it was where people in the housing units were assigned. Most facilities in the public housing were black, and most senior citizens' complexes were white. This was not merely the luck of the draw. It was partially the result of illegal admission procedures. Lawyers concluded that segregation was so widespread that it violated the civil rights of the 8,000 residents.

What to do? The housing management could have taken an authoritarian approach, in which their tenants were shuttled about like so many sides of beef. "You, Mrs. Jones, and your family, into that tower there. You, Mr. Papilowski, into that apartment on the other side. And I don't want to hear any complaints!" Since the tenants already feel powerless in a public housing situation, this would have made these emotions even stronger.

The second approach was unanimously approved by the authority's board. It called for incentives for those willing to move into projects where their race was outnumbered. No coercion or arm-twisting would be needed.

As in most public housing, there is a waiting list to get the right kind of apartment. Those who rise to the top of the list were to be offered the size apartment they had requested—chosen randomly from all available apartments. They could also get a similar apartment in any project where their race was represented in a smaller percentage than the authority-wide average. For example, suppose the percentage of whites (or nonminorities) in Complex A was 30 percent, and the overall fraction of whites in the housing authority was 50 percent (these are hypothetical figures). Then apartments in Complex A would be the second choice of apartments offered to whites.

Ordinarily tenants would take the first of the two choices. To ensure that the second choice is made a significant part of the time, incentives were attached to it. Tenants taking the second choice, which would tend to even out racial distribution, would have received incentives worth up to $1,000, or an apartment with one more bedroom than they would be entitled to otherwise. For example, if they had been allotted a two-bedroom apartment based on their family size, by taking the second choice they would have gotten a three-bedroom residence.

The incentives would not have been cash—I suppose housing authorities do not trust their tenants with dollars, fearing they will spend it on booze or worse. Instead, they would have been such items as security systems, ceiling fans, and new appliances. Many would be home related.

The money for these incentives would have only totaled $500,000. This means that if 500 tenants had taken them up on their offer and received the maximum amount per family, the fund would have been exhausted. Still, the program would have reduced racial segregation significantly in Buffalo public housing.

We often think of environment as so many parts per million in the air or water. Ultimately, "environment" means *all* our surroundings, taken as a whole. Tenants in public housing frequently have a much worse environment than those in middle-class suburbs, regardless of what is in their air or water.

Added to the inadequate environment is often segregation, not by law, but *de facto*. With an imaginative incentive plan, one housing authority has shown how segregation can be eliminated.

Catching Terrorists

When we walk though an airport and nothing happens to us, we may think that the calm stroll has nothing to do with the environment.

If we had a machine gun fired our way, our environment would be greatly disturbed.

In that sense, the reward that the Federal government pays to those who help thwart a terrorist act—$2 million—is an incentive for improving our environment. According to the State Department, the money can be paid to "any person who furnishes information that leads to the prevention, frustration or favorable resolution of a terrorist act against U.S. persons or property." The bill was signed into law by President Bush.[35]

The concept is the same as Post Office "reward" posters. Everyone is against terrorism, and we should all be on the lookout for it. Without this incentive, a handshake from the President is all we would get for risking our lives. For some, that would be enough. Unfortunately, there are not enough of these selfless souls to go around.

Not being blown up in the sky is as much a part of our environment as clean air and pure water. The massive reward offered by the government helps preserve that part of our surroundings.

In 1990, the National Science Foundation wanted to develop a new world-class magnet laboratory. In the ordinary course of events, the NSF would send out requests for proposals to existing laboratories. It would then evaluate the proposals it received solely based on scientific criteria, and make a decision.[36]

That's not what happened this time. According to David Hamilton, who wrote an article entitled, "Magnet Lab: Science to the Highest Bidder?," economics entered into the decision. Florida State University was willing to put up $58 million to secure the lab for the Sunshine State. The Massachusetts Institute of Technology could only come up with $36.5 million. The lab went to Florida.

MIT officials were nonplussed, especially since their university already had the major magnet lab in the country. They noted that the advisory committee to the NSF had recommended the new lab be built at MIT, saying that Florida State "has no demonstrated capability in magnet technology."

Florida State officials did not see it that way. Provost Gus Turnbull said it was "about time" for the southeastern U.S. to get a major science facility. "The people of Florida contribute a lot to the Federal treasury. The whole region has been shortchanged in terms of federal support."

The people of Florida were compensating the rest of the country for siting the lab in their state. Whether Florida was wise to do this is for them to decide. The rest of the nation did not have to spend the money that Florida reimbursed.

AIDS Research

Some of the major studies of AIDS take place in Africa, where the disease is common. Getting people to take part in epidemiological studies that offer them no direct benefit can be difficult.

Thomas Quinn, a researcher at the National Institute of Allergy and Infectious Diseases who has worked extensively in Africa, says that monetary compensation is not appropriate in this context, but that some type of compensation is necessary.[37] He offered African mothers who participated in one of his studies a picture of their child, and in another study a bottle of milk.

Not all compensation has to be in cash. It can be by lower taxes, increased services, or other forms that do not have a check attached to them. Quinn and other researchers in AIDS realized that it is ethically unfair to ask people to take part in research without giving them something in return.

Compensation, thy name is legion! While some of the examples described above are only proposals, the following are or have been on the books. The Black Thunder Mine in Wyoming built housing, schools and other community facilities, as well as paying out cash grants to the community.[38] Basin Electric, also in Wyoming, guaranteed school bonds. In France, as I noted before, the national nuclear utility gave price concessions on electricity to residents near its power plants. In addition, a system was set up to train and hire local workers. A significant share of the contracts from their power plants was awarded to local firms.

In Idaho, two small hazardous waste disposal facilities were developed on the site of abandoned Titan missile silos. The private developer's offer to the local community included free waste disposal services, additional fire protection and medical training.[39]

A group wanting to build a Missouri Basin Power Project dam offered the state of Nebraska and four conservation groups a cash settlement to head off their opposition to construction of the hydro site. They were rejected. When the money was re-offered as a trust fund to benefit whooping cranes that might be adversely affected by the facility, it was accepted. Sometimes the form, not the cash amount, of the compensation is vital.

In Massachusetts, a curious example of a quasi-auction took place. The town of Haverhill was offered $1 per ton to host a resource recovery (recycling) facility. It accepted. Later, the town rejected the offer, since people there felt that the price was not high enough for its trouble. Still later, Haverhill reversed itself again and accepted the offer. If it had not, the adjacent town of North Andover would have taken the facility. After the first reversal, Haverhill residents realized that they would have trucks passing through their town on the way to North Andover, without getting any compensation at all for the psychological effects of these trucks.

In Tennessee, a $2 million trust fund was established for communities that accept a hazardous waste facility that includes both a landfill and an incinerator. At least 25 percent of the fund must be used for facility monitoring and regulatory enforcement. Localities can, in addition to receiving this money, levy fees of up to $5 per ton for disposal facilities and $2.50 per ton for treatment facilities.[40]

New Hampshire communities receive $6 per ton. In California, towns receiving wastes get 10 percent of a facility's gross receipts. In Connecticut, communities get the greatest of 5¢ per gallon, $3.50 per cubic yard, or a specified fraction of gross receipts. It is clear from this brief description that many states allow or require compensation for towns or counties with landfills.

Polling on Compensation

Most of the above examples deal with actions that have been taken by officials and governments. What do their masters, the citizens, think about all this?

Polling has defects. The main one is the divergence between willingness to pay and willingness to accept. However, if people are polled primarily on the question of the acceptability of compensation we should obtain valid answers.

Wisconsin residents were polled on a potential high-level nuclear waste site for their community. Since no such repository had ever been proposed for Wisconsin, the questions were clearly hypothetical.[41]

This poses problems for pollsters. People often say one thing when a decision is far away, and another when the choice has to be made on the spot. You may prefer vanilla to chocolate ice cream generally, but settle for chocolate if a vanilla cone is a quarter more.

In any case, 22 percent of the respondents said that they would favor a repository in their area, even without incentives. Seventy-one percent opposed it. The rest did not know.

The term *no incentives* deserves some clarification. The respondents were being asked about a repository in their own community, so some jobs would have been created even if there were no cash payments from the government. Some of the respondents may have hoped to get some of the jobs, or have their businesses expand under the influx of highly paid scientists.

In other words, there would have been some economic incentives even without government checks. Since the pollsters did not get to this level of detail, we will never know the motives for saying "yes" in this poll. Most experts in the field of opinion on nuclear waste facilities would be surprised at the high level of acceptance in this community. A margin of 71 percent against to 22 percent in favor would be regarded as a large defeat in most contexts. But the support for these allegedly dangerous facilities is so low nationally that a vote of 22 percent in favor seems remarkable.

People in other parts of the Dairy State were not part of this poll. It is almost certain that the support level for the repository would have been even lower among the "out-staters" than the 22 percent recorded for the people around the hypothetical site.

The history of nuclear waste siting has been almost invariably of a community for which the site is suggested being somewhat disposed toward the facility or neutral. The rest of the state is hostile in their dislike, sometimes violently so.

Differences of opinion depending on distance from the site are logical. The rest of the state, whether we are talking about the hypothetical situation in Wisconsin or the real one in Tennessee, would get little or nothing from the project, under the present siting system. As a result, they are usually opposed. People around the site at least have the chance for some jobs or increased economic activity, so a considerable proportion is often willing to consider the facility.

People around the proposed Wisconsin site were quizzed after incentives were added to the package. This time, the proportions that were favorable rose to 42 percent, almost double the previous value. Those who were opposed fell to 47 percent, with the rest undecided. In other words, the respondents were about evenly split on the waste site after incentives were offered. *Before* the incentives, those in favor were outnumbered by over three to one.

This result gives the lie to those who claim that incentives will not work, that people's attitudes toward undesirable facilities are set in concrete. Incentives do the job they are supposed to—get people to reconsider what is in their best interest.

What was lacking from the poll was any indication of how the opinions of other Wisconsites might have changed under an incentives package. As I noted above, the conflict between those near a potential site and those far away has been the downfall of most proposals for these sites. The attitudes of people a long distance from the site, but still within the state, are ignored, at least initially. This disregard continues until lawmakers from other sections of the concerned state rise up in arms. Then the proposal sinks like a stone.

Conducting an Auction by Poll

The word *auction*, to my knowledge, was not used in the Wisconsin poll. Yet the questions were framed like an auction.

Respondents were asked, in effect, "Would you favor the repository without *any* incentives? Would you favor it if we threw in incentive A? What would you think if we gave you A *and* B?" There was a total of six incentives, so there was a crude type of auction happening.

Obviously, the more incentives, the greater the proportion of favorable answers. The interviewer continued down the list until he or she got a "yes" answer, or until the list of incentives was exhausted.

What were the incentives? Only one dealt directly with economics, and was specified as "substantial payment to your community." The meaning of "substantial" is unclear. As well, this payment does not guarantee that a penny will end up in a respondent's pocket. The "substantial" amount could be spent by local government in a way that does not benefit a specific person.

The other incentives included independent monitoring of the waste site, the power of the community to shut it down, representation of the community on a governing board, and so on. However, at least one of the incentives, independent monitoring, requires money. Those funds could derive from a bonus or direct financial incentive to the community.

Nonfinancial incentives could be used as extra incentives if a site auction were held. For example, suppose that the level of the bonus had risen to $100 million for a hazardous waste site, and siting officials thought that any more would bankrupt them. They might say, "In addition to the $100 million cash payment, we will grant the local community the right to shut down the facility under certain specified conditions. *Now* will a volunteer come forward?"

The example show that even during an auction, siting officials could sweeten the pot with nonfinancial measures. It would be analogous to an art auctioneer trying to sell a picture and facing dispirited and weak bidding. He might tell the crowd, "to get the bidding going faster, I'm going to throw in this small Picasso with the Renoir." Tossing in some extras is legitimate in the context of finding a site acceptable to its neighbors.

Polling on Compensation

Portney performed a poll in five Massachusetts towns on a hazardous waste treatment plant. Portney told respondents that the mythical plant would try to change hazardous waste to safe waste.[42]

With this assumption, the Massachusetts plant meets Prof. Kasperson's criterion for a "good" facility—it produces something of benefit. Thus, at least in principle, it should be regarded more favorably than a plant with nothing "good" coming out of it.

The hazardous waste plant did not receive much approval. About 31 percent favored a hazardous waste plant in their town without specific incentives. About 62 percent were opposed, and 7 percent did not know.

When respondents were asked about building a treatment plant of this type elsewhere in their state, as opposed to their own community, results were radically different. More than half, about 56 percent, were now in favor, 38 percent were opposed, and the rest were undecided. NIMBY had prevailed.

Not everyone was part of the NIMBY group. About a quarter of respondents changed their mind when the possibility of building the plant elsewhere in the state was raised. This is a substantial fraction—but far from 100 percent.

Massachusetts is small, so even building it elsewhere in the Bay State might make the waste plant uncomfortably close for many respondents. If the question had been asked of Texans, the proportion in favor would have been greater.

Portney listed a total of eleven incentives. Two were risk-related. One was having public officials and citizens inspect the facility on a regular basis. Another was to have state officials "do their best" to prevent accidental spills.

The financial incentives were wide ranging. One was direct and universal—a payment of $50 to every family in town. Others were in the nature of governmental or societal benefits. One was to repave the city's streets, in recognition of the increased truck traffic around the proposed facility. Another would have the developer pay for increased fire protection, assuming that the plant would have some risk of explosion.

Some of the economic incentives would benefit only a few people. One was to have the developer hire at least 15 local residents; another was an award of five college scholarships to local high school seniors annually.

In calculating the effect of incentives in changing minds, the subgroup that was opposed to a hazardous waste plant *anywhere* in the state was excluded. The implication was that these people had fixed ideas. Nothing would budge them.

Of those who favored a plant of this type somewhere in the state, but not in their town (that is, those with the NIMBY syndrome), 43 percent had their attitudes changed by one of the eleven incentives. If respondents could choose more than one incentive, 52 percent would change their mind.

For these respondents, the most attractive incentives were those dealing with safety. Yet in the risk analyses and environmental impact statements that invariably accompany proposed waste sites, the hazards are invariably estimated as low. Respondents obviously think they could and should be made lower.

The most popular economic incentives out of the nine that were offered were those that would have benefitted only a small proportion of the population. For example, the five college scholarships were deemed to be the most desirable of all.

This may be due to American's infatuation with education, more than a serious evaluation of the merits of the incentives. Only a tiny fraction of the town's residents would receive any benefits from this inducement. We tend to think that anything improving education is an unmitigated good.

The direct payment of $50 ranked poorly among the economic incentives in changing minds. This might suggest that offering direct compensation, into citizens' pockets, is not the best way to find a site.

That conclusion would be invalid for at least three reasons. First, there was no indication of the relative value of the nine financial incentives. A $50 bill may seem like a paltry sum in exchange for living next to a waste site for a generation, and a college scholarship a handsome gift. Suppose there are 5,000 families in town, and a college scholarship is worth $20,000. A $50 bill to every family in town is worth $250,000 under these assumptions, and five scholarships are worth $100,000.

It is difficult for most people, even in this age of pocket calculators, to gauge the relative size of widely differing economic incentives unless the total values are described in black and white. This was not done in the Massachusetts survey.

Second, the bonus in an auction would allow for scholarships, property tax waivers and even re-paving of the streets—all from the same pot of money. If a town were considering entering an auction, its leaders could say to its voters, "We will offer fifty town-sponsored scholarships. Further, we will wipe out half the property tax bill of town residents for the next decade. The money for these wonderful acts will come from the bonus we get, at the level we will make the bid. We know that we won't get a penny less, because we won't bid any lower than that."

Third, and perhaps most important, it is not possible to determine in advance how much money that people would accept in compensation. O'Hare says that direct responses to questionnaires of this type, although revealing in non-economic areas, are "useless" as indications of price and value.

A Poll in Tennessee

Bill Lyons, a political scientist at the University of Tennessee, conducted a similar poll of Tennessee residents. He and his colleagues quizzed almost 600 people about yet another hypothetical facility—a hazardous or radioactive waste plant.[43]

A total of six incentives was considered. Three were safety-related or administrative in nature—would a local committee monitor the plant's safety? Would the plant be operated by the Federal government or a private contractor?

The other three had some relation to compensation. One was a statement that the plant would provide 1,000 new jobs (probably much higher than most installations of this type). The second was that lower county taxes would be levied. No definition of "lower" was supplied. The third incentive said the plant would pay for county fire protection—presumably only for the plant itself, not for the county as a whole.

Lyons asked if respondents would be more or less favorable to a plant accompanied by an incentive. For the new jobs, 34 percent said they would be more favorable; 6 percent said, 'less favorable." Presumably this tiny group would oppose any compensation.

For lower taxes, 28 percent became more favorable, and 5 percent less so. With the lack of definition of what "lower taxes" meant, it could imply 1 percent less, or their complete elimination. The pollsters left it up to the respondents to decide exactly what was intended.

For the third question, county fire protection, 30 percent were more favorable, and 5 percent were less favorable. Again, the exact monetary value of this compensation was far from clear.

The results show that in Tennessee, about a third of the population become more favorably inclined when compensation was offered. If the questions about compensation had been written so that respondents could set their own amounts, as in an auction system, the proportion would certainly have been much higher.

What We Learn—and Don't Learn—From Surveys

Surveys show that minds can be changed if the proper incentives are offered. Not all, admittedly, but a substantial proportion. We are not frozen in our attitudes toward undesirable facilities.

Some incentives can be related to safety. Others are based, either directly or indirectly, on money. We cannot tell with precision just how high the bonus in an auction will rise by polling people. Yet economic incentives *do* work in getting people to reconsider immovable views. As the bonus rises, the change in public opinion within a town, county or state that is considering accepting a site may be startling.

Conclusions

Dollar bills and the environment can mix, without adverse effects on either side. Yet undoubtedly some will say, "The whole basis of finding a site should be to minimize its risk and environmental harm. Everyone, whether they favor compensation or not, is in favor of that. Why bring in an entirely new factor, crass economics? Let's just concentrate on making it as safe as possible."

This would be an eminently sensible way to proceed, if most people were scientists or engineers, versed in the ways of risk analysis—and believed its answers. The building of a repository—perhaps the most controversial LULU of all—would then long ago have been consigned to an obscure inch-long squib in the *New York Times*:

Nevada (or Montana, or Maryland) Completes Repository

State officials opened the nation's first high-level nuclear waste site today. The system was built in the record time of two years. Although some thought that the repository would be embroiled in legal problems, no lawsuits were filed in the course of construction. This came as a surprise to Jim Walters, an attorney who had participated in many previous legal battles over wastes. "I'm amazed," Mr. Walters said, "I thought there would be a basketful of injunctions. But everyone seemed satisfied."

Environmentalists and nuclear industry officials gave speeches at the ceremony, praising each other and state personnel. The speeches tended to be highly technical, dwelling on details of probabilistic risk analysis such as fault and event trees. This may have been because almost all speakers held a doctorate in science. The crowd was small, reflecting the lack of interest in the state since the project was announced. One placard held up by a member of the crowd showed a series of differential equations, which one of the speakers solved on the spot. All agreed that the site would be safe, and would continue to be so for millennia.

Alas, that news will never appear. Since we are not a nation of analytical scientists, our attitudes toward undesirable facilities tend not to be technical in nature. Agreement between those who know the chemical table of elements and those who do not has receded into the distance.

The best way to solve the dichotomy of feelings is to show that it can be to our benefit to consider these facilities. Adam Smith, author of *Wealth of Nations*, noted that the baker and the butcher do not bake bread or slaughter cattle because they want to feed their neighbors. They do it out of self-interest. Compensation by means of an auction is the simplest and most appropriate way to appeal to that self-interest, and still preserve environmental standards.

Notes

1. Science Advisory Board, *The Report of the Strategic Options Subcommittee, Relative Risk Reduction Project* (Washington, D.C.: Environmental Protection Agency, September 1990) report EPA SAB-EC-90-021C, Appendix C, 67.
2. Ibid., 68.
3. Ibid., 73.
4. Ibid., 80; Environmental Protection Agency, *Policy Options for Stabilizing Global Climate* (Washington, D.C.: The Agency, 1989) executive summary, 12; and Environmental Policy Institute, *Project 88: Harnessing Market Forces to Protect Our Environment: Initiatives for the New President* (Washington, D.C.: The Institute, December 1988).
5. William H. Macleish, "Where Do We Go From Here," *Smithsonian* 21 (1) (April, 1990): 58.
6. Science Advisory Board, *Report of Strategic*, 85.
7. "Time to Get Your Nickel's Worth," *Los Angeles Times* (July 13, 1989): II–6.
8. Science Advisory Board, *Report of Strategic*, 95.
9. Ibid., 99.
10. Ibid.
11. Jon Laidler, "In Gloucester, It Will Cost Cash to Dispose of Trash," *Boston Globe* (30 September 1990): N–10.
12. Michael Weisskopf, "A Clever Solution for Pollution: Taxes," *Washington Post* (21 December 1989): A27.

13. Jay Mathews, "California Car Pools Mean Fast Cash," *Washington Post* (11 February 1990): A3.
14. David S. Hilzenrath, "Free Health Spa Privileges End Hotel Dispute," *Washington Post* (10 February 1990): B1.
15. "Spa-Mail," *Washington Post* (22 February 1990): A16.
16. Peter Simon, "Curiosity Unlocks Prison's Potential," *Buffalo News* (2 May 1990): B1.
17. Robert G. Healy and Frank G. Popper, "Speeding Industrial Siting—The False Promise of Procedural Reform," *Sloan Management Review* (Fall 1980): 47.
18. Peter Simon, "Families Eager to Buy Canal Homes," *Buffalo News* (13 May 1990): A1.
19. "Host Depew Will get Recycling for Free," *Buffalo News* (18 May 1990): B5.
20. Michael Parrish, "Operating a Dump Keeps a Town from Wasting Away," *Los Angeles Times* (13 May 1990): 1.
21. Marvin G. Katz, "YIMBYism is Coming, But...," *Waste Age* (January 1990): 40.
22. Parrish, "Operating a Dump."
23. W. E. Blundell, "Firms Seek to Avoid Boomtown Problem by Providing Services," *Wall Street Journal* (12 August 1981).
24. Katz, "YIMBYism."
25. Blundell, "Firms Seek."
26. R. G. Shuff, "'Bribes' Work in Wisconsin," *Waste Age* (March 1988): 51.
27. Joseph A. Davis, "Super-Swap Possible Under Nuclear Waste Bill," *Congressional Quarterly* (31 October 1987): 2684.
28. C. T. Cory, "Shhh—It's a Noise Auction," *Psychology Today* 16 (12) (1982): 12.
29. Remy Carle, "Why France Went Nuclear," *Public Power* (July-August, 1981): 58.
30. "Fear and Loathing of Nuclear Power," *Science* 250 (4977) (5 October 1990): 28.
31. Constance Hornig, "WTE[waste-to-energy] Pioneers Enjoy Its Benefits," *Solid Waste & Power* (October 1989): 34.
32. Michael Winerip, "'Mr. Garbage' and His Million-Dollar Offer," *New York Times* (6 May 1986).
33. Macleish, "Where Do We Go."
34. James Heeney, "Desegregation Plan Provokes Criticism," *Buffalo News* (2 May 1990): B1.
35. "U.S. Raises Reward for Thwarting Terrorism," *Washington Post* (19 December 1989).
36. David P. Hamilton, "Magnet Lab: Science to the Highest Bidder," *Science* 249 (4971) (24 August 1990): 851.
37. Joseph Palca, "African AIDS: Whose Research Rules?," *Science* (October 12, 1990): 199.
38. Michael O'Hare, Lawrence Bacow, and Debra Sanderson, *Facility Siting and Public Opposition* (New York: Van Nostrand Reinhold, 1983) 119.
39. Ibid.
40. John Hodges-Copple, "State Roles in Siting Hazardous Waste Facilities," *Forum for Applied Research and Public Policy* (Fall 1987): 78.
41. Sam A. Carnes, Emily D. Copenhaver, Jon H. Sorensen, E. J. Soderstrom, John Reed, D. J. Bjornstad, and Elizabeth Peelle, "Incentives and Nuclear Waste Siting: Prospects and Constraints," *Energy Systems and Policy* 7 (4) (1983) 323, especially 335.
42. Kent E. Portney, "Allaying the NIMBY Syndrome: The Potential for Compensation in Hazardous Waste Treatment Facility Siting," *Hazardous Waste* 1 (3) (1984): 411.
43. William Lyons, Michael R. Fitzgerald, and Amy McCabe, "Public Opinion and Hazardous Waste," *Forum for Applied Research and Public Policy* (Fall 1987): 89.

10

The Rich and the Poor:
Will an Auction System Discriminate
against the Latter?

Some people assume that the poorest state or county eligible for an auction will always make the bid, that is, have the undesirable site on its territory. This could be the obvious guess, but it would be wrong.

There are three answers to those who would claim that an auction system is a cynical way to exploit the poverty stricken. First, the wealthy will always escape. Second, the poor are smarter than we think. And third, look at what the poor get now. The rest of this chapter will expand on these points.

If I could ensure that only wealthy states and counties bid on hazardous wastes, and poor ones sat on their hands, I would do it. The wealthy already live in better surroundings than the poor.

It is not going to happen. Wealthy communities are almost always successful in keeping noxious facilities away from them. Because these facilities have no other place to go, they tend to end up in poorer communities. All of this started long before siting hit the front pages.

Are there any landfills in Beverly Hills? Or debris in Fort Lee (a wealthy suburb of New York City)? Or waste in Wellesley (Massachusetts; a suburb of Boston)? Any giant incinerators proposed for Bal Harbour, Florida, recently? Or refineries going up in Hillsborough, the home of the Hearsts near San Francisco?

Anyone who expects "yeses" to these questions must live in air castles. These affluent towns have never taken in unwanted facilities. They never will, whether the present siting system or an auction is used. They are not equitably sited now, so a compensation system would not upset a delicate balance.

There is an unspoken assumption behind the contention that the poor would be stuck with LULUs under a compensation or auction system.

215

It's that the poor are not too smart, and would yield to the temptation of shiny silver dollars. The assumption may not always be phrased as blatantly as that, but that's what it means.

Is this true? I think not. The vast majority of the poor in any country do not yield to temptation all that easily. For example, even though all the poverty-stricken could use more money, they do not go out and steal it. Almost all work very hard, at legal enterprises.

To assume that all the indigent communities eligible for compensation would make a bid the moment an auction began is to demean them. They are wiser than many in the middle class assume. They are not some type of subhumans, fascinated by the smell and feel of money.

When the auction begins, I expect poor communities to make up their minds much the way that middle class ones do. They will weigh the costs and the benefits, and come to defensible conclusions. That's all anyone can ask.

An auction cannot guarantee that impoverished towns or states will not bid for a site. In some instances, they almost certainly will. But they will have the power, in Nancy Reagan's phrase, to just say no.

A Story of Cans and Bottles

I was discussing the problem of rich *versus* poor with an old friend, Herschel Spector of the New York Power Authority, one day. We were drinking soft drinks from cans when he pointed out something about those cans.

"Just look at this," he said.

"I am. But I don't see anything except a can."

"There's more to it. We have millions of poor people in this country. Suppose the government told them, 'We want you to work harder for your living. So we're passing a law that says you have to retrieve empty soft drink cans from the garbage. You'll earn a nickel, or dime, or whatever the deposit happens to be. This way you'll have more income'. What would you think of such a law?"

"Most people would think it was despicable. Imagine sentencing them to something like that," I responded.

"But isn't that what we do every day, by refunding deposits on cans and bottles? The difference is that people aren't required to do this."

"I guess you're right," I said.

"Even more interesting, environmentalists want the deposits to go even higher. This will make even more poor people rummage through garbage to make money."

The same effect was noticed by Michael Hurley of New York. He writes, "Since my arrival in New York City several months ago, I've noticed that many people pick through the garbage in search of redeemable cans. I saved a week's worth of cans in a plastic bag and 'threw out' the bag. Within 10 minutes, someone had 'found' my donation. Since this trial, every week's results have been the same."[1]

My conclusion? Forcing poor people to do unpleasant things, whether it's accepting a site or hunting through refuse for valuable cans and bottles, is unethical. Giving them the choice, to rummage or not, to approve a site or not, *is* ethical.

Which Rich Towns are Avoiding Waste Sites?

Do undesirable facilities go to the rich now? I reproduce some income data.[2] Tables 10.1 and 10.2 show the richest places in the United States, arranged in order of both household and *per capita* income. The two lists are not exactly the same, because the average number of persons per household varies from place to place.

TABLE 10.1
Highest Per Capita Incomes, in Thousands

Palm Beach, Florida	42.3	Newport Beach, California	27.9
Bal Harbour, Florida	37.1	Summit, New Jersey	26.9
Milburn, New Jersey	35.3	Creve Coeur, Missouri	26.9
Beverly Hills, Calif.	33.9	Annandale, Virginia	26.6
Oak Brook, Illinois	32.7	Highland Park, Illinois	26.2
Westport, Connecticut	32.2	Alexandria, Virginia	26.1
Frontenac, Missouri	32.0	Lower Merion Twp., PA	26.0
Greenwich, Connecticut	31.0	Hinsdale, Illinois	25.9
Bethesda, Maryland	30.2	Saratoga, California	25.9
Watchung, New Jersey	30.1	Livingston, New Jersey	25.7
Bloomfield Twp., Mich.	29.5	Los Altos, California	25.7
Fort Lee, New Jersey	29.3	Lexington, Massachusetts	25.6
Ridgewood, New Jersey	28.9	Wellesley, Massachusetts	25.3
Falls Church, Virginia	28.5	Wilmette, Illinois	25.2
Garden City, New York	28.0	Edina, Minnesota	25.1

TABLE 10.2
Highest Household Incomes, in Thousands

Frontenac, Missouri	81.4	Bowie, Maryland	59.7
Northbrook, Illinois	81.4	Lexington, Massachusetts	59.7
Watchung, New Jersey	71.9	Wellesley, Massachusetts	59.6
Westport, Connecticut	71.9	West Bloomfield Twp., Mich.	57.8
Saratoga, California	70.0	Rancho Palos Verdes, Calif.	58.1
Milburn, New Jersey	68.1	Creve Coeur, Missouri	57.6
Garden City, New York	68.0	New City, New York	57.6
Bloomfield Twp., MI	66.9	Paramus, New Jersey	57.4
Danville, California	64.9	Orange, Connecticut	57.3
Ridgewood, New Jersey	64.4	Trumbull, Connecticut	56.4
Los Altos, California	64.2	Cupertino, California	55.8
Livingston, New Jersey	64.0	East Brunswick, New Jersey	55.7
Plainview, New York	62.4	Merrick, New York	55.4
Bridgewater, NJ	60.7	Des Peres, Missouri	55.3
Bethesda, Maryland	60.2	Port Washington N., New York	55.3

For example, Beverly Hills has a very small number of persons per household. While it has one of the highest *per capita* incomes in the country, it does not show up on the list of places with highest total household incomes.

Are any of these places being considered for new undesirable facilities, such as prisons, toxic waste installations, mental hospitals, and the like? I would wager not. For example, the "Battle of Braintree," to which I refer in chapter 3, was an attempt to put a hazardous waste site in a working-class suburb of Boston. Did the developers dream, for even a second, of siting it in Lexington, Wellesley, or other wealthy Massachusetts towns? Anyone who believes that probably has faith in the Tooth Fairy.

Is there any evidence for poor communities rushing forward to get the almighty buck, other than an intuitive feeling?

There *is* evidence, but in the other direction. In a thesis, Jeffrey Himmelberger of Clark University in Worcester, Massachusetts, studied compensation for landfills in Wisconsin. Would wealthy communities would demand greater compensation than poorer ones?[3]

Towns in the Dairy State are paid by landfill operators for the privilege of operating these facilities. The landfills are located in both relatively well off and poor towns. If affluent towns would require a large bonus to bid on a landfill, then they would demand higher compensation than poverty-stricken towns for the privilege of operating a landfill. At least, that's the conventional logic.

Himmelberger found this was not so. In the statistical language often used in dissertations, "[T]he data was unable to reject the null hypothesis that compensation is unrelated to the socio-economic status of the host county."

In other words, the amount of money demanded for landfill sites does not vary much with the wealth of the community in which they are located. It is then possible that the successful bid in an auction may not come from the poorest community or state. Himmelberger's work overthrows the standard wisdom on this subject.

O'Hare on Rich and Poor

O'Hare has written extensively on unpleasant installations and their relationship to the income and wealth of the communities that get—or avoid—them. In the following, he is describing a type of auction.[4]

What he calls "low bids" would be called "successful bids" in auction terminology. Any bid that is not a low bid would be an unsuccessful bid, in fact a bid that is never made. When he wrote, public concern about noxious facilities was usually about refineries and similar installations, rather than waste dumps and AIDS treatment centers. However, the principle has remained the same:

[One prediction is] that when noxious facilities are auctioned off among towns of varying wealth, the poor towns will bid less and acquire the facilities. Why should rich people be allowed to buy their way out of their "fair share" of regional disamenity? For discussion purposes, the idea can be expressed as "Should we site a disamenity in a wealthy town that made (or would make) a high bid, even though a poor community is willing to accept it for a lower total compensation payment?" The issue obviously evaporates in cases with a low bid from the wealthy town.

In general we [O'Hare] favor schemes to redistribute income from rich to poor, but imposing a refinery on the residents of an occasional wealthy community is a clumsy way to do it, as are most redistributional schemes grafted onto policies whose fundamental purpose has nothing to do with income distribution. There seems to be little to recommend giving poor people an amenity (freedom from the refinery) they are anxious to sell, and only vengeance to recommend taking from the rich that which is relatively worthless to others.

> While forcing a refinery on Scarsdale may be, however crudely, *vertically* equitable, it entails a mindless horizontal inequity: Why Scarsdale and not Oyster Bay [both affluent and environmentally clean communities near New York City]?

There are a number of points made in the preceding long quotation that deserve further explanation. First, O'Hare is talking about towns, not states. Siting can affect states, as in the case of the proposed high-level nuclear waste repository, or counties, towns or neighborhoods.

States vary in their wealth, as much as towns do. Delaware and New Jersey have traditionally led the nation in *per capita* income, with Mississippi and Alabama on the bottom. Yet few who have driven along the "refinery corridor" in New Jersey would want that string of chemical tanks in their state.

Second, O'Hare points out correctly that pursuing the rich around the countryside with threats of waste sites, mental health facilities and prisons is an inefficient way to punish the wealthy, if that's what we have in mind. Setting higher tax rates would be a lot easier. In any case, even if we moved a penitentiary to Scarsdale or Beverly Hills, the people there, by definition, have enough money to move away. We'd never achieve our goal of penalizing the rich with dumps next door.

Devising *any* system to guarantee that needy communities will never get unwanted facilities seems close to impossible. There may not be a logical way out of the dilemma.

Race and Poverty

The problem of siting is not confined solely to the question of rich *versus* poor. Race often enters into the equation. It has been described as a battle with a new front in gritty ghetto streets."[5]

This was the claim of the Commission for Racial Justice, a civil rights group associated with the United Church of Christ.[6] Their 1987 study was one of the first to link racial bias to siting of undesirable facilities.

According to the group, three of the largest commercial hazardous waste landfills were located in predominantly black or Hispanic communities. Reverend Benjamin Chavis said, "The results of our research conclusively show that race has been the discriminating factor of all those tested in the location of commercial hazardous waste facilities in the U. S."

The report went on to say that 60 percent of blacks and Hispanics live in communities with uncontrolled toxic waste sites. It concluded,

"We believe that this situation across the nation reveals an insidious form of institutionalized racism. It is, in effect, environmental racism."

All of this took place before any auction was ever held. Supposedly scientific factors were often used to find the best sites, yet somehow the wastes ended up mostly in minority communities. What a coincidence.

This was nothing new, of course. Afton, North Carolina, made world news headlines.[7]

Warren County, where 64 percent of the population was black, was the chosen site for polychlorinated biphenyl (PCB) disposal. Predominantly white counties were somehow not suitable.

The PCBs had been spread on state highways to avoid the cost of proper disposal, and now the state was collecting it all in one place.

Over one hundred demonstrators marched two miles to the entrance of the site. Almost half were arrested after refusing orders to disperse. Eventually almost 400 mostly black demonstrators had been arrested. They included Reverend Joseph E. Lowery, president of the Southern Christian Leadership Conference, of which Martin Luther King, Jr. had been the first leader. Representative Walter Fauntroy of the District of Columbia, then chairman of the Congressional Black Caucus, was also taken into custody.

None of this was provoked by an auction. Black people thought that they weren't being heard. They did not have a legal right to say no, as they would in an auction situation.

On the South Side of Chicago

In the far South Side of Chicago, the black ghetto of Altgeld Gardens contains a dilapidated housing project, according to John Elson writing in *Time*. Built atop a former landfill, its "fetid odors still rise from the basements after more than 60 years.... [there are] tons of pollutants from a nearby sludge plant, a steel mill, a paint company, a huge incinerator and an 80-foot high landfill." A few miles away are mounds of trash, broken glass, rusty nails and construction debris.[8]

There are three main characteristics to Altgeld Gardens and the other terrible conditions described in Elson's article. First, the poverty-stricken residents never had a say over whether wastes would be put in their town or neighborhood. Second, it's obvious from the description that just about every environmental regulation and law is being broken. Third, few if any of the neighborhoods described in the article ever got a nickel from landfill developers, governments or anybody else.

None of these conditions would continue under an auction system. First, no community, rich or poor, would make a bid for wastes or any other undesirable facility unless there was a consensus to do so. The day of "dump and run" would be over.

Second, an auction system, as well as most other compensation methods, does not require even the loosening of any environmental rule, let alone breaking it. Any waste facility would be properly engineered and approved, not the old "over-the-back-fence" type that plagues Altgeld Gardens.

Finally, if a poor community did decide to accept a waste site, they would receive precisely the price they wanted in compensation, not a penny less. What could be fairer?

All residents in a town, county, or state will receive economic benefits under an auction system. A few will undoubtedly use their check to move away. The vast majority will stay, and spend the money on better things.

The city fathers of Chicago are of course concerned about this inequity. They are planning to move much of this debris to the Playboy Mansion in Chicago, home of the millionaire publisher High Hefner. Sure they will.

Not far from Love Canal in Western New York is Forest Glen. This is another minority area, contaminated with various types of hazardous wastes. The trailer park may be even worse than the infamous Canal.[9] In recognition of the unfairness this causes minorities, politicians in Western New York are planning to transfer some of the mess to Lincoln Parkway in Buffalo, site of some of the largest mansions in the region. Sure they will.

Reservations and Wastes

The movie *Dances with Wolves* revived the almost forgotten Western genre. The wide-open scenes on the plains were memorable. Just a few miles away from where some of the movie was shot, a solid waste landfill was being proposed for the Rosebud Sioux Reservation. Engineers from Connecticut suddenly took an interest in South Dakota. Senator Tom Daschle of South Dakota called it "Dances with Garbage."[10]

The reason a landfill was being considered there was, of course, financial. Mary Hager of *Newsweek* writes that the Cabazon reservation near Palm Springs, California, now has an incinerator. The Indians there are much poorer than the nearby wealthy white people. To be equitable, the mayor of Palm Springs will ensure that some of the incinerator smoke blows over some of the prominent residents of the town, such as Bob Hope. Sure he will.

In Mississippi, the Choctaw Indians, who have a *per capita* income of about $3,000, perhaps one-sixth of the national average, negotiated a contract for a toxic waste site. They were planning to get $8 million yearly from it.

Are the Indians really being dumped on? Not really, although some outsiders think they are. All contracts have to be approved by the Bureau of Indian Affairs. As well, companies operating landfills and incinerators on reservations can't avoid national standards for these operations. The EPA rules still apply. So the rules of an auction system still hold here; environmental regulations are not to be dispensed with.

Some conditions of an auction prevail today on reservations. For example, the Choctaw Indians held a referendum on the proposed waste site (it was defeated). The people should always have a say; off the reservation, they often don't.

The Choctaws were able to prevent an undesired facility on their reservation. This shows that wastes will not always end up on Indian land.

I spent considerable time in chapter 2 describing the nuclear waste riot in Allegany County, in Western New York State. From the viewpoint of the siting commission, the riot was inexplicable. They had spent huge sums on the scientific side of siting, such as ensuring that the clay soil of that county had low water permeability. They had also chosen a site with a low population density, so if the installation ever leaked, few if any would be harmed.

Such crass aspects as the economic level of the inhabitants apparently never crossed their mind. Subjects like that would have corrupted the purity of the science, and perhaps destroyed the whole basis of the selection procedure.

But one news report quotes Carol Muhleisen, of Muhleisen's Fine Food and Cocktails in the town of Almond: "We're very poor." Allegany County has the lowest income of New York's 62 counties. Could this have entered the siting commission's considerations?[11]

If the commission wanted to put the site in an area of low population density, they could have chosen the far reaches of Westchester County, just north of New York City, There the manicured lawns seem to roll on forever, and the population density is considerably lower than that of Manhattan or Queens. Of course, the residents of Rye and other Westchester towns are considerably more affluent than Allegany

Countians. Would they have considered accepting a waste site? How many ways are there to translate the word "No"?

To be fair to all concerned, the siting commission will also propose a second site in Pocantico Hills, not far from the Rockefeller estate. Sure they will.

Needles and Low-Level Waste

Although Congress passed its original law on low-level radioactive wastes in 1980, a decade and a half later the planned-for system of regional waste sites hadn't appeared, due to public opposition.

That is, except for California. The Golden State had a site picked out.[12]

The site is to be located in Ward Valley, twenty-four miles west of Needles, in the Mojave Desert. While it is difficult to find the economic level of Needles in reference books, I have driven through it myself. Although more prosperous than Alabama or Mississippi, Needles doesn't have many Mercedes or BMWs cruising its streets. One hardly has to be an economist to recognize it as one of the poorest California towns.

One of the many aborted systems for dealing with high-level nuclear wastes was the so-called Monitored Retrievable Storage (MRS) scheme. Under it, the wastes would be temporarily stored, until a final resting place could be found.

Opponents of the MRS said, "How do we know it will be temporary?" As one of the governors involved in nuclear waste siting once said, "Nuclear wastes are subject to a special type of physics. In this equation, temporary equals permanent."

That was the question faced by residents of Welch, West Virginia, when they considered an MRS for their town. Why Welch? According to David Corcoran, publisher of the Welch *Daily News,* "We need jobs right now. If we do not get jobs right now, then the human misery, which is the real tragedy in this county, will continue and get worse."[13]

Along downtown streets, shops were boarded over. A medical team documented instances of starvation in the county. Four suicides were recorded in five months, possibly because of the economic depression there. As publisher Corcoran says, "The thing that disturbs me the most, and probably makes me more open to new ideas such as the MRS, is the fact that I see so many lives shattered by unemployment."

All of this took place before an auction system was in place. And to make up for the MRS possibly being located in a poor West Virginia town, the authorities will place a similar facility next to the house of Senator Jay Rockefeller, who represents the state in Congress. Sure they will.

Prison Towns

Will future prisons have Rolls Royce dealerships in the next block? Not likely. If experience is any guide, they will continue to be located in economically depressed areas, regardless of which method is used to choose the site.

In Taylorsville, Illinois, then Governor Jim Thompson was greeted with joy on a visit. He wasn't announcing a new road program or lowered county taxes, but the next best thing as far as Taylorsville was concerned: a new prison. This would create 300 permanent jobs and 200 temporary building jobs for the have-not town.[14]

In Georgia, the Department of Corrections was slated to be the second-largest part of the state government by 1992.[15] According to news reports, prisons are welcomed as economic boons by Peach State communities. One of them was to be built in Union County, which has the lowest income in the state.[16]

And to avoid any charges of economic unfairness, the largest prison in Georgia will be built just down the street from Ted Turner's house in Atlanta. Sure it will.

In California, Avenal, just south of Fresno, was dying on the vine. In the words of the *Washington Post,* it was a "onetime boom town bust, a dusty, two-bit slice of nowhere traveling at warp speed toward oblivion...by 1980, Avenal, never a garden spot, was three-fourths of a square mile of dusty streets and rundown clapboard houses, populated by about 5,000 oil company pensioners and migrant farm workers." Not exactly material for a Chamber of Commerce brochure.[17]

Enter Nick Ivans, who ran the Tomer Drug Co. in downtown Avenal for four decades. He saw a news item in an out-of-town newspaper, saying that the California Department of Corrections had a half-billion dollar budget for prisons, but nowhere to spend it. Ivans saw the opportunity, and started advocating a prison for his town.

None of it would have made any difference if the people of Avenal didn't want the chance to build a prison. They did. The news article says that Ivans "is a local hero."

The facility employed 1,000 people, of whom 700 are guards. There haven't been as many new residents in town as had been anticipated. This probably will change as new housing is built, after a hiatus of many years. Most importantly from the viewpoint of the town, the prisoners are counted as residents for tax purposes. As a result, the town gets an extra $200,000 in revenue from the state every year. Some of it was used to light and landscape the main street, put in sidewalks, gutters and perform all the other maintenance that had disappeared during Avenal's fallow years.

Was this a good deal for Avenal? I wouldn't presume to tell them what they should have done. They thought the prison was to their advantage.

The Golden State is full of people who believe in equity, as well as being the home of such figures as Michael Eisner, head of Walt Disney Studios, and Bill Cosby, the entertainer. Both had incomes of tens of millions annually in the 1980s and 1990s. As a result, the state plans to build prisons just up the street from both Eisner and Cosby. Sure they will.

West Virginia Landfill "Civil War"

"We need it," said Kenneth Dadisman, president of the Barbour County, West Virginia county commission. He was referring to a proposed landfill in that poverty-stricken county that would accept 10,000 tons a day. The largest in the world, Fresh Kills in Staten Island, New York, takes in 16,000 tons daily.

The landfill would provide 200 permanent jobs, and send about $5 million in revenues into the county treasury. That's about four times the county's $1 million annual budget. In a time when Federal budgets are measured in the trillions and annual Federal budget deficits in the hundreds of billions, a budget of $1 million for a county seems tiny. That's all that Barbour can afford.

Volunteer firemen in the county weren't even in the budget; they had to ask for charity for three years. The county's forty-two employees hadn't had a raise in six years. Unemployment was over 15 percent in August 1990, twice the state's average rate.

The landfill wouldn't go into Barbour without its say-so. The contention is fierce, with one report describing it as a "civil war." Yet what they are doing corresponds to a major aspect of an auction system. If the people don't accept a site, for whatever reason, there is no point in sending it their way.[18]

The Pullman District is located in Chicago's far Southeast Side. It is described as made up of 1890s-vintage working-class housing, and only two miles from already existing landfills.[19]

Waste Management, Inc., the giant waste-handling company, wanted to put a new landfill in the area. Rather than merely battle the firm, the residents of the district decided to ask for compensation.

"It is inevitable," said Thomas McMahon, president of the Pullman Civic Organization. "The garbage problem will not go away. We as a community have to face that fact. Our voices will not be heard if the rest of the city wants landfills here. If that happens, we feel that we are entitled to reimbursement."

Banker James Fitch agreed. "It is a matter of people deciding what is just and fair, and at what price they are willing to accept the continued operation of a controlled landfill development."

To be fair to all residents of Chicagoland, Waste Management will also build a gigantic landfill somewhere on the Gold Coast, the expensive area extending north of the city. Sure they will.

Bridgewater Gets an Incinerator— and Likes It

Most towns considering a unwanted installation within their boundaries have one developer or siting agency pursuing them. East Bridgewater, a small town twenty miles south of Boston, had two companies trying to site an incinerator.[20]

According to Cynthia Beach, a member of the town's solid waste committee, "People say if you [turn down] Wheelabrator or BFI [Browning Ferris Industries] [the two companies involved] that taxes will go up. People were sympathetic to the idea incinerators were noisy and had trouble, but they are really worried about taxes."

To Selectman [town official] Peter Sprague, the matter was simple: "That's a way of doing business, no matter whether you are in waste-to-energy or real estate."

Browning-Ferris Industries already has a landfill in the town. It pays the community about 15 percent of its revenues for the privilege of running it, or about $2 million annually. According to one report, the competition for perhaps the last incinerator allowed in Massachusetts "is delighting some East Bridgewater officials, who think competition will bring economic benefits to their town."

If East Bridgewaterites could think of these economic benefits before an auction is instituted, there is no reason why they shouldn't think of them afterwards. Of course, town residents have to weigh the benefits against potential harm, just as they would in an auction.

The Emelle Story

Over the years, Richard Bullard and others concerned about siting justice have made much of the situation in Emelle, Alabama, as mentioned in chapter 5. Some have claimed that it illustrates why compensation for handling wastes is about the worst possible policy. Others have countered by noting the progress that Sumter County, on the Alabama-Mississippi border, has made over the years. In a *Wall Street Journal* article in the summer of 1995, Greg Jaffe evaluates both claims.[21]

Why Emelle, of all places? It has a chalky, virtually liquid-impermeable subsoil. In the low-technology days of the 1970s, this was wonderful. Hazardous wastes could be put in the ground without the need for plastic liners. The wastes would not flow into the water table, it was believed.

Before discussing the good and bad of Emelle, it should be remembered that the story began in the mid-1970s, before the reverse Dutch auction had come into being. There was compensation, as with many waste sitings, but compensation is not equivalent to a Dutch auction.

The population of the county, about 16,000, has remained almost the same from 1980 to the present. The percentage that is black has also remained about constant, at about 70 percent. The percentage of the population living below the poverty line has decreased somewhat, from 42.5 percent to 39.7 percent, but it is obvious that Sumter County remains one of the poorest in the nation. Compared to the rest of Alabama, in 1980 it ranked fifty-eighth out of sixty-seven counties in terms of median household income. In 1995, it was sixty-fifth, so there had been a relative decline.

So the compensation had failed, in the words of the article's headline, "to lift Alabama county out of poverty." Therefore compensating people to accept undesirable facilities is a failure, right. Not quite.

There is little question that Emelle was a volunteer, in the sense that the waste facility was not foisted on it by a bureaucracy in Birmingham, the state capital, or Washington. As Joe Steagall, the former mayor of York, one of the county's towns, said, "We had to be realistic. We were not going to attract high-tech industry with our work force."

Was this discrimination against the poor? If other poor Alabama counties had had the chalky soil that Sumter did, they probably would have competed for the facility as well. Anyone who has ever driven down a dusty Alabama road, as I have, seeing the broken-down houses, would recognize that chance of getting any type of new facility in these backwater areas is close to negligible. So in that sense, there could be no discrimination if there was a volunteer.

The Emelle situation again differed from the Dutch auction in that there was no fixed amount that was to be paid to the residents. While the article does not go into detail on Emelle's economics, it says that the Alabama tax on hazardous waste was only $5.40 a ton in 1988. This rate was presumably smaller in the late 1970s, when the facility opened.

As well, the article does not specify exactly how much money came to the county, as opposed to the state. If the bulk of any compensation goes to the state as opposed to the local community, that community will be more reluctant to volunteer under a reverse Dutch auction system.

Nonetheless, the amounts that flowed to Sumter County were substantial in proportion to what already existed there. Tom Tart, the current mayor of Livingston, the county seat, says that "the tax revenue was without a doubt the biggest thing to ever hit Sumter County." The taxes accounted for almost 30 percent of Livingston's annual budget. It bought new police cars and a library. It built a small art museum in York and a day-care facility.

Given all this, why hasn't Sumter County lifted itself out of the poverty that has engulfed it for decades? The article traces it to school segregation, and the almost complete separation of the two racial communities. While legal segregation ended long ago, de facto school segregation continues. The public schools are more than 99 percent black, and almost all white students go to private academies. To its credit, the waste facility operator, Chemical Waste Management, a unit of WMX Technologies Inc., proposed plans for desegregation. They suggested a new public school that would be so advanced that students of both races would attend. However, they were unable to get the black-majority school board to agree. As George Autry, the head of a North Carolina think tank, observed, "You can't attract industry until you bridge the gap between the races and integrate the schools."

The efforts of the waste company to bring Sumter County into the 20th century went beyond what could be expected from a reverse Dutch auction. In the auction, what the community does with its money is its own business. Some communities will use the money wisely, propelling themselves forward, and others will have little to show for it after the facility eventually closes.

So it was in Sumter County. The county seems little better off than it was when the facility opened, according to the article. However, it points out that for a variety of reasons, the county missed golden opportunities. This was not the fault of the compensation system, but rather of the people who received the money.

What happened to the facility? In 1988, the Environmental Protection Agency ordered 47,000 tons of PCB waste sent from Texas to Emelle. Governor Guy Hunt opposed this, saying that Texas should handle it. This was in spite of the fact that tens of thousands of tons of hazardous waste were already in Emelle, and that it was probably the lowest-risk site in the nation for this type of waste. The acronym "PCB" was like a red flag to the Governor. He persuaded the legislature to raise the tax per ton from $5.40 to about $51.

Anyone with even a rudimentary knowledge of economics could have predicted the events. The weight of hazardous waste coming into Emelle dropped precipitously. Employment at the facility plunged by 60 percent. The taxes paid to Livingston now constitute 18 percent of its budget, rather than 30 percent.

How did this happen? There was really no binding contract between the state, the waste facility and the community. As a result, when one man, Governor Hunt, became enraged, he was able to change the terms of the situation.

Under the reverse Dutch auction, there would be a binding contract between all parties, so that a potential volunteer community could determine, in advance, just how much compensation they would get from accepting the facility. The people of Emelle had never heard of Guy Hunt before they agreed to the facility.

Some have pointed to Emelle as a horrible example of what takes place when compensation is offered to a poor community. True, the results did not fulfill the expectations of some in Sumter County. However, some points should be kept in mind. First, the county might have been even worse off, if such an event can be imagined, without the waste facility. Second, compensation itself cannot guarantee that a community will lift itself up out of the poverty hole. Apparently the county missed its main chance to break the cycle of segregation, which went hand-in-hand with its poverty. This was due to the people of the county themselves, rather than any system of compensation or Dutch auctions.

Into Africa

Because of the NIMBY syndrome, some waste handlers are shipping garbage to the Third World. As James Brooke writes,

From Morocco to the Congo, virtually every country on West Africa's coast reports receiving offers this year from American or European companies seeking cheap sites to dispose of hazardous wastes. Fees offered African recipients have gone as low as $3 a ton.... Guinea-Bissau would receive a yearly payment of $120 million—slightly less than the gross national product of $150 million [to accept 15 million tons of toxic wastes].[22]

Is this the inevitable consequence of compensation for siting? Not necessarily. First, almost all the proposed schemes were formulated in secret. Autocratic African rulers would cut a deal behind closed doors with European companies, perhaps keeping most of the proceeds for themselves. The people of their nations never found out until the waste-bearing ships were just off the coast.

This couldn't happen with a proper auction system. The people would have to be informed of what was going on. While the auction system can't produce democracy where it hasn't taken root, if a dictator tried to accept wastes in an auction system without consulting his people, he would hear about it, loud and clear. The rising bonus would be announced over the radio, which even impoverished Africans own. A properly designed auction system would ensure widespread publicity about the rising bonus.

Would African or other Third World countries have adequate environmental rules for such wastes, if they decided to take them? Only they can determine exactly what regulations they need or can afford. If Western countries who generate the wastes want to ensure that safety measures were employed, they could specify that the environmental rules of the country of origin were followed at the final destination.

In any case, the problem of shipping wastes to Africa was quickly resolved. Communities in the affluent originating countries, such as Holland and Italy, felt guilty about what they had done to the Africans. They decided to take back the wastes and bury it in their own back yards. Sure they did.

Notes

1. Michael Hurley, "Trash that Pays," *Christian Science Monitor* (7 June 1985): 16.
2. *1991 Commercial Atlas and Marketing Guide* (Chicago: Rand-McNally, 1990).
3. Jeffrey J. Himmelberger, *The Practice of Compensation and Facilities Siting: A Case Study of Wisconsin's Recent Experience*, master's thesis presented to Department of Environment, Technology and Society, Clark University, Worcester, Massachusetts, 1990.
4. Michael O'Hare, "'Not in *My* Block You Don't!'—Facilities Siting and the Strategic Importance of Compensation," *Public Policy* 25 (Fall 1977): 407, especially 453.
5. John Elson, "Dumping on the Poor," *Time*, 136 (7) (13 August 1990): 46.
6. Timothy Aeppel, "Civil Rights Group Links Race with Siting of Toxic Waste Dumps," *Christian Science Monitor* (16 April 1987): 5.

7. "N.C. PCB Disposal Protested," *Facts on File World News Digest* (8 October 1982).
8. Elson, ibid.
9. Ibid.
10. Mary Hager et al., "'Dances With Garbage," *Newsweek* (29 April 1991): 36.
11. Sam Howe Verhovek, "Nuclear Dump Plan Ignites Rural Protests," *New York Times* (19 September 1989).
12. Shawn Hubler, "Siting of N-Dumps is Tale of Almost Total Opposition," *Buffalo News* (22 May 1991): A9.
13. Laurent Belsie, "West Virginia Courts Nuclear-Waste Dump Site," *Christian Science Monitor* (17 July 1987): 3.
14. Rick Pearson, "New Prison Lifting Central Illinois Hopes," *Chicago Tribune* (28 July 1989): 2C-4.
15. Richard Whitt, "Prison Construction has Become Boom Business in Georgia," *Atlanta Journal* (8 October 1989): B-l.
16. John Harmon, "3 Rural Areas Likely to Become Prison Sites," *Atlanta Journal* (13 December 1986): B1.
17. Guy Gugliotta, "Pharmacist's Rx for a Dying Town: Take 1 Prison," *Washington Post* (16 June 1990): A3.
18. Laurent Belsie, "Town Trenched in Dump 'Civil War'," *Christian Science Monitor* (1 November 1990): 6.
19. Casey Bukro, "Southeast Siders See Some Green in Landfill Plans," *Chicago Tribune* (2 February 1988): 1.
20. Andrew J. Dabilis, "Rivals Wooing E. Bridgewater with Bids for Incinerator Site," *Boston Globe* (16 November 1989): 92.
21. Greg Jaffe, "In the Dumps: Landfill fails to Lift Alabama County out of Poverty," *Wall Street Journal* (2 August 1995): S1 (Southwest Journal).
22. James Brooke, "Waste Dumpers Turning to West Africa," *New York Times* (17 July 1988): 1.

11

The Reverse Dutch Auction Offers
an Exit from the Maze

The present way we choose sites for hazardous and radioactive wastes, and other locally unwanted land uses, replete with elaborate environmental impact statements and risk analyses, is necessary, all right. It is not sufficient. If it were, we would not have run into so much trouble.

If Helen's was the face that launched a thousand ships, the "scientific" process of finding sites is the system that has launched a thousand raucous public meetings, in which scientists, engineers and public officials are denounced and cursed. How can these installations be built without setting off riots, or generating public meetings in which the most common term used is "I'll see you in court!"?

A "Deep and Profound Dread"

Professor Kai Erickson, in an article in the *Harvard Business Review*, ascribed these public concerns as "a deep and profound dread." Yet ascribing these adjectives to the phenomenon is to give it a name without saying anything useful about it.[1]

The dread—of toxic and radioactive wastes, of nearby prisons and half-way houses for mental patients—is clearly common. Is there a way to deal with it, or must we continually chant "NIMBY, NIMBY"?

There *is* a way out of the contradiction of everyone favoring burying wastes and building undesirable facilities, as long as it is at least a hundred miles away from them. It involves simple—and proven—market principles. Environmental standards, cumbersome as they sometimes are, do not have to be diluted or reduced.

Sergeant Friday on *Dragnet* used to intone that all he wanted was "Just the facts, Ma'am." As a risk analyst myself, I cannot quarrel with the scientific studies. Yet more is needed.

233

The picture was put into perspective for me by an eminent scientist, who had studied the New York situation. He told me, "They say that Marxism would be an ideal system if people were not involved. About the same can be said about New York and, for that matter, many others. If nobody lived in the Empire State, the present site-finding system would be just fine."

The solution envisioned by most siting agencies is education. Who could be against that?

To carry this out, public meetings are held, in which the potential host communities are lectured by scientists and administrators. They are usually told that the risks are very small (which they are) and that the chances of environmental damages from a well-engineered facility are almost negligible (also true). They then sit back and wait for nods of agreement from the locals.

The nods never come. As Elihu Katz has noted, "In spite of the blind belief of advertisers, politicians, some academics and the public that media campaigns are capable of inducing massive changes in opinions, attitudes and actions—always somebody else's, not one's own—the research evidence continues to say otherwise."[2]

While educating the public on any technical subject is a good idea, in the case of hazardous and radioactive waste it has rarely worked. That is because the attitude of the technicians at the podium often is perceived as, "Here is the story. There is no appeal, because we know what the truth is. If you have any sense, you would accept what we say."

Piling On the Scientific Way

While the siting problem is rarely a wholly scientific one, it is often approached that way. The difference between the "scientific" approach and what really happens can be visualized by figure 12.1.

In each of the four drawings, the left-hand side represents the scientific requirements, as expressed in regulations or other rules. The right-hand side of each diagram represents how the public perceives the regulations. There is a horizontal dotted line, indicating when the public has given its general approval.

In the first of the four diagrams, there is a moderate number of regulations. However, the approval level of the public is small, a long way from the dotted line of acceptance.

The requirements do not exist in a vacuum. They are devised to get public approval. The seemingly logical next step is to *add* to the re-

FIGURE 11.1
An Avalanche of Paper

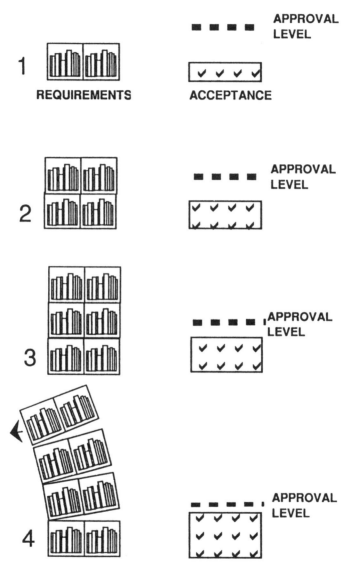

The presumed objective of the risk and other studies done on LULUs is to convince potential neighbors of the safety of the facility. In Part I, two volumes are shown stacked up, with a level of acceptance well below the approval level. In Part II, there are four volumes. The acceptance level has increased only slightly. In Part III, there are six volumes. Acceptance is up again, but only marginally. In Part IV, the stack of eight volumes topples over, but acceptance is still below the approval level.

quirements, in the hope of boosting approval, as shown in the second diagram. The approval level rises only slightly with the addition of new requirements.

The third diagram continues the process. More requirements, but the public still has not crossed the dotted line.

The fourth diagram shows the culmination of the process. So much paper has been piled on paper that the mountain of requirements topples. The National Academy of Sciences, in a report on the U.S. Department of Energy high level nuclear wastes program in the summer of 1990, said much the same.

They remarked that the DOE program was becoming muscle bound, as requirement was stacked on requirement, regulation upon regulation. While all of this was presumably to convince Nevadans that the repository proposed for their state was safe, there was no evidence that Silver Staters were paying the slightest attention. A dance was being put on for an audience that had gone home.

Much of the debate ultimately centers on risk, with the risk analysts saying that the hazards are small, and the people in the affected areas saying "We do not believe you." Part of the disparity in viewpoint is normal, deriving from who is performing the risk analyses, and who is expected to understand them.

Chauncey Starr, the former head of the Electric Power Research Institute in Palo Alto and 1991 winner of the National Medal of Technology, is one of the few in the scientific community who has an appreciation of both sides of the risk issue. He used to tell a story about bread cutting. He said,

> Go to the grocery store and buy a loaf of unsliced bread. When you get it home, start slicing. Note how far your thumb is from the knife. Now call in your spouse, a neighbor, or even a stranger walking down the street. You again grasp the loaf, but this time let the other person hold the knife. Now see how far your thumb is from the knife. Chances are it is much farther away.

When you are in charge of your own risk, you are perhaps nonchalant. If somebody else is controlling the hazards, you are a lot more cautious.

All the above may have given the impression that the public is somehow irrational about hazardous waste sites near them. They are not.

Determining Whether Consumers are "Reasonable"

Those around a potential waste site are exercising a type of rationality, although it may not be readily apparent to the beleaguered scientists and engineers dodging verbal bullets on the platform. Humans have survived as a species for hundreds of thousands of years by exercising the normal reaction of "fight or flight" when a perceived risk comes into view. "Fight or flight" was the appropriate choice when confronted by a saber-toothed tiger.

Consider how this reaction, or form of rationality, applies to a proposed hazardous waste site. Most people do not want to leave a community they may have lived in for decades when a new potential risk comes over the horizon. They do not plan to flee, in the dichotomy posed by the Neanderthal part of our brains. Instead, many of them fight. We have seen this in riots and raucous meetings.

If our only possible reactions are to fight or flee, then no sites will ever be built, anywhere. What to do?

Gail Bingham says that the best way to deal with this situation is to "change the incentives that motivate people's behavior."[3]

The rush to the barricades begins. "You cannot mix the environment with money," the cry arises. "The health of people and ecological quality are too important to be rung up on a cash register."

Perhaps the best response to this viewpoint was given to me by a fellow risk analyst, a professor at a Southeastern university:

> In a perfect world, environment and dollars might be in separate compartments, kept apart by an impermeable barrier. In the real world, they are already intermingled, whether or not the neighbors of a waste site get a penny themselves. The funds to "educate" the people that the risks are smaller than they imagine have to come from somewhere.
>
> They are taken from the pockets of the rest of us, of course. And the various siting commissions spend freely. I should know—some of my research is paid for by them. The states have spent tens of millions of dollars, if not hundreds of millions, to develop new sites without an ounce of low-level radioactive waste being permanently buried. The Federal program for high-level radioactive wastes has spent billions, with about the same results.
>
> So let us not pretend that there are no incentives in the hazardous waste siting process. There are plenty of them—but they go to government bureaucrats, university types like myself, and consulting firms. The people whose lives would be most touched by the waste site see precious few of these incentives.

As a one-time consultant myself, I believe in being well paid. Yet it always seemed strange to me that I and my fellow consultants could make money from a NIMBY controversy, but the people who were most affected had empty hands.

Bribes are, by Definition, Bad

The word "incentives" often has "bribes" following hard on its heels.

Does the use of incentives for accepting wastes constitute a bribe to the local population?

In a word, no. As I explained in Chapter 8, bribery has three elements that a properly designed incentive system does not. First, it is only used in pursuit of an illegal act. Finding a site for hazardous wastes is not only legal, everyone favors it—as long as it is not in their backyard.

Second, it is almost always done under the table. An auction system would avoid closed doors. The bonus would be publicly and widely known.

Third, bribes are always targeted. An auction does not zero in on any specific county, town or other political jurisdiction, as is often done under the "objective" procedure now in place.

Many people might say, "Why go to the trouble of an auction? The simplest way is negotiation between the affected community and the siting agency. We use this all the time in labor-management contracts. Why not for siting?"

While at first glance the two situations appear similar, in reality they are quite different.

First, in a labor-management dispute, the two parties are usually rough equals, and are so specified by law. Before the passage of the Wagner Act in the 1930s, the two sides were usually highly unequal, with management in a dominant position. Labor now has many legal rights that it did not have then.

In a waste siting situation, the two sides are often unequal legally. (This depends on the operative law, the state, and other factors.) The siting authority can make a "take it or leave it" offer. In many cases, that offer has already been made by the state legislature or Congress.

Second, in a labor-management dispute, the factory is already there. The argument is over the rate of pay of its workers.

Contrast this with finding a waste site. By definition, the site does not exist at the time of the proposed negotiations. As a result, it is difficult for both sides to decide what they are negotiating. It is much simpler for the community being targeted to invoke the NIMBY doctrine.

Secrecy Sinks the Process of Negotiation

Third, negotiations involve secrecy. This silence has sunk most of the projects for finding waste sites. People generally do not like their representatives going behind closed doors on such a touchy issue.

Labor-management negotiations take place behind closed doors. Secrecy is accepted. Why not for waste sites?

Under U.S. law, the proposed contract has to be submitted to a vote of the workers. That is, secrecy is followed by full democracy.

In Britain until the Thatcher years, labor leaders could approve or disapprove a contract completely on their own, without reference to the workers they represented. Many observers, otherwise sympathetic to labor, found this to be one of the major defects in British labor law. It has since been corrected.

Contrast this with waste siting negotiations. To my knowledge, there is no requirement in any siting legislation in this country that a referendum be held in the affected community after an agreement is reached.

This is not merely an oversight by legislators. Rather, the lack of referendum mechanisms is because state legislatures and Congress think that such referendums would fail. That is, the waste sites would be rejected in the proposed communities. They are probably right.

In most important issues facing counties, a vote of some type is held. A prime example is bond issues. Votes are confined to the issues the community thinks are vital.

Yet when it comes to waste sites, citizens are told, "This is important, but your elected representatives will settle it behind closed doors. No vote will be held." It is little wonder that citizens, even those with an open mind on this issue, become suspicious.

A site auction works better than negotiation. It is not secret. There is no "Big Brother" looming over the negotiations. The community handles it on their own, and when they are satisfied with the price they make a bid. There will undoubtedly be some small-scale clean-up negotiations after the auction is over, but the major part should be as an auction. The siting process is too different from the labor-management model for the latter to be used.

The auction is practical for situations where, as Ralph Cassady says, there is "no standard value" of the detriment. Each hazardous or radioactive waste site is a unique combination of calculated risks, geology, nearby population, engineering design and, most importantly, the attitudes of potential surrounding neighbors. For this reason, an auction is the best way to decide the appropriate level of compensation.[4]

Although almost everyone has participated in an auction at one time or another, we may be unfamiliar with their use in public policy. One recent example was the debate over the superconducting supercollider. The largest scientific project in history, an indirect (and non-sanctioned) auction among the competing states produced the eventual winner, Texas.

As well, almost everyone who has flown has taken part, at least by listening, to the auction held to get rid of excess passengers from overbooked flights.

The Sound of an Auction

The reverse Dutch auction is the only type that takes account of the undesirable feature of waste sites. It would sound about as follows:

> Counties, we have all this hazardous waste we want to bury forever. We know that none of you want it, and we are not going to make any of you take it. The arm-twisters who formerly ran this agency are all gone. They are working as professional wrestlers, we think.
>
> We will let the market, rather than complicated regulations and court orders, do the talking. If you are not interested, you do not have to participate. The rising price may draw your attention after a while. If you wait too long, of course, you do not get any of the bonus.
>
> We are not going to choose the site—you are. Since you counties usually do not employ too many scientists and engineers yourselves, hire all you want, and send the bill to us. But do not hire them to prove you should not have the site in your area. If you do not want the site at any price, do not bid.
>
> The first month of the auction, we are offering a $10 million bonus to a county that volunteers. After that, the bonus will rise $10 million monthly, until a county comes forward.
>
> And we know that one will volunteer, when the price is right. That should end, conclusively, the hazardous waste controversy in our state. In the last two years, there have been three riots, 16 lengthy lawsuits, and dozens of newspaper and TV editorials pointing with alarm. All of that unproductive activity can now end. We have found the key to making the volunteer county happy that they have decided to step forward.

Is all this just a nefarious technique for foisting a waste site on the poorest community in a state? Not really. Chances are that the distribution of these facilities will be about the same as before the auction took place, with the wealthiest communities avoiding them. Some activists may derive pleasure in trying to stuff undesirable facilities down the throats of well-to-do towns and cities. But this is simply not going to happen in any siting system that I or anybody else can imagine.

If a poor county volunteered in the auction, they could anticipate a substantial bonus heading their way. It might be of the order of millions or tens of millions, depending on the wastes, the size of the state, competition in the auction, and other factors. Modern Landfill Inc. offered every citizen of Lewiston, New York (near Niagara Falls) $960 annually for twenty years for the right to expand a landfill, from which hazardous wastes would be excluded. The price per citizen could very well be higher for hazardous and radioactive wastes, although the bonus could only be decided as the auction continued.[5]

Who Will Pay the Compensation or Bonus?

Where would the money for the auction come from? There is only one source—the waste generators. Ultimately, the costs will be passed on, in one form or another, to the rest of us. As a nation, we have been crying, "NIMBY, NIMBY," without paying for the privilege. But the right to live 10, 100 or 1,000 miles from a site surely has an economic value. Whatever the level of the bonus in the auction, it is the true social cost of the facility. Put another way, it is the price the rest of us have to pay so the wastes are not in *our* back yard.

Waste generators will not like new taxes—who does? At least they would be getting something for their money. No bonus would be paid until a real site was found and approved.

Contrast this with the search for a low-level radioactive waste site in New York State. According to Roberta Lovenheim, who has been active in the so-far fruitless quest, $37 million has been spent to date. They are a longer distance away from finding a site than they were at the beginning of the process, now that they have alienated two potential counties. The Federal government has spent billions on a site for high-level waste, battling Nevada and the governors of other states. The nuclear fuel rods still wait patiently in their pools at the reactors scattered throughout the nation.

The moral? It is better to pay for a Mercedes, if you are definitely going to get it, than a Yugo that never appears.

What About Existing Sites?

Everything written so far has been about future sites. What about existing hazardous waste sites, like those supposed to be cleaned up by Superfund? Can an auction do anything about them?

Richard Stroup, of the Political Economy Research Center in Montana, came up with an idea that might take care of this legacy. [6]

In 1980, Congress passed what became known as the Superfund law, based in large part on the events at Love Canal. The idea was commendable: Over the decades, hazardous and toxic chemicals had been dumped all over the country, in thousands of sites. In many cases, the people and companies who had done this—often without breaking any laws or regulations of the day—had left town, gone bankrupt, or both. This was in some distinction to what happened at Love Canal, where everybody knew that Hooker Chemical had put the chemicals in the ground. These then were, in the terminology, "orphan" sites.

In some cases, the chemicals from the drums or cans were leaking, causing environmental damage. What to do? Congress delegated the task of clean-up to the Environmental Protection Agency, and gave them a substantial budget to carry out the task.

The Superfund program has accomplished little, at least according to Congressional and other independent reports. The number of sites cleaned has been minuscule in comparison to the billions of dollars spent.

Much of it has to do with legal complications, as the EPA tries to track down just who was responsible. The lawyers have made much money, but the pollution level has not decreased by much.

The Stroup proposal says: "The government could [induce a private firm to take over an orphan waste site] by auction. In some cases, there will be a positive price—that is, companies will offer to pay for the site. In the more difficult cases, the government will have to pay for transferring the site. The 'auction' will be won by the low bidder—the company or person who accepts the lowest payment for accepting ownership."

What Stroup describes is, in essence, a type of auction. The siting agency would say:

> We have a site containing chemicals. Our analysis of the hazards is contained in this report we are distributing. We want a volunteer firm to take over the site, and clean it up.
> If this land were chemical-free, it would be worth $1 million, in our estimation. Obviously, it is worth less—perhaps even a negative amount—by now. So we will start the bidding at $500,000. Is there anyone who will bid at that figure? Nobody? How about $300,000? $100,000? Take the site for nothing?
> This is obviously going to be a little difficult. We will offer half a million to a firm that takes the site. No takers? How about a million? Any interest yet?

Chances are that the siting agency will have to pay a firm to take the site, rather than being paid for it.

There may be some sites that have a positive, rather than a negative, value. How could the accounting be done in black, not red, ink? If there were a hazardous waste site in Manhattan that did not have too many chemicals, a firm might pay to own it, rather than having to be paid. If they were successful at cleaning it up, they might have a valuable property on their hands.

What Type of Auction is the Stroupian System?

The Stroup system is clearly a Dutch auction, since there is only one bidder. Once one firm raises its hand, the auction is over.

The Stroup system is also a reverse auction, since it starts with a high value—the worth of the land before the chemicals were dumped on it—and decreases. However, it is different from the ordinary reverse Dutch auction in that it is "bipolar." That is, both positive and negative values are allowed.

Why would a firm ever want to bid to own a Superfund site? Stroup says,

> There will be competition for such a site from firms who believe they can protect it at a reasonable cost. Firms with the best technology will underbid [i. e., require a smaller payment from the government] those with more expensive or less certain technology...
>
> This approach would create an incentive to find cheap and effective ways to deal with hazardous waste. Companies currently in the waste management field, chemical companies with containment expertise, biotechnology firms with microorganisms that destroy waste—these and many others would have an incentive to develop and test new techniques...no bureaucratic or political approval of the results would be needed.

The auction should cut through the labyrinth of delay and obstruction. It allows firms to solve the problem of hazardous waste sites conclusively.

The main problem with the Stroupian system is that companies have finite lifetimes, sometimes short. No American firm has the longevity of the Hudson's Bay Company, still running after three centuries. What happens if, after getting started on clean-up, a company goes bankrupt or is liquidated? How can the public interest in completing the job be protected?

Stroup takes account of this possibility: "The government does need a guarantee that the new owner [of the site] will not walk away from the job.... It should require the firm...to post an interest-bearing bond large enough to match the potential danger of the site. The bond would remain in the hands of the government though its real income (above inflation) will go to the firm. The bond remains with the government agency as long as the danger exists—possibly indefinitely, if the waste on the site is contained rather than destroyed or removed."

Setting the size of the bond will not be easy. If it is set too high, only a few large firms will be able to raise the money. Small innovative firms will be disqualified. If it is set too low, the deterrent effect of the bond will be diluted. Nonetheless, in principle these problems could be worked out in time.

In a typical Superfund site, the surrounding public urgently wants a cleanup or at least removal of the wastes. The local community would welcome a firm attempting to destroy the wastes immediately. They are tired of waiting through years of legal wrangling without any action. Minds do not have to be changed, since they are already made up—"get that stuff out of here!"

So the Stroup system forms a neat fit with the auction proposed here. It can take care of the waste sites that already exist, which in almost every case are more environmentally harmful than new waste facilities. The reverse Dutch auction can handle the next generation of hazardous waste sites, some of which will take the wastes retrieved from the old Superfund locations. It can also deal with a host of other sites, ranging from trailer parks to mental health facilities to prisons. Between the two of them, the days of LULU controversies are numbered.

Are the Canadians Wiser?

In Canada, a different approach has been taken. The federal siting Task Force on Low-Level Radioactive Waste Management has said, "The voluntary participation of communities is the cornerstone of the process...[c]ommunities are indeed prepared to listen and participate, once they are confident that nothing is being foisted on them and that they are truly an equal partner in the process."

One of the Task Force's pamphlets is entitled, "Voluntary Participation—How It Works." As a result of this emphasis, twenty-six communities requested the Task Force to hold initial information meetings. After these meetings, fourteen communities wanted to go on to the next stage, setting up liaison groups.

Compensation has been considered by the Canadians as well, although the precise method by which it will be set is still undetermined, according to Geraldine Underdown, director of the Task Force. The group writes,

> The community should receive compensation to offset unmitigatable impacts, and to enhance local benefits.... The Task Force does not accept the assumption that expending more effort and money on impact mitigation [e.g., building a more

secure installation, improving local roads, etc.] somehow negates the need to address the imbalance of costs and benefits that inevitably accompanies siting decisions. Even with the best of mitigation, there will be impacts that cannot be avoided or reduced to acceptable levels. These should be compensated by both financial and non-financial means.

The Task Force responded to claims that compensation equals bribery by saying, "Such accusations (and there have been some) have been answered by indicating that a bribe is something offered as an illicit payment and that it induces a betrayal of trust. The 'reward' proposed in this process is well deserved. It is an explicit component of the...guidelines."

Perhaps as a result of these attitudes north of the border, in 1987 the Province of Alberta in western Canada was able to site a new hazardous waste facility at Swan Hills. This marked one of the few such installations to open in North America in recent years. The magazine *Hazardous Waste Consultant* writes, "[T]he [U.S.] federal role is limited to one of cleaning up past sites, not actively supporting projects that will prevent future Superfund sites. Ten years from now, we fully expect U.S. governments to still be bemoaning the need for better hazardous waste management facilities, while Canadian governments will have long since resolved the problem."[7]

The Alberta system was also voluntary. The Swan Hills site was put to a referendum, receiving 79 percent approval.[8] In most regions of the U.S., managers of hazardous waste siting commissions would be pleased if they could get an approval rate in targeted communities that was the *reverse* of the Swan Hills vote, that is, 21 percent in favor.

Wastes and other unwanted materials are here, right now, whatever we may think of them. James Wall, writing in *The Christian Century,* says, "I offer an analogy to sewage: it is not a product any community is eager to have, but no civilization can survive unless it finds a way to dispose of human wastes. We might want to argue with the Divine Creator who dreamed up the notion of bodily waste, but until we win that argument, we have to find a place to put it."[9]

The Present System is Broken

In our school days, most of us dreaded the teacher's finger pointing our way, demanding that we recite or solve a problem on the blackboard. That attitude still persists. Counties or towns slated for hazardous or nuclear waste sites resent the finger of the siting commission aimed at them. That irritation is eventually reflected in litigation and sometimes rioting.

People who cry "NIMBY!" have some rationality behind them. They are telling us that the cost, real or perceived, of a waste site in their vicinity is high *to them*.

Compare the way in which that outburst is received with the attitude of someone from a seemingly different area. Nigel Finn, director of food services for the giant British retailer Marks and Spencer, says of complaints, "We believe what customers tell us, and we don't try to be legalistic and defensive."

The present system of finding waste sites *is* legalistic and defensive. One critic has labeled it DAD, perhaps in honor of its paternalistic nature: "Decide, Announce and Defend." An auction allows site neighbors to set their own price for acceptance. At the same time, not one environmental or safety law, regulation, standard or guideline would have to be dropped.

Retire Sisyphus

According to legend, the Greek king Sisyphus had offended the gods. They set about thinking of the most exquisite punishment they could devise. Eventually, they came up with the never-ending boulder torture.

Sisyphus was condemned to push a gigantic rock, about all he could manage, up a hill. When he got to the top of the hill, the gods would make it roll down. He had to descend and start again. And this task would last till the end of time.

Figure 12.2 shows his problem in a schematic manner. In the first part, the rock is at the bottom of the hill. In the second part, Sisyphus has pushed it up part way, with enormous effort. The third part shows the boulder near the top. Success is at hand. But the fourth part shows that some unexpected event, such as a slippery spot, has rolled the rock down to the bottom again.

Managers in agencies trying to find sites must feel a lot like Sisyphus. They prepare their organization charts, hire their scientists and engineers, and print their elaborate reports. It looks as if they are just about to achieve their aim.

Then the gods—in the guise of the general public—thwart them. Public meetings are held in which the detailed plans are denounced as a creation of the devil. In some cases, demonstrations and even riots break out. The managers have to abandon their piles of paper, and restart everything.

FIGURE 11.2
The Sisyphus Effect

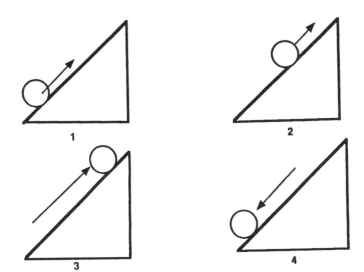

The Sisyphus Effect - Rolling a Boulder Uphill

According to the ancient Greeks, King Sisyphus was condemned for eternity to roll a giant boulder up a hill, only to have it roll down as soon as he reached the crest. The four diagrams shown here chart his progress.

I do not know if the original Sisyphus is still on the job. But it is time to retire the new Sisyphus, who has adopted the guise of the search for hazardous and radioactive waste sites. The reverse Dutch auction allows him to take his ease in a senior kings' home.

Notes

1. Kai Erickson, "Toxic Reckoning: Business Faces a New Kind of Fear," *Harvard Business Review* (January-February 1990): 118.
2. Quoted in Robert M. Adams, "Smithsonian Horizons," *Smithsonian*, 19 (2) (May 1988): 10
3. Gail Bingham and Daniel S. Miller, "Prospects for Resolving Hazardous Waste Siting Through Negotiation," *Natural Resources Lawyer* 17 (3) (1984): 473.

4. Ralph Cassady, *Auctions and Auctioneering* (Berkeley, Cal.: University of California Press, 1967), 20.
5. "Modern Offers Lewiston $64 Million Landfill Deal," *Buffalo News* (8 August 1990): B-5.
6. "Integrated Hazardous Waste Management Facility Opens near Swan Hills, Alberta," *Hazardous Waste Consultant* (January-February 1988): 1-1.
7. Ibid.
8. Jennifer McQuaid-Cook and Kenneth J. Simpson, "Siting a Fully Integrated Waste Management Facility," *Journal of the Air Pollution Control Association* 36 (9) (September 1986): 1031.
9. James M. Wall, "Storing Nuclear Waste: My Backyard or Yours," *The Christian Century* (9 November 1988): 1003.

Index

Parrish, Michael, 195
Patriotism, 20, 158
PCB-polychlorinated biphenyl, 221
Peckinpaugh, Timothy, 57, 181
Perception. *See* Public opinion
Persian Gulf War, 22, 95
Pertinax, 127
Ph.D.s, 129
Physicians, 105
Piasecki, Bruce, 76
Picasso, 209
Planning, 94. *See* also Waste planning
Playboy Mansion, 222
Pointing, 20, 240
Political Economy Research Center, 127, 241
Polling, 85, 89. *See* also Voting; economic aspects, 138; false answers, 206; Gallup, 161; landfills, 109; New Mexico, 198; nuclear power, 199; Pacific Northwest, 147; repository, 163; Tennessee, 211; trust measurement, 102; waste-to-energy, 176; Wisconsin, 206
Pollution, general, 129
Poor, the, 240. *See* also Fairness; bidding, 215; can retrieval, 216; intelligence, 216
Popper, Frank, 93, 118, 192
Poppins, Mary, 172
Portney, Kent, 209
Post Office, 66, 204
Praetorian Guard, 127, 139
Preservationists. *See* Activists
Prisons, 27, 107, 117, 133; Illinois, 225; incentives, 192
Professors, 121, 130
Provenance, 179
Psychological aspects, 11, 199; compensation, 176, 182; experiments, 82; repository, 168; risk, 19; verification, 45
Public health, 81
Public meetings, 28. *See* also Public participation; avoidance, 75; data, 28; description, 90, 105, 108; participants, 117; Tennessee, 15, 169
Public opinion, 90, 131, 157, 234. *See* also Polling
Public participation, 36, 42, 56, 58, 100, 107, 111
Public relations, 108

Que Sera, Sera, 104
Questionnaires. *See* Polling
Quinn, Thomas, 205

Racial discrimination, 202. *See* also Racism
Racism, 79, 221, 228. *See* Fairness: racial
Radiation, 113, 166
Radioactive waste. *See* Waste, radioactive
Radon, 32, 187
Randomness, 122, 144
Rationality, 122, 236
Reactors, nuclear. *See* Nuclear reactors
Reagan, Pres. Ronald, 173
Records: falsification of, 102
Recycling, 4, 76, 78, 186, 194; Massachusetts, 205
Referendums, 86, 96, 131, 201. *See* also Voting; approval levels, 136, 146; Indians, 223; not required, 239; West Virginia, 226
Refineries, 220
Regulated monopolies, 76
Religious aspects, 246
Repository, 159. *See* also Nevada; Nevada: repository; Waste, high-level radioactive; hypothetical opening, 212; study, 167
Republicans, 85
Reverse Dutch auction, 1, 11, 23, 81, 84, 86, 102. *See* also Auctions; advantages of, 60; alleged inequity, 144; approval levels, 64; bonds, 51; compared to Clarke, 150; compensation, 43, 62, 65; compensation cap, 62; disadvantages, 62; fairness aspects, 61; multiple locations, 134; no coercion, 139; operation, 49; origin of, 43; political consensus, 52; self-adjusting, 148; sound of, 240; trust fund, 50
Reversing decisions, 51, 130
Rhode Island, 67; Central Falls, 196
Rich: escape LULUs, 215; largest towns, 217
Rich and poor. *See* Fairness
Ride-sharing. *See* Car pools
Riots, nuclear waste, 16, 90, 115, 223
Risk. *See* also Educational aspects; analysts, 97, 99, 104, 105, 175, 233; aversion, 92, 133; communication, 37; comparative, 28, 147; delayed,

114; diffusion of, 96; dread, 99, 233; familiar, 109; fight or flight, 237; minimization, 212; perception, 26, 60, 63, 233. *See also* Psychological aspects; rate of change of, 111; social aspects, 72; toleration, 92; uncertainty, 112; undetectability, 113
Risk analysis, 13, 14, 22, 41, 94, 130, 169; caveats, 26; low-frequency and high-frequency, 104; mathematical models, 60, 112, 179; probabilistic, 212, 213
Risk-benefit analysis. *See* Benefits
Rockefeller, Sen. Jay, 225
Rockefellers, 224
Rogers, Kenneth, 20
Roman Empire, 127
Roosevelt, Pres. Franklin, 89, 172
Ryan, Mike, 5
Rydant, A. L., 109

Salad dressing, 158, 183
Sandia National Laboratory, 198
Sandman, Peter, 94, 96, 99, 107
Sasser, Jim, 61, 85
Scampas, Phil, 8
Scholarships, 65
Schuler, Richard, 91
Scientific aspects, 221, 233
Scientists. *See* Experts
Scott, David, 82
Secrecy, 59, 62, 140, 152, 170, 231. *See* also Negotiations: secrecy
Segregation. *See* Racism
Sheward, Michael, 9
Shuff, Richard, 197
Sibley, Elaine, 6
Sierra Club, 117, 195
Simmins, Dorla, 192
Simon, Julian, 44
Simon, Peter, 192
Sioux, 94, 222
Sisyphus, 246
Siting authority, 59, 61, 64, 67, 103, 107, 166; control, 101; lawsuits, 181; offers, 238; trust, 102
Skiing, 97
Slavery, 125
Slovic, Paul, 18
Smith, Adam, 213
Smith, V. Kerry, 62, 109
Society for Risk Analysis, 14, 18, 29

Sorensen, John, 66
Source reduction. *See* Waste minimization
South Carolina, 181
South Dakota, 222
Southeast Regional Compact, 57, 72
Southern Christian Leadership Conference, 221
Soviet Union, 95
Spector, Herschel, 216
Speed limits, 27
Speedy Trial Act, 183
Speiser, Dr. Roy, 7
Sprague, Peter, 227
St. George, 1
Stark, Rep. Pete, 190
State Planning Council on Radioactive Waste Management, 171
Steagall, Joe, 228
Stewardship, product, 188
Stress, 101
Stroup, Richard, 127, 241
Sturdy, Robert, 7
Subways, 191
Sulfur dioxide. *See* Oxides of sulfur
Superconducting Supercollider, 9, 130, 198, 239
Superfund, 32, 127, 241
Supply curves, 132, 146
Supply-push, 55
Surveys. *See* Polling
Susskind, Lawrence, 82
Szymanski, Jerry, 93

Taipower, 37, 200
Taiwan, 37, 200
Tart, Tom, 229
Tax Reform Act of 1986, 187
Tax relief, 65, 196, 205
Taxes, 162, 168, 173, 211, 241; Alabama, 229; Connecticut, 201; Japan, 200
Temple, Jim, 4
Tennessee, 14, 60, 85, 89, 105, 111, 206; Attorney General, 182; neighbors of, 167; Oak Ridge, 14, 58, 111, 138, 167; polling, 211; Roane County, 58
Terrorists, 203
Tevye (milkman), 20
Texas, 130, 230
Thatcher, Margaret, 239
Theme parks, 93
Third World, 187, 230